Experimental Education Series

EDITED BY M. V. AND H. E. O'SHEA

THE DIAGNOSIS AND TREATMENT OF

BEHAVIOR-PROBLEM CHILDREN

EXPERIMENTAL EDUCATION SERIES

Edited by M. V. and H. E. O'SHEA

CHILD PSYCHOLOGY.

By George D. Stoddard, Ph.D., Professor of Psychology and Director, and Beth L. Wellman, Ph.D., Associate Professor of Psychology, Iowa Child Welfare Research Station, University of Iowa.

THE DIAGNOSIS AND TREATMENT OF BEHAVIOR-PROBLEM CHILDREN.

By Harry J. Baker, Ph.D., Director, and Virginia Traphagen, M.A., Mental Examiner, Psychological Clinic, Detroit Public Schools.

ENRICHING THE CURRICULUM FOR GIFTED CHILDREN.

By W. J. Osburn, Professor of School Administration, The State University of Ohio, and Director of Educational Research, Ohio State Department of Education, and Ben J. Rohan, Superintendent of Schools, Appleton, Wisconsin.

FITTING THE SCHOOL TO THE CHILD.

By Elisabeth Irwin, Psychologist, Public Education Association of New York City, and Louis A. Marks, Member Board of Examiners, Board of Education, New York City.

THE FUNDAMENTALS OF STATISTICS.

By L. L. Thurstone, Ph.D., Bureau of Public Personnel Administration, Washington, D. C.

GIFTED CHILDREN: THEIR NATURE AND NURTURE.

By Leta S. Hollingworth, Ph.D., Associate Professor of Education, Teachers College, Columbia University.

HOW TO EXPERIMENT IN EDUCATION.

By William A. McCall, Ph.D., Associate Professor of Education, Teachers College, Columbia University.

MODERN PSYCHOLOGIES AND EDUCATION.

By Clarence E. Ragsdale, Ph.D., Assistant Professor of Education, The University of Wisconsin.

PRINCIPLES OF MUSICAL EDUCATION.

By James L. Mursell, Ph.D., Department of Education, Lawrence College.

SPECIAL TALENTS AND DEFECTS.

By Leta S. Hollingworth, Ph.D., Associate Professor of Education, Teachers College, Columbia University.

VOCATIONAL GUIDANCE AND COUNSELING.

By Alanson H. Edgerton, Ph.D., Professor of Industrial Education and Chairman of Courses in Vocational Guidance, Vocational Education, and Industrial and Applied Arts, The University of Wisconsin.

THE
DIAGNOSIS AND TREATMENT OF BEHAVIOR-PROBLEM CHILDREN

By

HARRY J. BAKER, PH.D.

DIRECTOR, PSYCHOLOGICAL CLINIC, DETROIT PUBLIC SCHOOLS

AND

VIRGINIA TRAPHAGEN, M.A.

MENTAL EXAMINER, PSYCHOLOGICAL CLINIC,
DETROIT PUBLIC SCHOOLS

NEW YORK
THE MACMILLAN COMPANY
1935

PREFACE

THERE is need of better diagnostic techniques and remedial measures for children who are behavior problems. There is less scientific procedure in diagnosis for behavior cases than for any other type of handicapped child. For the mentally handicapped or for the mentally gifted there are mental tests and accurate means of measurement; for the visually handicapped there are refined measures of vision; there are, too, measures of hearing and of defects of speech. But behavior cases have tended to remain in the realm of individual opinion and of guessing which is sometimes shrewd and sometimes wide of the mark.

The need for accurate diagnosis in behavior maladjustments is more urgent than in many other types of difficulties. When a child is crippled, his condition is more or less obvious and is recognized as a defect; but when a child begins to defy the teacher, fight with his classmates, or steal from others, he is usually considered a perfectly normal social being, merely afflicted with badness which should be removed as easily as putting glasses on the child who cannot see normally. It is most desirable to understand the causes of his difficulty, how serious they are, and what must be done to remedy them.

The successful diagnosis of behavior problems should include the quiet, retiring, timid, and introvert types of individuals who create no disturbance, as well as the overt, aggressive, dominant, and disagreeable mischief-makers. The mental problems of children of the quiet types are as difficult, if not so dangerous to others, as are those of children of the overt types.

Not all behavior problems have been solved in the past, because there were all degrees of maladjustment and little attention was paid to the milder types. They were supposed to be unavoidable evils which must be endured. The most acute cases were sent to the juvenile court or to special behavior schools and removed from the worry and responsibility of the teacher and even of the parent. Such agencies will continue to function in these extreme cases; but many of the less severe cases may be diagnosed and treated in their usual school and home environments by means of the techniques which are outlined in this volume.

Not all behavior problems have been solved in the past, for the mental mechanisms of problem children are not so easy to fathom as is the degree of hearing defect with the audiometer. However, there are intellectual differences which have been successfully measured by mental tests, and the emotional fields underlying behavior problems should not prove to be too difficult. True, it is comparatively easy to determine accurately the income of the citizens of a state and to know their ages, heights, and weights; but interpreting their feelings, emotions, and political philosophies is not so simple. It is easy to know how old a child is and to judge whether he can run slow or fast, but it is more difficult to know how he feels toward his teacher, his father, or his best chum. These difficult traits, however, are the very ones which must be measured if behavior adjustments are to be made.

The measurement of behavior motivations is not and cannot become a simple, mechanized process. It is not expected that the procedures of this volume may become easily routinized; at best they tend to narrow down the vast regions of guesswork to less expansive limits than heretofore. There are certain advantages in providing specific scores in any field of measurement; mental measurement owes much of its success and popularity to the magic of mental age and I.Q. Abuses and misinterpretations by the untrained and uninformed have by no means offset the good which has resulted. The faulty interpretations of the behavior scale will be only a molehill to the mountain of good which may result from intelligent interpretation.

The behavior scale is dedicated to unfortunate and unhappy children who may benefit from its use. It is not the inspiration or work of a moment or even of a few months but has been in the process of preparation for about six years. Some of the techniques have been employed in social work for many years, but they have all been gathered up and placed together in organized form in this volume for convenience in administration.

Many workers besides the two authors have contributed directly or indirectly to the work. The staff of the psychological clinic of the Detroit Public Schools has been of constant aid in furnishing specific materials such as appear in Chapter V, "Detailed Items of Diagnosis." Much credit is due especially to Dr. Charles Scott Berry, who was formerly Director of Special Education in the Detroit Public Schools, for inspiration in the ideal of successfully diagnosing and training *all* types of handicapped children.

Grateful acknowledgment is made to various authors and their publishers for permission to quote from studies, which we trust are verified and strengthened by our findings and conclusions.

HARRY J. BAKER

VIRGINIA TRAPHAGEN

EDITOR'S INTRODUCTION

NOTHING affects the destiny of individuals or of great groups of people more than the balance and adjustment of a human being. The vast panorama of present and past human society shows clearly a piling up of extensive benefits from interactions with great personalities and a dropping into deep crevasses of trouble and disaster from the activities of warped, unbalanced, antisocial personalities.

It has gradually become a recognized reality that adult behavior flows from the experiences and behavior of childhood and youth. The agencies which society has used in the past, jails, penitentiaries, mental hospitals, have made little headway in controlling or counteracting adult manifestations of inferior youthful behavior patterns; at least have met with little success in preventing outbreaks of misery in the next succeeding adult generation. It is in the earlier years that genuinely dependable steps can be taken forward towards a more equable, a more satisfying, a more enjoyable, and, in short, a sounder adult society.

In this volume the authors present a powerful instrument for appraising the problems and difficulties of children. Just as the careful physician keeps on his desk an outline of the physical characteristics of a human being which he wishes to investigate thoroughly in the case of each patient, so also the psychologist, the psychiatric social worker, or the school home visitor needs to have a skeleton list of human relationships and various other aspects of human life which he must survey in detail for the young person whose life he is studying. A psychologist or a social worker may form incorrect hypotheses concerning a child's struggles and needs if he has forgotten to study some one of the relationships in which the child is involved with the various people surrounding him.

The authors have brought together for the reader and the worker a comprehensive picture of the crucial elements in the life of a child. Any child who is in need of help can be viewed against this remarkably complete analysis sheet of a human life. No cooperation with a child can be genuinely constructive for him, except by the merest chance, unless his adult friend knows with the highest accuracy possible what demands are made upon the child, what insecurities threaten him, how his organism has thus far molded itself to meet the special stresses and strains of his particular life.

Dr. Harry J. Baker has long been the Director of one of the most important and largest city-school-system psychological clinics in the United States and as such has developed policies and procedures of significance for any psychological clinic. Miss Virginia Traphagen is an able member of his staff. The accumulated wisdom of years of dealing with hundreds and even thousands of children and their parents in the city of Detroit has been organized and condensed by the authors in the present guide to diagnosis and compendium of treatment for distressed children.

Students of child nature and of human society will find in the volume stores of wisdom concerning the intricacies of human motivation. Research workers will find emerging on every page some question inviting further systematic measurement and evaluation. Implicit in the whole volume is a philosophy of social courage, of human sympathy, which will warm the heart of the reader and which may bring reassurance that there is a way for society to lift itself out of its enmeshing difficulties, proceeding towards an adult society in which individuals and the whole of society shall find opportunity for fuller realization of their powers.

HARRIET E. O'SHEA

PURDUE UNIVERSITY
October, 1935

CONTENTS

LIST OF DIAGNOSTIC ITEMS

LIST OF TABLES

PART I

INTRODUCTION AND HISTORICAL BACKGROUND

CHAPTER I

INTRODUCTION: SIGNIFICANCE AND INCIDENCE

OF ALL the types of handicapped and maladjusted children whom the schools are attempting to educate, behavior-problem children offer the greatest challenge. Their handicaps create problems for them in school, on the playground, and in the home. Often their problems persist into adulthood; some people eventually become mentally ill while others join lawless gangs of thugs and gangsters. As a class, behavior-problem children are outcasts—unhappy themselves, as well as the cause of woe, destruction, insecurity, and great expense to society. The case of T. M. will introduce the problem.

THE CASE OF T. M.

T. M., twenty-two years of age, was arrested for stealing tires, gasoline, radiator caps, and other accessories from automobiles. He was sentenced to three years' imprisonment, after having failed to make good on probation following an earlier arrest on similar charges. His parents were in despair and reported that he had always been a problem in school and at home. He had not responded to any reasoning, kindness, or punishment from early childhood. He had left school at the age of sixteen years, having reached only the seventh grade, with a history of chronic repetition of grades, poor scholarship, and truancy after the age of twelve years. His mental examination had disclosed an I. Q. of 85, which was not sufficiently backward for a class of subnormal pupils; yet there was enough mental retardation to make competition with average children difficult. He had been more or less

3

of a problem to all teachers after the first grade, but in the earlier years they had been able to control him because of his size and immaturity. When he became truant, he fell in with two older boys who had had similar histories and in them found a sympathetic and understanding audience.

His home life had been equally unhappy. His older sister, who had been a brilliant and model student, was continually held up to him as an example; but instead of being inspired he cordially hated her, and she in turn had become ashamed of his record at school and his reputation as a bad boy. His father had had great aspirations for a college education for him and had tried to drive him to study and to develop responsible habits. These attempts had brought about open rebellion and his leaving home at the age of seventeen years. His mother had attempted to shield him, to cover up his inadequacies, and to keep his school record a secret; but all this resulted only in a feeling that his parents were working at cross purposes.

In the five-year period before sentence he had hitchhiked to California twice, roamed about picking up first one tramp and then another, and finally joined a small gang that had made stripping cars a means of livelihood.

The case of T. M. could be multiplied manyfold. He presents a combination of factors, many of which could be remedied but which bring ruin when allowed to run to their logical conclusion. It is the purpose of this book to bring diagnostic and remedial science to the aid of such problems. The methods of procedure will be found in the later chapters.

General Characteristics of Behavior-Problem Children

Behavior-problem children differ from other types of handicapped children in four important respects which serve to explain some of their unique characteristics. First, they tend to arouse anger and resentment toward their actions in the minds of parents, classmates, playmates, and teachers. Their very acts often offend the dignity of others and bring about physical injury;

they challenge adult authority and generally upset the calm and composure of everyday living and acting. It requires great patience and self-control on the part of those dealing with them to keep from reflecting, as in a mirror, the very attitudes and actions which they have manifested. On the contrary the blind do not incite others to become blind, the deaf to become deaf, or the feebleminded to become feebleminded. Maintenance of a calm and impersonal attitude is a first requisite in the treatment of behavior-problem children.

A second characteristic, which is contrary to a popular but fallacious belief, is that behavior manifestations are rarely deliberate meanness. Whenever a child hurts another, he is often described as doing it to be vicious; but many such acts are done by children who are the victims of emotional tangles and blockings. The cruelty is an explainable and obvious outlet. When the offender is punished with a view to curing his meanness, the punishment fails to correct and his attitudes probably continue with a greater feeling of injustice and misunderstanding. If others ascribe meanness to the child in addition to being angry with him, their attitudes toward the behavior-problem child make it doubly difficult to re-educate him.

A third characteristic is that the child carries over his attitudes, feelings, and emotions from his home to school or from school to home; whereas unfortunately he too often sheds his arithmetic, reading, and spelling as soon as he leaves the school door. In the field of school learning or even of habit formation, at home he may put such activities on or off more or less at will; but behavior attitudes are apt to live with him twenty-four hours a day. If the school and the home wish to find common points of contact in their children, they may be found not so much in the fields of traditional learning as in the realms of feelings, emotions, and attitudes. This fact is true of the average child as well as of behavior, or behavior-problem, children.

The fourth characteristic of extremely aggravated cases is the subtle and misunderstood relationship between causes and behavior manifestations. When a child or adult is suffering from some unusual worry, fear, or shock, he may respond by lying, stealing, truancy, or other antisocial behavior. In making a tentative and informal diagnosis the teacher or parent attempts to treat these obvious symptoms, whereas they are really only symptoms of deep underlying causes. Naturally the treatment fails, and a further accusation of meanness and antisocial behavior is made. The child develops a vague and indefinite feeling of injustice, of not being understood, of resolving to do even worse instead of better, and of thereby living up to reputation. The teacher and the diagnostician, too, dealing with different phases of the behavior situation, may fail to understand each other's point of view. The teacher expects immediate cure of obvious outbursts of stealing; the diagnostician, not expecting to bring about such a speedy change, chides the teacher for not being more patient and for not being more impersonal and less excited in the situations which arise.

These four characteristics of behavior cases are important in understanding behavior-problem children. Other features will be discussed in more detail, but this introductory list serves to sketch the general nature of the problem. Thus far the discussion has shown the need for definite and detailed diagnosis of real causes in behavior cases and a knowledge of how to interpret them and how to treat them.

CAUSES OF BEHAVIOR MALADJUSTMENTS

The causes of behavior maladjustments fall into three classes, but with overlapping and complicating networks of cross-relationships running between and among them. These causes are presented in order.

The first class of causes are physical, sensory, and nervous factors or conditions in the child. Under this category falls a great variety of items, such as defective hearing, defective vision, defective speech, undernourishment, undersize, oversize, nervous disturbances, weakened heart, epilepsy, accidents, illnesses, and a host of similar conditions. Sometimes these factors do not create behavior maladjustments, but often they do. Their effect in the field of behavior is the result of a comparatively simple mechanism operating somewhat as follows: The child cannot see as well as the average child, he works under a constant strain, he cannot sit still as long as others, he cannot give full attention to school learning situations, he begins to play in school and to seek ways to get satisfaction in life outside of the traditional avenues. He irritates other children, he becomes impudent to his teacher. He finds a thrill in being able to get attention by these methods, whereas he cannot call forth the teacher's commendation by excellent school work. Originally he starts out with a simple cause having probably a physiological basis, but he soon carries it over into fields of feeling and emotion. It is no exaggeration to say that every type of physical or sensory defect, mild or severe, has in it the germs of behavior maladjustments as well; it is only when all other factors are favorable that no such symptoms occur. It is an irony of fate that when such behavior patterns have been firmly entrenched, the correction of the physical defect frequently does not abate the mischief of the derived effects. Fighting the original cause of a fire does not necessarily extinguish the conflagration if it has been fanned by strong winds and spread into far locations.

A second class of causes lies in the temperaments and emotions of children. Some individuals are endowed with calm and well-organized emotional tones, others are not. The latter are sensitive to the buffeting of social contacts. Fear, rage, anger, domination, dread, anxiety, and similar traits cause large and foreboding issues in their lives. In this field are to be found causes which are often traceable to a hereditary trend or weakness. Whenever this condition is coupled with an unfortunate environment, the results in terms of behavior maladjustments are disastrous. Just at present there is probably an overemphasis upon the possibilities of a hereditary basis for much poor behavior; it is a usable but dangerous alibi for excusing the child and for absolving teachers, parents, and others from giving the best that can be offered by way of treatment.

The third type of cause has to do with the social and environmental forces acting upon the child. These causes are more common than the first two types. Since they arise from forces over which the child has little control but over which society can exercise some jurisdiction, they are responsible for a rather pathetic picture. A child may have no physical defects, he may have no basic emotional disturbances, but he may be the victim of a repellant and misunderstanding home atmosphere; or he may become the suggestible tool of a gang of irresponsible outlaws. He may have grown jealous of the attentions given by his parents to a baby in the family and be living an unhappy and miserable life. The classroom teacher or the parent may not realize that these attitudes and feelings, which are arising and growing out of ordinary events, may produce a profound and lasting effect upon his particular temperament. A perusal of the behavior factors which will be presented in later chapters will show the great number of factors which operate in these fields and some of their malicious effects upon children.

The Number of Cases

There are several complicating factors in estimating the number of behavior-problem children. On account of the extreme severity of a few cases the impression may prevail that hundreds of cases are to be found in any neighborhood, school, or community. A small group may spread terror and demoralization, so that their exploits remain magnified long after they actually live only in memory. It is undoubtedly true that communities vary in the number of cases of behavior difficulty. In certain declining areas of large cities the numbers are relatively large, and in small residential cities the numbers are few. Furthermore, a child may be no problem in one community or environment and a serious one in another. The environment of the home and of the neighborhood has a profound effect upon him. The atmosphere and attitude of a home or a school may be such that problems in some cases are minimized, but in other instances they may be increased. Standards of conduct vary so greatly that a child who is considered as scarcely any problem at all in one school is branded as a very bad boy in another, or *vice versa*. All these conditions bear upon the problem of behavior children and make any statement of the number ambiguous and confusing rather than clear-cut.

With these limitations in mind estimates of the number of cases vary from one to five per cent. Naturally if only one per cent of all children is the estimate, only the most severe and aggravated cases are included. If five per cent or more are considered the estimate, many of the milder cases are taken into the classification. If the percentage is extended to a higher figure, the cases average much less severe. Logically, if this process were carried to its theoretical limit, all children below the median in behavior would be considered problems to some extent; and finally the child next to the top of a scale of perfection would be a behavior problem of some degree with respect to the most perfect child. The estimates of five per cent or higher have been based chiefly on surveys by behavior clinics in certain large cities and include the negativistic and retiring types of personality, whereas the more conservative estimates of one per cent have been based on the listing of behavior problems by teachers in the public schools of Chicago and Detroit. In these instances only the more severe cases of the moment were probably considered; undoubtedly the schools did not want to be in the position of openly admitting that they had too many difficult problems. In any event the number is much too great in an enlightened society which boasts of so many mechanical inventions and perfections. Every community should know its own number of cases, what standard is set in calling them cases, and what must be done to bring about a favorable change.

If adults are considered as well as children, the numbers of cases with either mental disturbance or with criminal and antisocial trends mount to appalling figures. Even among children one per cent of those of eligible age are annually brought under the jurisdiction of juvenile courts or houses of detention. Two hundred thousand babies are born out of wedlock annually, many of whom eventually reflect an inherent instability which may have existed in either or both parents. The half million citizens who are sentenced to jails or penitentiaries each year, represent, it has been estimated, only one tenth of the number that have actually committed some criminal or civil offense. In the field of mental disorder the number of cases exceeds the combined total of all other kinds and types of illnesses. A certain percentage of these cases generate their problems from the home and environmental factors in their childhood. Some of the adult maladjustments cannot be traced directly back to childhood, but education and the social agencies of a community should still feel a vital responsibility for them.

Cost to Society

The numbers which have just been cited give some clew as to the appalling price society is paying for its mistakes in the education of children and for the conditions under which certain classes live in adulthood. Every inmate of every type of hospital or institution costs from fifty cents to one dollar per day. For children on detention farms or in schools where more supervision is required the costs range from five hundred to one thousand dollars per child annually. In addition to this item of maintenance the loss to society of what otherwise might be productive workers is difficult to estimate. At least it amounts to hundreds of dollars annually per person.

There are also many intangible costs, such as individual unhappiness; disgrace to parents, brothers, and sisters; and fear that similar mental conditions may afflict others in the family. Remorse over lack of understanding what factors could have operated to prevent these situations leads to further misery in the family. These feelings reach deep into the lives of parents and relatives, who are disgraced in the neighborhood perhaps, since children carry gossip about neighbors in an exaggerated and garbled form.

From the standpoint of financial saving alone the annual expenditure of millions for the study and prevention of malbehavior and delinquency would be justified by its later returns to society. The movement has often lacked force; it could not always be made definite or be understood by teachers, parents, and the community. This treatise on behavior diagnosis is dedicated to making the behavior factors more clearly understood so that a better program of prevention can be undertaken.

CHAPTER II

HISTORY OF TREATMENT AND CONTRIBUTIONS
TO THEORIES

THE history of civilization is paralleled by the evolution of behavior. Within the past fifty or one hundred years there have been phenomenal changes in both civilization and behavior. Behavior even in its unusual deviations and manifestations has had a tremendous influence upon civilization and the vicissitudes of mankind. Consider the mad Nero, who screamed in glee as his orders to burn Rome were carried out. When positions of high political, military, financial, or industrial power were held by those whose behavior drives became abnormal, the consequences and upheavals were nothing short of devastating. The very reasons for achieving great power were often to be found in some unusual drive in the persons concerned, people with thwarted early lives or people of small stature—Napoleon, for example—whose physical limitations drove them to find some compensatory outlet.

Many difficulties have arisen along the way in solving the enigmas of behavior. In the early days of civilization abnormal behavior was sometimes considered to be a divine gift which must not be opposed. It proceeded peacefully on its way with a passport signifying license to almost any sort of outrage or indiscretion. At other times these same patterns were thought to be the work of the devil and therefore called for execution by burning at the stake. Abnormal behavior was so often associated with fear and superstition that no sane scientific approach or study could have been made. Those in authority who were afflicted with various dementias were lauded as possessing traits characteristic of their office and necessary to the fulfillment of their duties. It is not strictly necessary to speak only in the past tense about these matters.

In the rank and file of the population the mentally ill were cared for by their families; unless they did violence, they were tolerated by their neighbors. There were fewer causes of distraction than in the modern complex social order, particularly in our large cities; and while as many disorders probably existed then as now, they were more easily assimilated into society. It is possibly true that more behavior situations develop and more breakdowns occur in our day on account of the complexities of environment, although that will always be difficult either to prove or to disprove on account of the meager and inaccurate records in earlier times.

In the history of civilization group forces of unusual constitution have at times been actuated by a mob psychology of unique but ghastly character; for example, the Children's Crusade in 1212 A.D. A belief arose that children could wrest the Holy Land from the Moslems, a feat which had not been permanently accomplished up to that time by a series of military expeditions. The results were beyond description. A twelve-year-old shepherd boy named Stephen from France, and Nicholas, a lad from Germany, went throughout their lands preaching this message; gradually fifty thousand children assembled and were led by Stephen to Marseille and by Nicholas into Italy. Pope Innocent III tried to send them home and a few returned; but the majority embarked on trading vessels which proved to be slave ships taking them into a Mohammedan slavery from which they never returned. Such tortures and cruelties inflicted upon children were somewhat more spectacular but scarcely less sinister than the white-slave trade in modern large cities, than industrial slavery in Europe of less than one hundred years ago, or than recent child labor which better working codes seek to bring to a happy and merciful close.

AUTHORITY OF THE HOME

The conception of parental authority, particularly of the patriarchal despotism of the father, in the family has been the source of many behavior troubles for children. In the early tribal days of society and in the pioneering days of our country the father took a very active part both physically and socially in protecting, guiding, and rearing his family in the midst of enemies and physical dangers. Absolute authority was vested in him in all matters of discipline, beliefs, and social customs. To a large extent this attitude is still predominant in Europe, and our own country is by no means exempt; in fact, parental authority has much sanction in courts of law whenever problems of discord over children arise. Any attempt to evolve a theory of child training which is not based solely on the principle of absolute parental authority, either through general social custom or through individual revision, brings clashes to which parents do not adjust themselves. Parents have in their background a type of tradition respecting their authority which it is difficult to overcome; they subconsciously indorse it as having been painful but satisfactory in their own lives; they believe that there should be no easier program for their children. The recent immigrants to America among the laboring and artisan classes have suffered most from making the sudden change; their children try to break away into new social traditions. The delinquency areas of large cities are mute testimony to the workings of this process. Even though the populations of slum districts change from one nationality to another, the percentage of juvenile maladjustment and delinquency remains about the same for all groups.

Society is probably in a general transition with regard to child behavior, and the period of transition is one of distressing growing pains. Much physical torture and punishment have disappeared, but the mental agony from ridicule, scorn, nagging, and sarcasm continues to reign. The problem will not be solved until these phases are understood and wholesome conditions incorporated into the educational program for children and for adults.

CONTRIBUTORS TO BEHAVIOR DIAGNOSIS

A brief résumé of the contributions of the four men who stand out as important contributors to theories of behavior throws light on the evolution of behavior concepts. While some of their contributions seem rather theoretical and somewhat removed from the immediate question of what to do with certain types of acute maladjustment, it is important to understand the broad underlying principles of mental mechanisms which they have discovered.

The first of these is Sigmund Freud (3 and 4 [1]), who believes that the keynote to all behavior is the motive for race preservation. This drive, expressed in sexual thinking and activity, is deeply repressed in childhood by parental training and social taboos. The very process of mental repression and restriction in itself became an object of Freud's study, and its mechanisms are important in the understanding of sexual and other repressions. Freud's real contribution probably lay in the field of behavior mechanisms, although he was roundly criticized for making application chiefly to sex life and activity.

It is desirable to examine Freud's general mechanisms of behavior. He divides the mind into three levels of activity. The first is the level of the usual "conscious" activities, of which we are aware and which we can control to a large extent or can consciously guide in this or that direction more or less at will. The second level is known as the "foreconscious." It lies just under the threshold of consciousness, subject to less control than the first and guarded by a censor, which is largely the will. It is illustrated when a person resolves to forget some extremely unpleasant and humiliating experience. The third level of mental activity, which is buried or "unconscious," rarely comes to active consciousness. The censor acts here most completely and suppresses sexual desires, possible hatreds of this or that person, and countless other situations. Yet all these buried motives or drives exercise a great influence upon the lives and actions of a person.

[1] These numbers indicate references at the end of this chapter.

The presence of these drives may be detected in slips of the tongue or of the pen, in personal mannerisms toward the objects or persons of interest, and in the content of dreams.

Ordinarily the "unconscious" drives are not very strong and few conflicts arise. But when too strong repression has been used, then the buried mechanisms dominate the outward or overt behavior in ways which may be expressed as unusual behavior. This behavior is not understood by the child or by his parents or teachers. The method of treatment is to analyze and to seek out these drives by the analysis of the dreams or by reviewing the unpleasant experiences and incidents of childhood. If these drives can then be understood and their influences determined and comprehended by the child, the emotional blockings and malbehavior tend to disappear.

Alfred Adler (1 and 2), like Freud from Vienna, has proposed a theory that the drive for self-preservation is the important motive in behavior. If this trend is thwarted in any way, the individual tries to break through with some kind of violent or spectacular behavior, which Adler terms the "will to power." He recognizes three kinds of motives due to barriers to self-realization: First is the drive to compensate for some organic or physical inferiority. If the child has lost the use of a limb or has any physical incapacity, he strives to compensate in other ways and, if necessary, will resort to bad behavior to gain his ends. The second motive is the desire of children to be grown up and strong like adults, particularly men. Adler also claims that certain women who are physically weak manifest the same drive in what he terms the "masculine protest." The third type of drive comes from children who feel rejected and unwanted by their parents. The lack of a sense of home security threatens their ego and the possibility of self-preservation. In attempting to surmount any or all of these blockings to self-realization, the individual may resort to unusual behavior to gain his ends. He frequently assumes an attitude of superiority to conceal his real feelings of inferiority, so that it becomes difficult to analyze and understand his real emotional predicament.

Carl G. Jung (7 and 8) outlines four steps in his analysis of mental mechanisms which lead to unusual behavior. The first is recognition of the problem. Recognition brings release from worry, much as when a noise in an adjoining room is found to be a vase blown off the table by the wind rather than the entrance of a house breaker. The second phase is the release from an emotional strain in which the patient feels no further blame. This release is accomplished by ascribing the fault to another person or to a combination of circumstances. The third phase is re-education to new ways of meeting the problems. Finally there is a transformation to a goal of perfection, in which every shadow has a light somewhere, a light that offers aid, comfort, and new inspiration. Jung's theory is somewhat more philosophical and idealistic than Freud's or Adler's and aims at mental self-realization, perfection, and contentment.

In the United States the contributions of William Healy (5 and 6) are most helpful in understanding behavior patterns. He shows that, when a child is suffering from fear, dread, rejection, or insecurity, he tends to respond by unusual or pathological behavior, such as lying, stealing, accusing others, and running away. If these basic drives can be removed before they have become too long-standing or deep-seated, the antisocial conduct will disappear; but if the motives persist for long periods of time, the effects, such as stealing, tend to remain from force of habit. This mechanism is not generally understood by parents or teachers, and when attempts are made to cure these undesirable traits by mental or physical punishment the results are disastrous. The child has a vague feeling that he is being punished for something beyond his own responsibility. The symptoms then persist in aggravated form with further and more severe punishments which continue to be ineffective. The actual treatment has to be an indirect one, requiring much time and patience and a sympathetic understanding upon the part of all concerned.

From these four contributors and many others it is apparent that society is becoming more aware of the need for understanding the mechanisms of behavior. The possible causes must be first found and then properly interpreted. This volume attempts to discover a large number of specific causes and to provide a means for evaluating them for degrees of severity. It also offers a discussion of each factor as to its possible significance in causing behavior maladjustments. Gathering the data as to the possible causes is relatively easier than making the interpretation. For example, two children may have had the same degree of poor health in their early years; but in one case it has caused behavior disturbances, in the other it has not. This fact cannot be explained by any simple formula or rule of thumb; the explanation must come from experience and insight into the basic mechanisms of behavior which have just been cited.

Naturally there are some dangers in putting diagnostic procedures into the hands of relatively unskilled and inexperienced workers. If great tact is not used in gathering some of the data, parents and children greatly resent intrusion upon the innermost secrets of their lives. At various places the authors have tried to indicate possible dangers and pitfalls. The risks involved are more than outweighed by the help which children may receive from a careful study and thorough analysis.

The scale for the analysis of behavior problems which is presented and discussed in the following chapters is offered with the hope that it will aid in removing diagnosis and treatment from the realm of subjective opinion. It offers specific numerical scores for definite facts to those who desire them. Many of the factors and causes have been known and discussed in child-study clinics in informal manner. This volume attempts to bring them together in convenient, organized form for practical use.

BIBLIOGRAPHY

1. ADLER, ALFRED—*The Practice and Theory of Individual Psychology.* New York: Harcourt, Brace & Co., 1924. 352 pp. (Translated by P. Radin.)
2. ADLER, ALFRED—*Understanding Human Nature.* New York: Greenberg, 1927. 286 pp.
3. FREUD, SIGMUND—*A General Introduction to Psychoanalysis.* New

York: Liveright Publishing Co., 1927. 406 pp. (Translated and with an introduction by G. Stanley Hall.)

4. FREUD, SIGMUND—*The History of the Psychoanalytic Movement.* Scranton, Pa.: Nervous and Mental Disease Publishing Co., 1916. 58 pp. (Translated by A. A. Brill.)

5. HEALY, WILLIAM—*The Individual Delinquent.* Boston: Little, Brown & Co., 1915. 830 pp.

6. HEALY, WILLIAM—*Mental Conflicts and Misconduct.* Boston: Little, Brown & Co., 1917. 330 pp.

7. JUNG, CARL G.—*Psychological Types.* New York: Harcourt, Brace & Co., 1923. 654 pp.

8. JUNG, CARL G.—*Psychology of the Unconscious.* New York: Dodd, Mead & Co., 1916. 566 pp.

PART II
THE DETROIT BEHAVIOR SCALE

CHAPTER III

THE DETROIT SCALE FOR THE DIAGNOSIS OF BEHAVIOR PROBLEMS

THE Detroit Scale for the Diagnosis of Behavior Problems consists of sixty-six items (possible causes) which are known to be significant in the diagnosis of behavior maladjustments.

TABLE I. SIXTY-SIX ITEMS OF THE BEHAVIOR SCALE

I. Health and physical factors. (See Chapter VI.)

1. Child's early health
2. Child's present health
3. Children's diseases
4. Serious infectious diseases
5. Accidents

6. Degree of speech defect
7. Degree of vision defect
8. Degree of hearing defect
9. Degree of orthopedic defect
10. Size for age

11. Motor control and muscular co-ordination
12. Convulsions, seizures
13. Nervousness

II. Personal habits and recreational factors. (See Chapter VII.)

14. Personal hygiene and clothing
15. Looks or appearance
16. Early self-care
17. Present self-care
18. Home duties

19. Conditions of eating
20. Eating habits
21. Time of sleeping
22. Sleeping conditions
23. Dreams

24. Early recreational facilities
25. Later recreational facilities
26. Playmates or companions

III. Personality and social factors. (See Chapter VIII.)

27. Social type
28. Personality type
29. Anger, rage, revenge, etc.
30. Fear, dread, anxiety, etc.
31. Excitement, shock, uneasiness, etc.
32. Pity, sympathy, enthusiasm, etc.

33. Intelligence
34. Interests or hobbies
35. Initiative and ambition
36. Vocational interests
37. General behavior

IV. Parental and physical factors of the home. (See Chapter IX.)

38. Father's intelligence
39. Mother's intelligence
40. Father's education
41. Mother's education
42. Father's age at birth of child

43. Mother's age at birth of child
44. Father's health
45. Mother's health
46. Father's personality
47. Mother's personality

48. Occupation
49. Economic status
50. Home language
51. Other adults in home
52. Number of and position in siblings

53. Adjustments to siblings
54. Legal status
55. Broken home

V. Home atmosphere and school factors. (See Chapter X.)

     56. General home atmosphere
     57. Ideals of home
     58. Religion
     59. Family recreation
     60. Parents' social adjustment

     61. Discipline
     62. Attitude toward child
     63. Child's attitude toward home
     64. School attendance
     65. Scholarship
     66. Child's attitude toward school

The Number of Items

Some explanation seems to be in order as to the number of items. This could have been reduced; some combinations could have been made, such as combining early health and present health into one item. But when such reductions are made, many important items begin to lose their individual significance. On the other hand the number of items could have been greatly expanded by splitting the present items into more subdivisions; but the scale then becomes unwieldy. For the present scale the gathering of data takes at least two hours at a minimum and often more. All things considered, the present scale strikes a moderate and practical medium between these two extremes.

Interpretation of the Items

In the chapters of Part III each of the sixty-six items is discussed with respect to its possible psychological and emotional implications for behavior. The remedies and preventions are also presented with a reasonable amount of detail. In Chapter V key questions and detailed questions or observations are given for each item. They are intentionally arranged so that, if the key questions disclose some difficulty in any particular item, the detailed questions may be used to pursue the problem with greater particularity. The scoring of each item is also given. It is the purpose of Chapter V to present questions and scoring together in a separate and usable form.

RANGE OF SCORES

In the discussion in Chapter V each item is scored in five possible categories as shown in Table II.

TABLE II. SCORING A BEHAVIOR ITEM

CATEGORY	SCALE VALUE
Very poor	1
Poor	2
Fair or average	3
Good	4
Very good	5

If a case should be found in which all of the sixty-six items were rated "very poor," a value of one point each, the total minimum score would be 66 points. If a case should be found in which all the factors were "very good," a value of five points each, the maximum perfect score would be 330 points. In practical use all children, from serious behavior cases to the model kind, fall somewhere between the extremes of 66 to 330 points. How such cases actually distribute themselves with respect to total score will be shown in the following chapter.

THE SCORING STEPS, OR CATEGORIES

The scoring for scale values of the sixty-six items set forth in Chapter V requires some comment. Not every item has been left merely to the worker's judgment as to "very poor," "poor," etc., but specific scores or descriptions are offered. For example, item No. 5, on accidents, is scored for the number of accidents. Other items, such as No. 18 on home duties, are necessarily stated in more general terms, yet they have sufficiently specific statements to be out of the class of general impressions. The location of the descriptions or numerical scores in the five categories was made after much discussion of each item by the entire staff of the Detroit Psychological Clinic, which consisted of twenty-five psy-chologists and social workers. Each item was fixed in its steps according to the pooled judgment of this group, and for each item problem cases were known in which the steps paralleled the final arrangement of the scale values.

In Item No. 11 (page 51) on motor control and muscular co-ordination a value of 2 points has been assigned to the unusually skillful and of 1 point, or very poor, for the exact opposite. It has been observed that unusual skill or unusual difficulty in motor control may cause behavior maladjustments. From the standpoint of normal adjustments, being about average in motor control seems to be more desirable than being unusually skillful. A similar situation exists with Item No. 10 on page 49 and Items 42 and 43 on pages 86 and 87.

NATURE OF THE ITEMS

As far as possible the sixty-six items are primarily basic causes of behavior difficulties. Symptoms or results of maladjustment, such as stealing, are not included since they are commonly results rather than causes. It is naturally impossible to make a definite distinction between causes and results in all factors in behavior. In the early stages some factors which would be classified as "results" eventually become major problems in themselves and in turn tend to become "causes." For example, in the early days of childhood the lack of responsibility for home duties (Item 18) fostered by parents may seem to be a result; but after this faulty attitude becomes firmly established so that no amount of later training seems to have much effect, neglected home duties and their psychological effects tend to become causes of other behavior maladjustments. In their present form the sixty-six items have proved to be a practical basis for the diagnosis of behavior maladjustments; any possible errors in the selection of items, in the number of items, or in the method of scoring seem rather outweighed by the practical nature of the entire scale.

Certain statistical evaluations and validations of the Detroit Scale for the diagnosis of behavior problems have been made on the Detroit Scale of Behavior Problems. A series of correlations has been computed between all the behavior causes and a discussion has been prepared reviewing evidence from a few of the studies of a similar nature. The discussion of these points is to be found in Chapters XII and XIII of Part IV since they contribute only indirectly to the practical application of the scale itself. For those who are primarily interested in these evaluations before proceeding with the administration of the scale it is recommended that these chapters be read before undertaking Chapter IV. For the practical workers who are not particularly interested in such validations less emphasis may be placed upon Chapters XII and XIII. However, they should be aware that such validations have been made if inquiries along this line are directed to them.

CHAPTER IV

ADMINISTRATION OF THE DETROIT BEHAVIOR SCALE

THERE are two important factors in the administration of the Detroit Behavior Scale which merit special comment. The first factor is the general background and training of those who wish to use the scale in practical diagnosis. Courses of training in psychology and social work are presupposed. It is conceded that occasionally a teacher or worker with a wide experience and of known insight into social situations may safely be entrusted with its administration and interpretation. The question of training is somewhat similar to the problem involved when teachers are permitted to administer the various intelligence tests with no further training than that offered by the manual of directions. It is not our purpose to discourage the use of the Behavior Scale but rather to stimulate its usefulness through a realization of its practical importance as a means of diagnosis. Persons trained in social work should find it of value in verifying their subjective opinions of individual cases.

The second factor is the tact with which the worker is able to proceed in securing and interpreting the information for the diagnosis. Many of the questions and factors, particularly in the latter part of the scale, are matters of private and personal concern to families and information cannot be demanded or acquired in any purely mechanical manner by following the questions and observations listed in Chapter V. Some items yield ready responses from children or parents much more easily than others. The items in the early part of the scale are easier to handle since they concern the health, development, and habits of the child. It might be added that workers with training and experience may be as susceptible to error in this matter as is the comparative novice; caution in the matter of tact should never be relaxed.

APPROACH TO PARENTS AND CHILDREN

Many children who will be studied by means of the Detroit Behavior Scale will be out of adjustment with the school and possibly with their parents when they first report for diagnosis; in fact, these are often the very reasons why the children are to be studied. The approach must be in terms of a desire to study and help with the problem, never in the spirit of trying to punish the child. Contrary to popular opinion the maladjusted child seldom delights in his bad reputation; oftener deep in his heart he feels very much disgraced and saddened by his experiences. He will usually respond to study and diagnosis as a means of improving his morale. Naturally he cannot be stampeded too quickly into a "confession" or even into a free discussion of his difficulties; time is required.

In dealing with parents the problem is equally difficult. Parents have often been disgraced by the child's actions and are beginning to reject him. The diagnosis and treatment should lead them back into a happier relationship. Many times they are resistant to the school, which is openly blamed as the cause of the child's troubles. Insult is added to injury if the worker is too aggressive in taking the inventory of home factors which have contributed to maladjustment. However, these are theoretical rather than practical difficulties, since experienced workers or even workers in training seldom find resistance lasting for any time when the real purpose of their mission is known. There is also a problem of dealing with the schools and particularly with the teachers if the child has been a difficult problem of discipline. Teachers cannot help being upset and disturbed, as are parents; in some cases it is probably well to transfer the child to a different school. Generally it is futile to censor either parents or teachers for the attitudes which they have developed from bitter experience with certain behavior children.

DURATION OF DIAGNOSIS AND TREATMENT

True cases of behavior maladjustment have usually arrived at their present degrees of difficulty after a long period of time. They cannot be brought out of these states overnight or with the waving of some magic wand, such as the administration of this scale or finding the I.Q. by a mental test. The behavior attitudes carry with them certain emotional feelings and blockings which continue to function after the initial causes have ceased to exercise their direct effects. In making the diagnosis the worker should not expect to be through in one interview or with one visit to the home. Answers to the early questions of the scale dealing with health may usually be acquired quickly; but such factors as ideals of the home and recreation of the family can best be determined only after more than one visit. Treatment of certain factors may begin before the diagnosis is completed. Whenever opportunity arises, treatment should begin. As a matter of fact the worker should realize that diagnosis itself is a part of treatment, since the child gets insight into his problems through diagnosis.

Certain cases of slight difficulty can be cleared up in a short time, and the number of cases which are greatly aided by one visit or interview is phenomenal. However, the chronic case may persist over weeks or months; in fact certain special schools for behavior children set a minimum of two or three years for the period of their treatment. There is no other substitute for time in the treatment of cases, although change of environment and a sympathetic understanding of problems operate to relieve the tensions. There is no intention to discourage work with behavior problems on account of their complexity or the length of time required for them. By placing diagnosis and treatment upon a more definite basis it will be possible to determine the nature and extent of the problem and what society must eventually do to raise itself and its unfortunate members above the present standard of behavior.

Problems of Interpretation

While there are difficulties in securing co-operation from parents and children and while there are problems in securing the information for the diagnosis, the interpretation in terms of behavior is the most difficult problem of all. In the diagnosis outlined in Chapter V certain items will be found rated 1, or very poor; others 2 or poor, etc. For example, a boy may be found to have very poor conditions of eating and be rated 1 for this item. The essential question still remains as to whether or not the poor conditions of eating are actually contributing to this boy's behavior problems. How can the effect be determined? Just the mere fact of having a poor rating on this item does not really establish the fact that conditions of eating are a real cause of maladjustment. The solution lies in studying his behavior and attitude when the question of eating is discussed with him. If he assumes a sudden silence and a sullen attitude, the chances are that he has some strong feelings about eating; or if he actually becomes perturbed, the signs probably indicate a disturbance. On the other hand, if he is prone to laugh off the problem of eating and seems to have no special feeling about it, the chances are that it is not of particular significance in his case. There is still a chance that eating may be a real emotional problem; but he does not recognize it as such, which throws the question back upon the intuitive judgment of the worker. Long experience and a special gift of insight are needed to solve these problems. In making interpretations of factors which score "very poor," the worker should avoid the extreme of believing and finding a serious emotional problem behind every factor or the other extreme of discounting all of the very poor factors as not contributing to the maladjustment.

It should be recalled that individuals respond differently to the same situation. One may be much upset, another may show some concern, and a third may be entirely indifferent. One person may be much upset about poor conditions of eating while another may not be. This should be kept in mind in interpreting factors for any individual.

Explanation of scoring. The method of scoring all items according to a five-point plan was shown in Table II of Chapter III. The detailed steps for scoring each of the sixty-six items are shown in Chapter V. The distribution of scores for items on a typical behavior case is shown in Table III.

TABLE III. SCORE OF A TYPICAL BEHAVIOR CASE

SCORE VALUE	NUMBER OF ITEMS	WEIGHTED SCORE
1	7	7
2	13	26
3	16	48
4	18	72
5	12	60
Total	66	213

The seven items rated "very poor," with a score of 1, are as follows:

No. 4 Serious infectious diseases
No. 11 Motor control and muscular co-ordination
No. 15 Looks or appearance
No. 25 Later recreational facilities
No. 44 Father's health
No. 51 Other adults in home
No. 57 Ideals of home

The thirteen items rated "poor," with a value of 2, are as follows:

No. 3 Children's diseases
No. 10 Size for age
No. 16 Early self-care
No. 20 Eating habits
No. 26 Playmates or companions

No. 28   Personality type
No. 33   Intelligence
No. 37   General behavior
No. 41   Mother's education
No. 49   Economic status

No. 56   General home atmosphere
No. 63   Child's attitude toward home
No. 66   Child's attitude toward school

The seven "very poor" items and the thirteen "poor" ones should become the basis of adjusting this child.

Significance of the total scores. The scores for the individual items are valuable in the diagnosis and treatment. The total score for an individual is significant in determining the general severity of the entire problem. In Table VIII (page 345) of Chapter XII the medians and score distributions for one non-behavior and two behavior groups are shown. Upon the basis of Table VIII a plan of letter ratings with their significance is shown in Table IV.

TABLE IV. SIGNIFICANCE OF TOTAL SCORES

RATING	SCORES	SIGNIFICANCE
A	301 to 330	Very model behavior motivation
B	285 to 300	Superior behavior motivation
C+	265 to 284	Good behavior motivation
C	236 to 264	Fair behavior motivation
C−	216 to 235	Poor behavior motivation
D	200 to 215	Decidedly inferior behavior motivation
E	66 to 199	Extremely poor behavior motivation

According to present knowledge and experience scores of less than two hundred points, rated *E*, characterize approximately the poorer half of the pupils enrolled in special schools for behavior problems. These cases are usually recommended for an extended term in such schools with occasional ones recommended for trial in regular schools. Those rated *D* constitute most of the better groups in behavior schools, many of whom are recommended for regular grade placement. Those rated *C* — occasionally find themselves in behavior classes; many of those selected for special study as problem cases from regular grades fall in this classification. Those rated C probably fall within the range of normal, average behavior, with the $C +$ group holding a slightly more favorable position. Those rated B are above the average for non-problem behavior, while the group rated A are ideal with respect to their behavior motivation.

No attempt has been made to determine a percentage distribution for these ratings such as obtains in intelligence measures. There has not been sufficient sampling of the entire range of the school population for this purpose. It is probably true that the percentages of A and B and of D and E are much smaller than in the case of intelligence measures, which include 20 per cent in the two ratings at each extreme. Possibly not more than from 2 to 5 per cent fall in the last two ratings at each extreme, although any estimate would be pure conjecture.

In Table IV the term *motivation* has been used in stating the significance of the various letter ratings. This concept seems much more to the point than considering the ratings as a final measure of behavior. It leaves open the challenge to improve the total score by improving the motivations. The problem is similar to stating that a ten-year-old boy is fifty-two inches tall, which is not his final height. The fifty-two inches contains potential elements of further development, such as his being only ten years old and having promise of food, exercise, and sunshine to stimulate the growth beyond that mark.

The authors are well aware of the fact that not all cases of maladjustment make a successful recovery. Glueck and Glueck (1) in a study of five hundred criminal careers found 82 per cent of the cases from a reformatory repeating in some penal institution or its equivalent in a five-year period; and the same authors (2) in a more recent study of one thousand maladjusted children found 88 per cent of repetition for this group. Later studies may show that the cases that are rated D or E in the Detroit Behavior Scale will continue to show lack of adjustment. In any event through the use of measurement more specific knowledge will be gained of these trends or drifts in children. If necessary, a new philosophy as to the gravity of maladjustments may have to be evolved. Merely hoping and wishing that problem cases will improve leaves us far short of the goal.

Range of ages to be studied.   Some mention should be made of the range of ages which may be covered by the Detroit Scale of Behavior. It may be used on children as young as five years or younger. For these cases the chief difficulty lies in trying to make distinctions between Items 1 and 2 on health, Items 16 and 17 on self-care, and Items 24 and 25 on recreational facilities. It is recommended that the second item of each of these pairs be scored like the first one unless more specific information is available on the second item.

Item 36 on vocational interests cannot be scored reliably on such young children. In the absence of information it is advisable to give the child the benefit of the doubt with a rating of 4 or 5. For young children in the case of Items 61 through 66, on discipline, home attitude, and school adjustment, there is little information available, and therefore these items should be scored rather high in fairness to the child.

The scale is usable throughout the range of school grades, including the high school. In fact it may be used to advantage with adults in the twenties, particularly if they are single and still living at home. Adults who are maladjusted might be rated with respect to what was true in their childhood, and contrasts be made with their more recent feelings on factors which cause behavior difficulties. There is a danger of course that adults may have forgotten some of their childhood experiences and attitudes or may believe that they were different from what they actually were.

At all ages it is important to gather accurate information on all sixty-six factors. To the extent that hurried guesses are substituted for facts or that the scale factors are arbitrarily rated too high or too low, results will be of little value.

Fidelity and accuracy of records.   A final word should be said of the importance of a complete and accurate record of items on the Detroit Behavior Scale. On the recording form * which is furnished with the scale there should be placed a complete and exact statement of conditions and factors, so that a second person can get a full picture of the problem. Care should also be exercised in scoring each item according to the steps in Chapter V. The interpretations in Part III should be consulted freely since they cover many types of situations. It is important to check for arithmetical errors computations such as those shown in Table III. Mistakes in addition or multiplication are more liable to occur than errors in estimating the score values of any item.

If the true spirit of social work is faithfully preserved, with honest use of the aids for specific diagnosis and remedy the Detroit Behavior Scale should prove to be an effective tool for solving maladjustments.

* Copies of the printed individual record form for use with the Detroit Behavior Scale may be procured from The Macmillan Company, 60 Fifth Avenue, New York City.

BIBLIOGRAPHY

1. GLUECK, SHELDON, and GLUECK, ELEANOR T.—*Five Hundred Criminal Careers*. New York: Alfred A. Knopf, 1930. 365 pp.

2. GLUECK, SHELDON, and GLUECK, ELEANOR T.—*One Thousand Juvenile Delinquents*. Cambridge: Harvard University Press, 1934. 341 pp.

CHAPTER V

DETAILED ITEMS OF DIAGNOSIS

THIS chapter presents the specific points of information to be gathered about each of the sixty-six items. There are three phases to each item.

First, for each item are given one or more brief but important questions to be asked of children and a similar set for parents. These key questions have been appropriately marked and are intended to bring out the pertinent facts. They are symptomatic of significant trends in each case.

Second, if these key questions bring out some important facts, there are additional questions and observations designed to disclose more details. Not all these supplementary questions are intended to be used for every item, but only for those items which the key questions have shown to be of some particular importance. These questions are by no means exhaustive but indicate the avenues of approach to the problems.

Third, the scoring is made on a five-step scale, ranging from one to five points. Detailed steps are shown which should assist in making an accurate diagnosis. It is hoped that many of the possible situations have been covered. The scheme of scoring is not intended to be arbitrary; it should be interpreted in terms of the emotional effects upon children. For example, if a child has had many illnesses but never any bad mental effects, the scoring should probably be at least one point or step better than the mere number of illnesses would indicate.

All these factors have proved useful in diagnosing and studying problems. It seemed desirable to bring them together in a convenient form. The interpretation of the items is given in Part III.

For recording the facts a special eight-page form * is offered known as "The Detroit Scale of Behavior Factors." One copy should be used for each child.

The first page contains identifying information as to name, sex, grade, school, and date of birth. The total score and rating are to be recorded and a recommendation made which will necessarily be suited to the local program of any community. The recommendation may be made in terms of a school adjustment; it may be for a placement under the direction of the juvenile court, for a change to a boarding-home environment, or for similar disposals. The agency or individual making the referral for study should be recorded. In the space entitled "Nature of the Problem" there should be recorded the type of problem which the child offers to the home or the school, the kind of trouble he makes, and the kinds of offenses of which he is considered to be guilty. Under the "Summary of Factors" should be summarized the number of items in each of the five categories with their weighted score, and below should be listed the numbers and names of the items which are rated as "very poor," or 1, and also the items which are "poor," with a rating of 2. On the remainder of this page are spaces for results of tests of intelligence and achievement, which will probably have been given or should be given for supplementary information. At the bottom of the page is space for a record of any physical examination and of recommendations as to physical corrections, such as defective vision. In some instances a separate medical and physical record will probably be available; it should be attached to this chart.

On the second page there is to be a listing of the members of the family, which should also include foster parents if there are any. The item "Heredity" should cover some statement as to grandparents and aunts or uncles, with particular note made of

* The Macmillan Company, 60 Fifth Avenue, New York City.

any evidences in them of instability, mental backwardness, or social maladjustment. The developmental history should cover the chief facts of the child's health and physical condition in early infancy, with particular attention to his being breast- or bottle-fed and to any convulsions, or seizures, or head injuries at birth.

On the third page the other agencies which have been active on the case or on the family should be listed, so that duplication of effort may be avoided. The school history should list the number of schools, grades repeated or skipped, and whether the general scholarship was good, fair, or poor. The worker's impressions should include the personal appearance of the child or of any particular phase of the problem which especially challenges his attention. The worker should also summarize the chief facts of the diagnosis and what seems to be necessary for successful treatment.

On the remainder of the third page and on the next four pages are given the sixty-six factors with space allowed for recording the chief facts. The amount of space varies depending on the kinds of factors. *It is suggested that the amount of information about any topic should never be limited to the amount of space which has been provided; additional facts should be carried over on to a supplementary sheet of paper with the items numbered. A note of such continuation should be inserted after the topic on the record blank.* If there is a long story behind any item, it should always be recorded. The final page may be used for subsequent record of later contacts or of suggestions for treatment.

In the following pages of this chapter the detailed questions and scoring are given.

1. CHILD'S EARLY HEALTH [1]

Children—How often were you sick when you were little or up to about two years ago? (Get his story as to number of times, length of time, and so on.)

[1] See page 118. See also Items 3 and 4.

Parents—Was he ill very much in childhood? Was he a constant care and source of worry from poor health?

ADDITIONAL QUESTIONS AND OBSERVATIONS

Find out the chief facts about colds, sore throat, discharging ears, and attacks of indigestion.

Was he afflicted by constipation and what was done to relieve it?

Was his vitality poor or good in early years? What was the cause of low vitality?

Did illness tend to make him more dependent upon others? Was he given too much satisfaction in this respect?

SCORING

Points   *Factors*

5.—Never or rarely ill; good vitality.

4.—Well except for occasional colds. Not more than one or two children's diseases. No upsets in habits of self-care.

3.—Ill from one to two weeks per year. Fair health, must avoid strenuous exertion. Not particularly difficult to re-establish habits after illness.

2.—Ill one or two months per year. Difficult to re-establish habits of self-care. Uses illness as alibi.

1.—Ill greater part of the time. Very nervous and dependent upon others. Refuses to accept responsibility. Must actually depend upon others to a great extent.

2.   CHILD'S PRESENT HEALTH [1]

Children—Have you been sick very much in the last two or three years?

Parents—Has he been sick very much in the last two or three years?

[1] See page 121. See Items 3 and 4.

Does he consider himself ill or well most of the time? Does he
   pretend or feign illness to avoid doing things?

Is his vitality low? Has there been any recent physical examination? What were the results?

Does he really tire easily? Does he look weak? Is his posture
   poor?

Is his appetite good or poor? (See also Item 19.)

Have illnesses seemed to make him more dependent on others
   for errands, helping to dress, and so on? What have the parents
   been able to do to offset these tendencies?

SCORING

Use the same points and factors as in Item 1.

3.   CHILDREN'S DISEASES [1]

Children—What children's diseases have you had? (Allow the
         subject to tell; but if he hesitates, suggest some listed
         under "Additional Questions and Observations.") At
         what age for each? How long were you sick? Were
         there any complications?

Parents—What children's diseases did he have? Have the parent
        tell; suggest some if necessary.

Suggested diseases: measles, whooping cough, chicken pox,
   mumps, tonsillitis, quinsy, mastoiditis, ear infection, boils,
   pinkeye, jaundice, impetigo, etc.

Get a complete medical or hospital report.

Make note of the effects upon habits of self-care, upon general
   initiative, or on change in personality pattern.

[1] See page 127. See also Item 4.

Points   *Factors*

5.—Has had none.
4.—Has had only one children's disease.
3.—Has had two or three children's diseases.
2.—Has had four or five children's diseases.
1.—Has had six or more children's diseases.

The degree or severity should have some weight. For example, if
the number was two or three but very severe, the item should
be scored two points instead of three.

If the mental effects seem pronounced, score one point lower; if
quite unnoticeable, score one point higher than the number of
diseases alone would indicate.

4. SERIOUS INFECTIOUS DISEASES [1]

Children—What serious infectious diseases or big sicknesses have
you had? (Allow the subject to tell; but if he hesi-
tates, suggest some listed under "Additional Questions and Observations.")
At what age? How long were you sick? Were there
any complications?

Parents—What serious infectious diseases did he have? Have
the parent tell, but suggest from the list if necessary.
Age? Length of time? Complications?

ADDITIONAL QUESTIONS AND OBSERVATIONS

Suggested diseases: scarlet fever, typhoid fever, smallpox, diphtheria, pneumonia, sleeping sickness (encephalitis), infantile
paralysis, tuberculosis, epilepsy. See also Item 12.

Get a detailed report on the length of time, severity, conditions
of care, quarantine, and so on.

[1] See page 129.

Find the effects on self-care, initiative, and changes in personality.

SCORING

Use the same points and factors as for Item 3.

5. ACCIDENTS [1]

Children—Have you ever had a bad fall or accident? Have you had more than one? If so, how many?

Parents—Did he ever have a serious accident or fall? At what age? What seemed to be the. mental or emotional effects?

ADDITIONAL QUESTIONS AND OBSERVATIONS

Is the subject inclined to be awkward and careless or were the accidents unavoidable?

What specific injuries were incurred, such as broken arm, broken leg, and so on?

Get a detailed report from the physician or hospital.

SCORING

Points   *Factors*

5.—No accidents.

4.—One accident; no particular mental effects.

3.—Two or three accidents; treated once in hospital.

2.—Four or five accidents; treated for about one month for one accident.

1.—Six or more accidents; was in hospital for six or more months with one of them.

If the mental and emotional effects seem to have been unusually pronounced, score one point less than the number calls for. If

[1] See page 139.

the effects seem negligible, score one point more than the number.

6. Degree of Speech Defect [1]

Children—Do you speak plainly and easily? Have you ever had any trouble with speech, such as lisping or stuttering?

Parents—Does he have any speech defect? What kind? Lisping? Baby talk? Stammering? Stuttering? When did it begin?

ADDITIONAL QUESTIONS AND OBSERVATIONS

Make your own observations from the conversation you have with him.

If there is any degree of defect, estimate how serious it is and of what type.

Lisping, baby talk, stammering, stuttering, indistinct speech? Is there a negative attitude toward speech?

Is the defect caused by a physical malformation or is it purely a mental problem?

Is he particularly disturbed and blocked by it? Do other children ridicule him? How does he take it?

Does he seem to be getting slowly better or worse? What is being done about it?

What seems to be the chief cause?

SCORING

Points　　　　　　　*Factors*

5.—No defect. Clear and distinct speech.

4.—Usually talks clearly; stutters a little when he gets excited.

3.—Has speech defect, such as lisping, from malformed organs of speech, but no bad mental effects.

[1] See page 135.

2.—Has defective speech much of the time; worse at some times than others.

1.—Chronic case; no particular hope of cure; has feelings of social inferiority.

7. Degree of Vision Defect [1]

Children—Did you ever wear glasses or do you now? Do your eyes hurt? Can you see the blackboard from where you sit? Do you have headaches from your eyes?

Parents—Do you know whether he has any trouble with his eyes? Does he squint? Is he fussy and nervous when he tries to read? Does he wear glasses?

ADDITIONAL QUESTIONS AND OBSERVATIONS

Check his obvious vision with a standard eye chart.

If necessary to consult an eye specialist, get exact prescription.

Is there a defect in mechanical condition, such as myopia, hyperopia, strabismus, astigmatism, or other type of heterophoria?

Is there any disease of the eye such as cataract, glaucoma, trachoma, or pinkeye?

How does the condition affect his school work; his play, such as baseball; his general nervous condition?

Does he seem confused in direction?

SCORING

Points   *Factors*

5.—Eyes apparently normal without glasses.

4.—20/30 or better in both eyes with glasses.

3.—20/40 to 20/50 in one or both eyes with glasses.

2.—20/60 to 20/70 in one or both eyes with glasses.

1.—Both eyes poorer than 20/70 with glasses.

[1] See page 138.

Score one point higher or lower if the mental condition seems to warrant it.

8.   DEGREE OF HEARING DEFECT [1]

Children—Do you have any trouble hearing people talk? Can you hear well in school? Do you have trouble with running ears?

Parents—Does he seem to have any trouble hearing? Do his ears run? If he does not pay attention, is it a habit or is it poor hearing?

ADDITIONAL QUESTIONS AND OBSERVATIONS

Check his hearing, if at all doubtful, by using a low conversational voice at distances of twenty feet or less. Keep the examiner's mouth hidden by a book or paper so that the subject cannot read lips. Note the distance where hearing occurs.

Does he seem slow to respond to questions or in conversation? Have the parents tried to test him in language uses?

Does he hold his head to one side in listening?

Are there any conditions of running ears? Mastoiditis? Has it been necessary to have a puncture of the membrane?

If an ear specialist has been consulted, what were his diagnosis and recommendation?

SCORING

Points	*Factors*
5.—	Hears conversational voice at twenty feet or further.
4.—	Hears conversational voice at from seventeen to nineteen feet.
3.—	Hears from twelve to sixteen feet.
2.—	Hears from six to eleven feet.
1.—	Hears from five feet or less or totally deaf.

[1] See page 147.

Score one point higher or lower if the mental condition seems to warrant it.

9. DEGREE OF ORTHOPEDIC DEFECT [1]

Children—Are you crippled in any way? Did you ever limp? Did you have any trouble with or defects of arms or legs? Of any other parts of the body? Can you run and exercise as well as other boys?

Parents—Has he any crippled condition? Can he stand up straight? Can he run and walk as well as other children? Have any bones ever been broken? Did they heal properly?

ADDITIONAL QUESTIONS AND OBSERVATIONS

Get a complete description of the nature of any crippled defect. What was the cause: accident, infantile paralysis, osteomyelitis, or something else?

Length of time: time in hospital, time in bed, how long on crutches, how long unable to walk or play actively?

If unable to play actively, what have been the emotional effects? What compensations does he cultivate?

Is he attempting to harmonize his defect to a suitable vocational and occupational choice?

SCORING

Points   *Factors*

5.—No orthopedic defect or condition.

4.—A defect but not affecting legs.

3.—Cannot run or play actively; uses a cane.

2.—On crutches or in wheel chair for most of time.

1.—Completely handicapped and cannot get around; attitude of helplessness.

[1] See page 153.

10. Size for Age [1]

Children—Are you small, large, or average for your age?

Parents—Is he large, small, or average for his age? Has he always been large or small?

TABLE V. Norms for Height and Weight

	Boys				Girls			
HEIGHT IN INCHES	WEIGHT IN POUNDS	AGE IN YEARS AND MONTHS	15 PER CENT UNDER-WEIGHT POUNDS	15 PER CENT OVER-WEIGHT POUNDS	WEIGHT IN POUNDS	AGE IN YEARS AND MONTHS	15 PER CENT UNDER-WEIGHT POUNDS	15 PER CENT OVER-WEIGHT POUNDS
27	21	1– 0	18	24	20	1– 0	17	23
28	23	1– 2	19	26	22	1– 2	18	25
29	24	1– 5	20	28	23	1– 5	19	26
30	26	1– 7	22	29	25	1– 7	21	29
31	27	1–10	23	31	27	1– 9	23	31
32	28	2– 0	24	32	29	1–11	25	33
33	29	2– 3	25	33	30	2– 3	26	35
34	30	2– 6	26	35	31	2– 7	26	36
35	31	2–10	26	36	32	3– 0	27	37
36	32	3– 2	27	37	34	3– 6	29	39
37	34	3– 7	29	39	35	4– 0	30	40
38	35	4– 0	30	40	36	4– 4	31	41
39	37	4– 4	31	43	37	4– 8	31	43
40	39	4– 8	33	44	38	4–11	32	44
41	40	5– 0	34	46	39	5– 4	33	45
42	41	5– 4	35	47	41	5– 9	35	47
43	42	5– 8	36	48	42	6– 2	36	48
44	44	6– 0	37	52	46	6– 8	39	53
45	48	6– 6	41	55	49	7– 2	40	56
46	51	7– 0	43	59	51	7– 8	43	59
47	55	7– 6	47	63	53	8– 2	44	61
48	57	8– 0	48	66	55	8– 8	47	63
49	59	8– 6	50	68	57	9– 2	48	66
50	61	9– 0	52	70	60	9– 7	51	69
51	64	9– 6	54	74	62	10– 0	53	71
52	67	10– 0	57	77	65	10– 6	55	75
53	70	10– 8	60	81	68	11– 0	58	78
54	73	11– 4	62	84	72	11– 5	61	83
55	76	12– 0	65	87	76	11–10	65	87
56	79	12– 6	68	91	80	12– 3	68	92
57	83	13– 0	71	95	84	12– 9	71	97
58	87	13– 6	74	100	89	13– 3	76	102
59	91	14– 0	77	105	93	13– 8	79	107
60	94	14– 4	80	108	98	14– 1	83	113
61	97	14– 8	82	112	104	15– 0	88	120
62	101	15– 0	86	116	110	16– 0	94	127
63	109	15– 6	93	125	118	17– 0	100	136
64	118	16– 0	100	136				
65	124	16– 6	105	142				
66	130	17– 0	111	150				

[1] See page 156.

If more than 15 per cent overweight, is there a glandular deficiency or is it a natural condition for him?

If more than 15 per cent underweight, is there a condition of malnutrition?

See Table V for norms on height and weight. They are the averages of all norms available from various studies. Interpret first in terms of height and second of weight. A ten-year-old boy, 55 inches in height, is said to be the height of a twelve-year-old with a weight of 62 pounds and is more than 15 per cent underweight for his height. In computing the general size for the scoring consider both height and weight. Give more consideration to height for age comparison but more to weight for general physical condition.

SCORING

Points   *Factors*

5.—Less than one year's deviation from average for age.

4.—One to two years undersized for age.

3.—One to two years oversized for age.

2.—Two or more years undersized for age.

1.—Two or more years oversized for age.

11. MOTOR CONTROL AND MUSCULAR CO-ORDINATION [1]

Children—Do you think you are more or less awkward in your actions and movements than other boys or just average?

Parents—Does he seem more or less awkward or graceful in actions and movement or average? How was he when a small child?

Is his handwriting acceptable for his age and grade? Better or poorer? Is he left-handed or right-handed?

[1] See page 160.

Is his work in the school shop good, fair, or poor? In art?

Does he handle himself well or poorly in the gymnasium?

Is he handy with tools around home, in dressing himself, and in running, swimming, and other sports?

If he is poor, does he feel inferior about it?

The Whipple-Healy Tapping Test is a simple device for measuring one's elementary skill. It consists of half-inch squares, ten to a row with fifteen rows; it is sold by C. H. Stoelting and Company, Chicago. The score is the best of two half-minute trials in tapping one dot to each square with a pencil. The norms are as follows:

Months	Years											
	5	6	7	8	9	10	11	12	13	14	15	16
0	21	33	41	46	51	58	64	68	72	76	80	84
3	24	36	42	47	53	60	65	69	73	77	81	
6	27	39	43	48	55	62	66	70	74	78	82	
9	30	40	44	49	56	63	67	71	75	79	83	

SCORING

Points   *Factors*

5.—Apparently normal.

4.—About one year accelerated above chronological age.

3.—About one year retarded below chronological age.

2.—Unusually skillful and adept for age.

1.—Obviously extremely backward in these respects.

12. Convulsions, Seizures [1]

Children—Do you ever get dizzy or faint or feel unsteady on your feet?

Parents—Has he ever had dizzy spells? Does he faint easily? Is he unsteady on his feet? Is there any actual epilepsy, either petit mal or grand mal?

[1] See page 165.

Find out what spells or unusual comas existed in early babyhood.

Does he ever jerk violently and suddenly?

If there is actual epilepsy, what are the frequency and severity of the seizures? Is there stiffness, screaming, or subsequent exhaustion? What is the length of time?

Does he have an unusually cross and difficult disposition, which is frequently characteristic of epilepsy?

Was there any evidence of active sleeping sickness in childhood, or of unusual drowsiness?

SCORING

Points   *Factors*

5.—Apparently no evidence of any such symptoms.

4.—Suspected of such symptoms, but no one will admit it.

3.—Has had or does have occasional mild attacks.

2.—Frequent attacks of moderate severity or severe attacks infrequently.

1.—Violent attacks very frequently, many times daily. Light attacks with varying frequency but with serious emotional mental consequences.

13. NERVOUSNESS [1]

Children—Do you think you are more or less fussy and nervous than others of your age or about the average? Can you sit quite still and calm for short periods?

Parents—Does he seem to be more or less fussy and nervous than other children of his age or average? Has he been better or worse than now in early years of childhood?

[1] See page 168.

Can he sit still? Does he always want to be fussing with something with his hands?

Do his eyes water easily or twitch or blink? Are there any jerking muscles or tics about his face? Does he bite his nails much?

Is he impatient or does he lose his temper easily? Does he cry easily? Does he talk or walk in his sleep? Must he go to the toilet often? Does he wet the bed (enuresis)?

Did he ever have any severe shock or scare or sickness which seemed to make him more nervous? Is he afraid of anyone, particularly in the family or among neighbors?

A simple test is to observe whether he can remain calm and steady when asked to stretch out his fingers with outstretched arms in front of him and hold them very tense for a moment or so.

Is he too calm and composed, too cool and calculating?

SCORING

Points *Factors*

5.—Calm and comfortably composed most of the time.

4.—Has short periods of some restlessness.

3.—Quite restless at times; tires easily; does not concentrate well in school or on easy tasks at home.

2.—Has considerable tremor of muscles of eyes.

1.—Constantly on the move; playing or fussing with hands; in a state of trembling and restlessness.

14. PERSONAL HYGIENE AND CLOTHING [1]

Children—Do you think that you keep your clothing looking as neat as other children of your age do, about the same, or better? Do you keep your hands and face as clean as others do? How often do you get clean clothes?

[1] See page 175.

Parents—Is it easy or difficult to keep him as clean as other children of his age? Compare children of the same sex. Does he take responsibility for washing, changing to clean clothes, and washing his face and hands?

ADDITIONAL QUESTIONS AND OBSERVATIONS

Note the actual condition of his clothes to-day. Are they clean or dirty? Do they fit fairly well? Does he take any pride in his appearance?

Does he have regular habits of washing his hands? Does he have a regular place for a towel and a wash cloth of his own?

How often does he brush his teeth? Does he comb his hair regularly? Does he brush his shoes and his clothes?

Does he look better, poorer, or the same as the average of his neighborhood group?

With young children who are lax, suggest a chart of gold stars to be awarded at home by parents for improvement in these factors.

SCORING

Points   *Factors*

5.—Well dressed; neat and clean as to body and clothes.

4.—Has good clothes, but poorly cared for. Has rather poor clothes but very well cared for.

3.—Has fair clothes but keeps them in only fair condition. Is rather careless about personal cleanliness.

2.—Rather dirty clothes; wears clothes handed down from older children; no pride. Careless and rarely washes hands.

1.—Chronically dirty and ragged; no self-pride; no one in family takes any interest in his appearance.

15. LOOKS OR APPEARANCE [1]

Children—Do you think you are good-looking? Are you better or worse than your playmates or are you average?

Parents—Do you think he is good, poor, or average in appearance? What effect does it have on his contacts with others?

ADDITIONAL QUESTIONS AND OBSERVATIONS

Study the facial features of the subject carefully. If there is anything unusual, analyze what it is and what its effect seems to be on others.

Do others quickly like him or are they repulsed?

Does he have good social qualities which tend to offset any unfavorable personal impression? What are they?

If he is very good-looking, does he take undesirable advantage of this quality by imposing himself upon his friends and playmates?

If he is unfortunate in appearance, does he tend to make himself disagreeable to gain some sort of unfavorable reputation?

Does he make friends easily or very slowly? Is his appearance the cause?

Are his mannerisms more noticeable to adults or to children?

SCORING

Points   *Factors*

5.—Quite good-looking and agreeable to others.

4.—Of average appearance, with fair traits.

3.—Extremely good-looking or pretty and spoiled easily on account of this fact.

2.—Rather unattractive on first acquaintance. Very attractive in appearance but capitalizes the fact in undesirable ways.

[1] See page 178.

1.—**Very** homely and repulsive. Has poor social traits and little hope of change.

16.   EARLY SELF-CARE [1]

Children—Did you wash and dress yourself all alone by the time you were in the first grade? Earlier or later?

Parents—Did he wash and dress himself at about the age of six? Earlier or later?

ADDITIONAL QUESTIONS AND OBSERVATIONS

Get a complete story from the parents, particularly the mother, on his early self-care.

When was he able to care for his own toilet habits? Did he do it willingly?

When did he learn to wait on himself at the table? Was he handy or awkward at it? See also Item 11.

Were there many problems of discipline growing out of these habit-forming situations? What were some of them? How were they handled?

Was he fairly rapid or did he dawdle and waste much time?

SCORING

Points   *Factors*

5.—Able and willing to dress himself at the usual age.

4.—Would try most of the time but occasionally refused to do it for himself.

3.—Spent too much time; needed much urging.

2.—Had to be coaxed a great deal; could not establish any regular habits; slow; no interest.

1.—Utterly refused; made a scene; was always in trouble with parents about it. Had a maid to do it or someone in the family who always did everything for him.

[1] See page 181.

17. PRESENT SELF-CARE [1]

Children—Do you gladly and quickly dress and wash yourself? Have you established regular habits?

Parents—Do you continually have to remind him to do things for himself? Describe his habits of self-care as to dressing and washing.

ADDITIONAL QUESTIONS AND OBSERVATIONS

The questions and observations must vary with the age of the subject.

Do you have a regular time and place for dressing and a regular place to keep your clothes? Do you keep them there?

Do you change to clean clothes often without being reminded?

Has he made a regular system out of these habits? Is it a nightmare of hit-and-miss efforts?

Do you have your own towel and wash cloth? Your own tooth brush? Do you use it regularly?

Is he good or poor about keeping his clothes clean at school? Does he willingly change his clothes when doing any dirty work?

SCORING

Points   *Factors*

5.—Takes full responsibility and seems to enjoy it.

4.—Tries to do pretty well most of the time but has lapses and is not entirely dependable.

3.—Does fairly well but needs constant supervision; no particular place or system of organization.

2.—Generally poor and haphazard except for occasional items or times.

1.—No system; needs constant urging; does the least possible; takes no pride in caring for himself.

[1] See page 181.

18. Home Duties [1]

Children—What regular jobs do you have to do to help around home?

Parents—What regular jobs does he have around the house? Does he do them without urging?

ADDITIONAL QUESTIONS AND OBSERVATIONS

Get a list of the regular and special things which he does around the house.

If he has none, whose responsibility is it?

Does he have a feeling of responsibility or must he always be urged?

What other jobs might be assigned to him?

Does he expect to be paid for doing them? What rewards are given?

If a girl, is she encouraged to buy the food and plan and cook some meals?

Does she help make her own clothes and care for her own room?

Are these things matters of discord and continual urging?

SCORING

Points   *Factors*

5.—Reasonable number of tasks, done regularly and willingly.

4.—Has to work most of the time; is fairly willing.

3.—Has some duties, not regular; very little planning or organization.

2.—Forced to work all the time; no time for recreation.

1.—No duties; encouraged to despise any work. Rebels and absolutely will not accept any duties.

[1] See page 185.

19. CONDITIONS OF EATING [1]

Children—How many times a day does the whole family eat together? Is there enough food for all?

Parents—How many times a day do all eat together? Does
everyone seem to enjoy it? Is there enough food for
all?

ADDITIONAL QUESTIONS AND OBSERVATIONS

Is there a good variety of food? Is there a balance of fruit and
vegetables? Are there chiefly starchy foods, as white bread and
potatoes? Is there milk or do the children drink coffee two or
three times a day?

Is the food well or poorly prepared? Does the mother have good,
fair, or poor ability as a cook? Are the children required to eat
when the food is poorly prepared?

Is the quantity sufficient or too little? Are too small helpings
given, so that the child feels slighted or unwanted? Is too much
put on the child's plate?

Is the food warm and do all eat together or is eating a continual
process?

Does the child eat between meals? Does he eat enough candy to
spoil his appetite? Does he eat just before going to bed? Does
he hurry the meal to get out to play?

SCORING

Points   *Factors*

5.—Regular time to eat; excellent variety of food; well prepared.

4.—One of foregoing three factors undesirable, such as no variety of food but well prepared and regularly eaten.

3.—Some irregularity; variable provision for variety; food
prepared rather indifferently.

[1] See page 188.

2.—Three factors rather poor or two very poor and one fair, such as fair food but very irregular and very poorly prepared.

1.—All factors very poor; no variety in food; poor diet for children.

20.   Eating Habits [1]

Children—What kinds of foods are there that you do not like very well? Do you eat just a few kinds of foods only?

Parents—What kinds of foods are there that he does not like? Is he very fussy or particular about his food?

ADDITIONAL QUESTIONS AND OBSERVATIONS

Does he make a scene about eating? Is he ever punished or sent away from the table because of his eating?

Does he eat too fast or too slowly? Does he chew his food well? Does he complain of stomache-ache or indigestion?

Will he try new kinds of foods? Does he persistently demand only a few foods?

If he is chronically malnourished, find out what food or diet is recommended. Does he faithfully carry out the instructions?

Is he neat about his eating habits or does he become careless and make messes of his food?

If possible, observe his eating at school or in home.

SCORING

Points   *Factors*

5.—Has good habits of eating; willing to try new foods.

4.—Fairly good, but not very willing to try new foods; sometimes hurries too much.

[1] See page 191.

3.—Eating habits only fair; insists on a few simple foods.

2.—Eats alone much of time; is unsupervised; eats very rapidly and is rather untidy about it.

1.—Continually creates scenes at table; nervous and irritable about foods; practically uncontrolled; no one interested in improving his habits.

21. Time of Sleeping [1]

Children—Do you usually get enough sleep? What time do you go to bed? Do you go to sleep quickly?

Parents—What time does he go to bed? Does he get enough sleep?

ADDITIONAL QUESTIONS AND OBSERVATIONS

Get a descriptive account of his time-of-sleeping habits.

At what time does he go to bed on school nights? At what time does he go to bed on other nights? Is he usually short of sleep for Monday? Is he usually short of sleep for any other day?

Is he slow about going to sleep? Does he sleep soundly or wake easily?

If the hours are late, find out why and see what can be done to remedy the situation.

TABLE VI. AVERAGE NUMBER OF HOURS OF SLEEP BY AGE GROUPS IN WESTERN UNITED STATES [2]

Age in Years	Number	Hours	Age in Years	Number	Hours
6–7	37	11.14	13–14	250	9.31
7–8	147	10.41	14–15	244	9.06
8–9	218	10.42	15–16	201	8.54
9–10	291	10.13	16–17	167	8.30
10–11	307	9.56	17–18	113	8.46
11–12	282	10.00	18–19	43	8.46
12–13	312	9.36	University students	51	7.47

[1] See page 194. See also Items 22 and 23.

[2] Compiled by Terman and Hocking. Quoted by permission of the publisher.

SCORING

Points   *Factors*

   5.—Regular hours, with plenty of sleep.
   4.—Usually good amount of sleep but with occasional marked variation.
   3.—Average hours of sleep but often varies from schedule.
   2.—Always a little short of sleep; stays out late.
   1.—Very short of sleep; no regular habits; always disturbed late in the evening or early in the morning.

22.   SLEEPING CONDITIONS [1]

Children—Do you sleep well or are you disturbed? Do you sleep alone? If not, with whom? Is the bed comfortable?

Parents—Does he sleep well or is he disturbed? Does he rouse easily? Does he sleep alone? If not, with whom?

ADDITIONAL QUESTIONS AND OBSERVATIONS

Get a description of the bed, type of springs and mattress, and kinds of bed clothes. Is there too little or too much bedding? Inspect it if occasion presents.

Is it clean or dirty? How often are the sheets and pillow cases changed? Are there vermin?

How is the ventilation? Is there too little good air? Is there a stove in the room? Is the heat always on?

Does he require a light? Must someone else always be in the room? Is he afraid?

Does he sleep quietly or snore? Does he toss around? Does his tossing cause trouble with others? Has he enuresis?

Who sleeps with him? Are they desirable or undesirable companions? Are they of the same age or of different age? Are they of different sex? Are there any suspected sex relations? Is there any self-abuse?

[1] See page 197. See also Items 21 and 23.

Points   *Factors*

5.—Comfortable bed; sleeps alone; never disturbed.

4.—Fair or good bed; others sleep in the same room in other beds.

3.—Fair or good bed; sleeps with other children of the same sex and age.

2.—Poor bed; frequently disturbed; sleeps with one parent, often of opposite sex.

1.—Miserable bed; crowded; sleeps with roomer or with adult of opposite sex.

23. DREAMS [1]

Children—Tell me about some dream you have had. Do you dream very much?

Parents—Does he tell of dreaming very much? What does he dream about? Do his dreams reflect any emotional conflicts?

ADDITIONAL QUESTIONS AND OBSERVATIONS

How often are there dreams? If every night, investigate such factors as being too tired, poor bed, or improper sleeping companions.

Does he have scary dreams of ghosts, goblins, or witches?

Does he dream of getting rich or being rich and what he would do with the money? Does he dream of what he would like to do best of all?

Does he dream of being chased by men in the dark, of being out on the street naked, or of falling?

Is he usually sad or happy in his dreams?

If he walks in his sleep, what are some of the causes?

[1] See page 199.

What does he think causes his dreams?
Is he afraid to go to bed? Is he afraid of being alone in the dark?

Points   *Factors*

5.—No dreams or occasional meaningless ones.

4.—Mostly negative or meaningless dreams but has them frequently.

3.—Dreams often; some of the dreams symptomatic; discusses them in the daytime.

2.—Disturbed practically every night by dreams; dreams of falling or of fears.

1.—Has night terrors; becomes hysterical; walks in his sleep.

24. EARLY RECREATIONAL FACILITIES [1]

Children—Did you have many toys to play with when you were small? What were some of them?

Parents—What toys did he have to play with when he was small? Did he take good care of them? Did he break them quickly?

ADDITIONAL QUESTIONS AND OBSERVATIONS

Did he have too few or no playthings? Did he always have to share with others so that he had no feeling of ownership?

Did he have too many playthings? Were they always around in the way? Was there any place for them? Did he try to put them away?

Did he seem to play with a purpose or was it sporadic and incidental?

Did he have constructive playthings, such as a workbench and tools?

[1] See page 202. See also Item 25.

Did he ever build a little shack, dig a tunnel, or have a sandbox?
Did he have swings or trapezes?
Did he get along well in playing with others or was there continual strife?
Did he play mostly at home or with others away from home?
What pets did he have?

Points   *Factors*

5.—A fair variety of playthings; kept them in order; played with a purpose.
4.—Had a fair number, but was not very good about order or purpose.
3.—Had a few things but no place for them; broke them and was careless with them.
2.—Had very few things; no regular place for them; played with no good purpose.
1.—No playthings; no particular place to play. Some playthings; always a source of trouble with others; no place for playthings and no organization in play.

25. LATER RECREATIONAL FACILITIES [1]

Children—How do you amuse yourself after school, on Saturdays, or during vacation? What do you have to play with?

Parents—What does he have to play with? How does he spend his playtime?

ADDITIONAL QUESTIONS AND OBSERVATIONS

What specific things does he have to play with? With what does he amuse himself?
Is there a purpose in his play or is it spasmodic and of no educational value?

[1] See page 202. See also Items 24 and 34.

Does he play at having shows or at make-believe school? Does
he play ball, skate, or build model houses?

Does he have a pet and does he care for it well?

Does he get any companionship with his parents through sharing
play and recreation with them?

Does he complain that time hangs heavy on his hands?

SCORING

Points   *Factors*

5.—Has a few well-organized things to do and desirable companions in doing them.

4.—Has good attitude but little opportunity to play or express
himself constructively with companions.

3.—Except for one or two things or for short periods, does not
know what to do.

2.—Has little to play with; is alone most of time; has no particular purpose or drive to activities.

1.—No purpose in play activities; no place to play; playthings
in poor shape; plays mostly away from home; no interest on parents' part.

26. PLAYMATES OR COMPANIONS [1]

Children—Who is your best pal or friend, either boy or girl? Do
you have more than one? What do you do when you
are together?

Parents—Who are his best friends? Are they desirable or undesirable? What do they do when they are together?

ADDITIONAL QUESTIONS AND OBSERVATIONS

Do they live near, next door, on the same street, or at a distance,
or are they seen only at school?

Are they in the same grade or class in school or in a different one?

[1] See page 206.

Are they older or younger? How much? Why were they selected
if there is much difference in age?

Who is the leader, your child or his friend?

What do they do? Do they play ball, listen to the radio, or work
at projects and hobbies or do they merely squander their time?

Does he play much with his own brothers or sisters? Are they
friendly or unfriendly?

Does he go to the houses of others or have them in his own
home? Do they often eat or sleep at one another's homes?

Does he have a gang with a regular meeting place? Is it considered undesirable by the police or the neighborhood?

Does he play alone? Why? What has been done about it?

The following questions on sex matters should be used, if at
all, with extreme care and caution. Workers of the same sex as
the children are recommended in preference to those of the opposite sex. It requires extreme care and tact to make successful
and constructive suggestions. Parents might well be consulted in
advance as to the desirability of asking any of these questions;
otherwise they may have legitimate cause for complaint.

Sex Questions for Boys

Have you a girl? In what school is she? How old is she? How
often do you see her? What do you usually do together? Do
you see her alone or in groups? Where do you see her? How
many girls have you had? How often have you changed? Do
the girls like you?

What trouble have you ever had with girls? Did you ever get
into any trouble with girls?

How many girls have you kissed?

Have you ever gone farther than kissing (have relations) with
girls? When was the first time? Did you ever do anything like
that when you were little? How many times have you done it
since? Did some other boy persuade you to try it? Did the
girl want you to? Did you ever force a girl? Did you ever pay
a girl? Did you ever go to a bad house? Were you warned

about venereal disease? Did you ever go to a doctor about venereal disease?

Do you want to get married? Do you want to have children? Why? Have you ever been in love with a good girl? Have you ever known a girl you wanted to marry? Did she turn you down? Did you hate all women after that? How did you feel?

Do you know any boys who go farther than kissing with girls? How do you know? Did they tell you about it? Is it with their friends or do they pay girls? Do they try to persuade you to follow their example? Do they go to bad houses? Do they try to get you to come, too?

Did any of your friends ever get a girl into trouble? What did they do about it? What would you do if you got a girl into trouble?

Where did you first get your sex information? Who first told you about where babies come from and all that?

Do you believe boys and girls should have intercourse or relations before they marry? Do you think men should have sex relations with other girls before they marry and settle down?

Sex Questions for Girls of Any Age

Do you generally play with boys or girls or both? What do you play together?

Have you a boy friend? How many boy friends have you? How often do you go with boys? Where do you go? Does your mother know where you go? How often do you have boys at your house? Do you have them alone or in groups?

Do any of the girls you know talk about dirty (impure) things with one another or with boys or write dirty notes or do evil (sinful) things?

Have they tried to make you do the same? How many times did you? When was the last time?

Who first told you about where babies come from? Did you ever discuss it with your mother or older sister? Have you a married sister or friend? Does she talk to you about married life? What does she tell you?

Sex Questions for Older Girls

How often do you go out with boys or have them come to your house? How old are they and what grade are they in? Have they cars? Where do you go with them? Does your mother know and approve of this? Do you go with boys alone or in groups?

How many times have you been kissed?

Have any of the girls you know gone farther than kissing (petting) with the boys?

Have you ever gone farther than necking? If not, why not? Have any boys tried to persuade you into going the limit? Have any men (boys) tried to force you into going the limit? Have any men (boys) offered you money for it?

Have any of the girls you know ever had intercourse with boys or men? Have they told you all about it? Have they tried to persuade you to do it? Were you ever a witness to such an act? Do these girls receive money? Have any of them ever had a disease? Have you been warned about venereal diseases?

Did any of your relations, sisters, or friends have a baby before they were married? Did they have to get married because they were going to have one?

Do you think girls should have intercourse with boys (men) before marriage? Why?

Do you want to get married? Do you want to keep house? Do you want to have children? How many? Why?

SCORING

Points *Factors*

5.—Several friends, apparently desirable, good, or wholesome; play projects.

4.—Several friends, some much older or younger, one or two of doubtful character.

3.—Mostly isolated; takes little interest in friends; prefers to work or play alone.

2.—Has many friends; plays away from home most of the time; parents know little of play activities.

1.—Entirely unsupervised; runs with lawless gang. Known to be practicing sex or homosexual relations.

27. SOCIAL TYPE [1]

Children—Do you get along with others well or poorly? Do you quarrel or fight? Do you run away from others? With whom do you get along best among your playmates? The poorest?

Parents—What types of people does he prefer and choose as friends? Does he seem happy or unhappy with his playmates?

ADDITIONAL QUESTIONS AND OBSERVATIONS

Does he make friends easily or with difficulty?

Do other children pick on him? Is he easily teased? Does he tease others? Relate actual incidents.

Does he seem to be shy and reserved or is he a boisterous type?

Is he a good sport when a joke is on him? Can he lose in a game with good grace or does he get angry?

Can other children get him into trouble easily? Does he get others into trouble?

How well does he get along with his brothers and sisters?

Is he very confidential with just one pal or playmate?

Does he ever pretend that he is the hero in a rescue or that he is a cowboy or a crook?

SCORING

Points	Factors

5.—Has a fine balance of social traits; not easily upset; does not quarrel.

[1] See page 213.

4.—Quiet, reserved, rather slow in making friends but does well after some period of acquaintanceship.

3.—Very boisterous; takes too much initiative; many others are a little suspicious of or offended by him.

2.—Extreme extrovert, crude; can make no real friends except one or two who are similar; classed as bad at school and in neighborhood.

1.—Very introvert; has no friends; distinctly antisocial. Repulsive, insulting, inconsiderate, uncouth.

28. PERSONALITY TYPE [1]

Children—Do you get upset and quarrel easily or do things seldom bother you very much? Relate some experience. Are you cheerful or gloomy?

Parents—Is he easily upset or do things usually go quite smoothly? Does he seem to be optimistic or pessimistic and, if variable, in what situations? Is he changeable in his moods or fairly uniform?

ADDITIONAL QUESTIONS AND OBSERVATIONS

Do you daydream very much and, if so, about what things?

Do you think hateful and revengeful things much of the time or do you seldom have such thoughts?

Are you cheerful most of the time or sad? Do you become easily discouraged? Do you worry about many things that never happen?

Are you changeable according to the time of day or as to how you feel about things in general or do you have little change?

Do you believe you have mostly desirable traits that make people like you or do you feel inadequate in this respect?

Can you concentrate well at school or in play or at any task or are you flighty?

[1] See page 219. See also Items 29, 30, 31, and 32.

Relate some experiences on the foregoing points of both desirable and undesirable situations.

SCORING

Points   *Factors*

5.—Well balanced in personality; not easily upset.

4.—Is somewhat upset and stirred up by an occasional situation. May be quite pessimistic on one or two topics but generally good balance.

3.—Is rather erratic and variable in moods; is upset easily in some situations.

2.—Extremely apathetic or unemotional in certain types of situations.

1.—Very emotional and flighty; easily upset; does many rash things upon the impulse of the moment.

29. ANGER, RAGE, REVENGE, ETC. [1]

Children—Do you have a quick temper? Do you get angry (mad) easily? Do you have a strong desire to get even with people?

Parents—Does he have a quick temper? Does he become angry easily? Does he always try to get even?

ADDITIONAL QUESTIONS AND OBSERVATIONS

How often does he get angry? How long does it usually last?

What situations or persons tend to upset him? Get details as to indirect relationships of causes.

Does he throw things, have temper tantrums, scream, or kick things?

Is he ever cruel to people? Does he ever try to harm them?

[1] See page 225.

Does he fly off the handle easily without particular cause or does he remain well controlled most of the time?

Does he remember grudges for a long time or are they soon forgotten?

Do the parents or others give in to him for fear of injury? How do they treat the situation?

If he cannot get even with someone, what does he plan or dream of doing to get even?

SCORING

Points   *Factors*

5.—Very calm and composed; rarely disturbed except for a righteous cause.

4.—Generally good poise but is easily upset in one or two kinds of situations.

3.—Harbors grudges; must be handled rather carefully or gets in fit of anger and rage.

2.—In trouble much of the time; looks for slights; tries to get revenge; seldom forgives.

1.—Lives in state of continual anger and rage; nothing is right. Upset by slightest provocation. No one seems able to improve matters.

30. FEAR, DREAD, ANXIETY, ETC. [1]

Children—Do you worry very much? About what things do you worry? Of what things are you afraid? Are you afraid of any persons? Who are they? Why are you afraid?

Parents—Does he worry much? Is he afraid of any persons or things? Is this something existing from early childhood?

[1] See page 230.

Is he afraid of certain persons all the time? What new types of strangers does he fear? What actual causes, if any, does he have for such fear?

Is he afraid of animals? Of what kind is he afraid? What are the reasons, such as scared or bitten by a dog?

Is he afraid of storms, of lightning, of the dark, or of being left alone?

Does he dread to start new jobs, to go to new places, to meet new people, or to start in a new school?

Is he likely to worry about things before he goes to sleep?

Does he ever get very moody and despondent over these worries? Has he ever talked seriously of killing himself?

Is he of the extremely opposite type? Are there no fears, dreads, or worries? Is he indifferent to everything?

SCORING

Points　　　　　　　　*Factors*

5.—Seems to have a desirable minimum of these traits but not alarmingly devoid of them.

4.—Is generally good but inclined to be quite upset over one or two things at occasional intervals.

3.—Variable; likely to be upset at any time. Worries about and dreads to start in new situations.

2.—Is worried and upset much of the time; has many fears. Apparently normal in a few unexpected and contradictory ways.

1.—Lives in a constant turmoil of dreads and fears. Cannot concentrate in school or at play.

31. EXCITEMENT, SHOCK, UNEASINESS, ETC. [1]

Children—Do you get excited and upset easily? What was the worst shock you ever had? How did it affect you?

[1] See page 236. See also Item 13.

Parents—Does he get excited easily? Is he very uneasy much of the time? What was the worst thing that ever happened to him?

ADDITIONAL QUESTIONS AND OBSERVATIONS

Is he usually calm and composed or of a nervous and unstrung temperament? Is it natural for him or just a temporary thing at certain periods?

Get actual illustrations, such as jumping when someone speaks loudly, a door slams, or someone's car muffler explodes.

Was he ever in much of an accident, such as a car collision, and what was the effect? How long did it last? What were some of the later effects, such as inability to sleep, dreams, or day-dreaming about similar incidents?

For boys—Did any other boy or a girl or man ever try to get him to talk about "bad" things? Has he told it about himself?

For girls—Did any man or large boy ever make advances of an improper kind to her? What happened? Was she actually attacked? Was she frightened? What has she said about it?

Does he (or she) worry about where babies come from? Has anyone in the family talked about it or answered questions?

See also the questions about sex, in Item 26.

SCORING

Points   *Factors*

5.—Has never had any serious shock; does not get upset easily.

4.—Usually quite calm but inclined to be rather badly upset by one or two kinds of things.

3.—Variable; alternates between extremes of calm and excitability. What is liable to upset him cannot be predicted.

2.—Lives in a state of considerable excitement; is constantly bribed by parents not to be that way.

1.—Constant turmoil; never at ease; no one tries to help.

32. PITY, SYMPATHY, ENTHUSIASM, ETC. [1]

Children—Do you sometimes feel very sad? Are you very sorry for someone or something? Do you ever become very enthusiastic about something or about some person?

Parents—What kinds of things make him sad or enthusiastic? Is he very sympathetic or does he lack sympathy?

ADDITIONAL QUESTIONS AND OBSERVATIONS

Is he considered kind or cruel by other children? If unkind, by whom? By younger or older children? By those of the same or the opposite sex?

Does he have some animal for a pet? Is he kind or cruel to it? Does he tease it? Does he tease pets belonging to others in the family or to others in the neighborhood? What kinds of things does he do to them?

For whom in the family does he show the most affection? Is it a constant or variable affection? Is affection entirely lacking and whose fault is it? Is he unsympathetic with anyone?

Does he ever become very enthusiastic about anything? About what and for how long? Is he able to translate his enthusiasm into effective action?

Does he get sad or cry easily? What things make him do so— seeing someone punished, feeling sorry for someone who is hurt, or grieving for the death of someone close to him?

Is he very considerate of sick people, of old people, and of the crippled or blind? Has he ever had much contact with any of them? Give details.

Does he get much excited about movies, the newspaper "funnies," stirring stories, games, or foods?

Is he dangerously apathetic about all these things?

[1] See page 240.

SCORING

Points   *Factors*

5.—Seems to have a normal balance and proper amount of these traits; under good control.

4.—Seldom upset; has an unusual amount of one trait, such as pity, but very good balance in others.

3.—Lives a rather negative and uninteresting life in these phases; shows these traits at times for some personal advantage in others.

2.—Is too much controlled by these traits; swayed too much at expense of reasoning and judgment; ineffective.

1.—Seems to be entirely lacking in these qualities; cruel; unsympathetic.

33. INTELLIGENCE [1]

Children—Administer some standard individual or group intelligence test.

Parents—Do you think he is brighter than most children of his age? Is he brighter than your other children? Relate some incidents or evidence.

ADDITIONAL QUESTIONS AND OBSERVATIONS

In school is he accelerated, retarded, or at the proper grade level for his age? Are his school marks good, fair, or poor?

Is there general promptness or response, insight into situations, and ability to answer promptly questions?

If he obviously is very defective, find out what he can do to care for his bodily needs, such as in dressing and at the toilet. How much of a care is he? Has an institution been considered? Explain the advantages of it.

[1] See page 244. See also Item 65.

If he is a little slow or below average, does he lose interest in school, take up with undesirable companions, or have more interest in mechanical or nonverbal things?

If he is superior or gifted, does he realize it and does he work up to capacity or does he take unfair advantage?

At any level does he work up to capacity or is he variable in mental effort and interest? Do you note any specially strong or weak traits, such as memory and vocabulary?

SCORING

Points   *Factors*

5.—I. Q. 100 to 130; average or superior; bright enough to succeed well in school; gets along well with companions and associates.

4.—Very gifted; I. Q. above 130; too much absorbed in mental interests; one-sided; not a good social mixer.

3.—Seems to have variable ability; difficult to measure; is linked with instabilities in Items 29 through 32.

2.—I. Q. 75 or lower; little initiative; is quite well supervised at school and home; not much chance to undertake and plan any delinquency.

1.—I. Q. 75 to 90 or 100. Not much interested in school; bright enough to make trouble; dull enough not to foresee outcome of undesirable behavior.

34.   INTERESTS OR HOBBIES [1]

Children—What do you like to do best during your spare time? What things do you like to read about or hear about most of all?

Parents—What does he do with his spare time? What seems to interest him most?

[1] See page 250. See also Items 24, 25, and 26.

What things are of most interest—movies, books, stories, radio, music, machines, or construction toys?

Is he most interested in baseball, football, roller skating, swimming, golf, hiking, the Scouts, or other similar activities?

Is his chief interest care of the garden, lawn, and shrubbery, care of pets, or helping at home with special jobs such as cleaning the automobile or painting?

Is he primarily interested in mechanics, as embodied in the construction of toys and model airplanes? Does he like to tinker with a car?

For girls—Is she fond of sewing, cooking, and general care of her clothes or of the house?

Have any of these things been particularly encouraged: taking music lessons or lessons in painting, reading books on animal care, or joining special clubs in school?

Are these interests well motivated or do they merely squander time?

SCORING

Points   *Factors*

5.—Has a few worth-while interests, well planned and well carried out.

4.—Possibly has too many interests; not very good in any of them; lacks ability for final completion.

3.—Follows one or two interests at times but without serious planning; lacks help or encouragement; possibly ridiculed for them.

2.—Has too many interests; is lost among them; no planning; general confusion; lost; no place or order.

1.—Has no interests; wastes time; has no encouragement; tries to play with belongings of others; never at home.

35. INITIATIVE AND AMBITION [1]

Children—Do you like to study or work very well? Do you think you are lazy or industrious? Do you take the lead?

Parents—Is he lazy or industrious? Does he help at home? Does he play hard with other children?

ADDITIONAL QUESTIONS AND OBSERVATIONS

Is he always looking for things to do or does he avoid work? Is he getting better or worse about this as he grows up?

On what does he exercise initiative?

Does he seem to have ambitions? If not, what are the reasons? Does he take after some other member of the family? Is he ill or physically incapacitated?

Does he make plans and then carry them out or does he change from moment to moment?

Does he work willingly or hurry through a task to get out to play? Does he have to be bribed to work?

How far does he want to go in school?

If he lacks ambition, was he waited upon too much as a child? Does his trouble carry over into a lack of initiative in school?

SCORING

Points   *Factors*

5.—Has a good amount of initiative and ambition; is well motivated.

4.—Has fair initiative but needs more sympathetic direction; feels unjustly rewarded or poorly praised for his best efforts; others take his work for granted.

3.—Entirely too energetic; lives under too much strain; does not follow any project through to a good finish.

[1] See page 254. See also Items 34 and 36.

2.—Interested only in amusements of the moment; demands pay and immediate rewards.

1.—Seems almost entirely lacking in initiative and ambition; has no motivation; squanders time; daydreams.

36. VOCATIONAL INTERESTS [1]

Children—What kind of job or position do you hope to have when you are through school and ready to go to work? How long have you thought so? Why?

Parents—What kind of job or position does he wish to have? What preparation has he made for it?

ADDITIONAL QUESTIONS AND OBSERVATIONS

Does the statement of ambition in vocation seem convincing and well grounded or merely an excuse?

Does the ambition match fairly well with his abilities and intelligence? Is it too high or too low?

Has he made an attempt to study the possibilities of such a job, visited places where this work is done, or read about it to any extent?

Do the parents sympathetically discuss his ambition with him; do they ridicule it; or are they merely indifferent?

Is anyone else influencing him unduly or helpfully?

Is there any one thing at which he is unusually good that is similar to what he wishes to do?

If the selection is a profession requiring much college training, has he the ability to complete such training, the financial backing for it, and the initiative to carry it on?

SCORING

Points   *Factors*

5.—Choice has been quite definitely decided upon; suited to abilities; serves as a good motivation.

[1] See page 258.

4.—Has decided on something below abilities; seems vaguely to realize the problem and is indifferent.

3.—Is partly decided upon something; choice is much beyond abilities or probabilities of realizing.

2.—Parents have made decision; subject has little or no idea of its possibilities or what effect their decision has on his attitude.

1.—Has no interests; living from day to day; no one is taking any interest in him in this respect.

37. GENERAL BEHAVIOR [1]

Children—What is the worst thing you ever did? What is your worst fault? How often do you get into trouble with your neighbors or family, at school, or with the police?

Parents—Is it hard to train or control him? What are his worst faults? Does he get into trouble with the family, at school, in the neighborhood, or with the police?

ADDITIONAL QUESTIONS AND OBSERVATIONS

Has he ever been in a detention home or arrested? For what charges? Has he ever been on probation? For what? How many times has he repeated there?

What things does he do that cause trouble? Does he fight or does he bully or disturb others? Is he insolent to the teacher or other adults? Is he given to lying, stealing, swearing, drinking, or sex assaults or approaches?

Is help being given to control him or are his tendencies allowed free rein? Why?

Is he given much corporal punishment? Is it beneficial or detrimental?

Is he getting better or worse? Was he always a problem?

[1] See page 261. See also Item 61.

Is he disciplined or ostracized by the school? Do others pick on him? Does he fight back?

Has he ever been examined mentally or physically with a view to understanding his problem?

Points *Factors*

5.—Is very well behaved; seldom in even any minor trouble.

4.—Generally good but has one or two bad faults that come to light from time to time.

3.—Only fair; not well understood or handled by his parents. Must be handled carefully or trouble occurs; not much self-control.

2.—Has been in detention home or on probation once; lies; steals; not at all trustworthy.

1.—Repeated offender with police; in constant trouble; seems to have completely antisocial behavior.

38 AND 39. INTELLIGENCE OF FATHER AND MOTHER [1]

Children—Your father is quite a smart man, isn't he? Does he get along well with other people? Did he ever say that his school work was hard or easy for him?
Ask the same questions for the mother.

Parents—Approach the problem cautiously as to direct questioning, depending more upon general impressions from conversation. If there is a foster parent, gather information about him or her relating to this and the following items.

Are they people with good vocabularies or very ordinary ones? How are their written notes if any are available?

[1] See page 264.

Do they have any insight into the mental problems of their children or do they deal with them purely on the level of food and clothing?

What do they read? What mental entertainment do they prefer?

Do they feel particularly conscious of any mental limitations, such as feelings of inferiority? How is it expressed or shown?

If they are rather superior, do they rely too much on intelligence at the expense of feelings and emotions? In what ways does this show?

Is there much or any discrepancy between them in intelligence? If so, in what direction and with what effects?

SCORING

Points   *Factors*

5.—Superior or gifted; seem to understand problem of their children.

4.—Have rather high intelligence but little training for parenthood; use too much reason, and not enough emotion.

3.—Have average ability or there is some marked discrepancy between them; child gets little helpful stimulation from them.

2.—Quite slow mentally; well meaning but have no idea of their own problems in child training.

1.—Have no conception of problems of children; feeble-minded; offer no help to children, who openly despise and defy them. Children should probably be removed from home.

40 AND 41. EDUCATION OF FATHER AND MOTHER [1]

Children—For how many years or through how many grades did your father go to school? Why did he stop there? Did he have a good school record?

Ask the same questions for the mother.

[1] See page 267.

Parents—How far did you go in school? Why did you quit? What kind of marks did you receive? Have you taken any night or evening courses since then? What were they? When did you take them?

ADDITIONAL QUESTIONS AND OBSERVATIONS

Get a detailed account of their school life if it was favorable. What line of specialization was followed? Is it still being pursued vocationally?

What kinds of courses did each like best? Least? Did they ever get into difficulties with teachers or school principals over poor work?

If the school career was meager, try to find out the parents' reason, such as that they were not interested or had to stop to go to work. Was the lack of interest apparently due to lack of mental ability but unrecognized as such?

Are the parents apologetic about their education or proud of it? What attitudes do they try to pass on to their children?

Do they try to keep up mentally by reading for culture, entertaining, or showing a mental interest in their children's schooling and general training?

SCORING

Points   *Factors*

5.—Had college or university training; seem to be able to apply knowledge and seek for more themselves.

4.—High-school graduates or equivalent; may not make enough effort to keep up with mental demands of their children.

3.—Have common-school or grade-school education; have little idea of problems of their children; feel quite inadequate. Discrepancies between them.

2.—Had not more than two or three years of schooling; almost illiterate; no help in stimulating their children.

1.—Practically illiterate; no stimulation to children; probably a demoralizing effect on them; resistant and rebellious about school's treatment of children.

42 AND 43.   AGE OF FATHER AND MOTHER AT BIRTH OF CHILD [1]

Children—About how old is your father? Your mother? If you are not quite sure, can you guess?

Parents—How old are you? (If the parent has been unwilling to answer many other questions, it would be well not to press this issue but to make a good estimate.)

ADDITIONAL QUESTIONS AND OBSERVATIONS

Do they seem young or old for their age? Upon what do you base your opinions? What are their general movements and what is their apparent strength in physical and mental work.

If there is any great difference between their ages, make note of possible reasons for the mutual attraction. Note particularly if the mother is older than the father.

Is either parent, if very young, seemingly immature and unable to handle the child? Does either lack experience and training to do so?

If either or both parents are comparatively old, are they adaptable to children or do they find the children a great responsibility? Do they seem usually patient and understanding of children?

SCORING

Points   *Factors*

5.—Average age 25 to 35 years; have good judgment in dealing with children.

4.—Rather young, 20 to 25; willing to learn; lack experience with children.

[1] See page 269.

3.—Rather old for children, 35 to 50; have some difficulty in making adjustment.

2.—Extremely young, 16 to 20; immature; cannot provide.

1.—Fifty years or older; difficult for them to adjust themselves to children.

Grade one point higher or lower than age suggests if the adjustment varies from the suggested places. For example, if the age calls for 2 points but maturity and training seem better, score as 3 or possibly 4.

44 AND 45. HEALTH OF FATHER AND MOTHER [1]

Children—Is your father well or ill? Your mother? How often are they sick? What is their trouble? Is it the heart, the lungs, the liver, the kidneys, rheumatism, or something else? Do they complain much?

Parents—Are you well or ill most of the time? What sicknesses have you had? What have you done about it? Are you getting better or worse?

ADDITIONAL QUESTIONS AND OBSERVATIONS

What diseases has each had?

What accidents did they have and how serious were they? Did either lose his position or become totally disabled for any accidental cause?

Are there any defects of vision or hearing? Does either ever wear glasses or a special hearing device?

Is there heart trouble? Are there fainting spells? How much time is each sick in bed?

Were any of the four grandparents in particularly poor health? If so, who was it and what was the nature of the trouble?

Was there ever any insanity, feeble-mindedness, epilepsy, or paralysis in the family? Who was affected and what was the nature of the illness?

[1] See page 272. See also Items 3, 4, 5, 6, 7, and 8.

What apparent psychological effects are any of these health or impairment factors having, such as need for being waited upon and expecting too much quiet?

SCORING

Points   *Factors*

5.—Good health and fine attitude toward work and children.

4.—Occasionally ill but no marked mental effects upon home or children.

3.—Many minor illnesses but much ado about them; affairs somewhat disorganized much of the time.

2.—Poor health; children are more or less repressed and seek recreation outside of home. Health very poor but not much mental effect.

1.—Very poor health; expect favors from children and others; a warped home atmosphere.

46 AND 47. PERSONALITY OF FATHER AND MOTHER [1]

Children—Is your father jolly or sad or between these extremes? Does he get angry easily? Is he too lenient or easy-going?

Ask the same questions for the mother.

Parents—Do things at home make you feel pleased or angry and impatient? Is the father (or mother) of an agreeable personality?

ADDITIONAL QUESTIONS AND OBSERVATIONS

In the main, information must come from observation in several interviews rather than from direct questions. Frequently one parent or the other will volunteer much information after the way has been opened.

---

[1] See page 274. See also Items 29, 30, 31. 32, 56, 57, 59, and 60.

What does the father do when he is at home to share his time with the children? Does he help with the housework and in caring for the lawn and the furnace or does he show no interest?

Which parent seems to be the aggressor and to dominate the other and the home? What effect does this condition have upon the rest of the family? Is there resentment or complete acceptance?

What specific personality defect is evident in either parent and what effect has it been having upon the child?

Is there a marked discrepancy between the father and the mother in personality?

SCORING

Points   *Factors*

5.—Seem to be well balanced and controlled; positive and desirable stimulation to children.

4.—Personality generally good; but they are occasionally upset by a few special situations.

3.—Variable and erratic; often upset.

2.—Severe and puritanical; colorless; the children are forced to conform to their parents' personality pattern.

1.—Very emotional; hysterical; no respect given by children. Children reflect parents' personality patterns.

48. OCCUPATION [1]

Children—Where does your father work? What does he do? How long has he worked there? What did he do before that? What did he do before he was unemployed?

These questions may apply to the mother if she is alone and works.

Parents—Where do you work? What do you do? What other things have you done?

[1] See page 276.

Get name of specific kind of work, not just a general statement, such as, "He works in the post office."

Does he ever discuss his work at home or does he talk about it all the time so that no one is interested?

Does he like or dislike his work? What are the reasons? Are his superiors pleasant or unpleasant? If he is over others, how does he get along with them?

Has he left many places of employment and for what reasons? Are the reasons, such as fighting with other employees, important?

What kind of work is he fitted for? Which job did he like best?

Is his present position suited to his abilities? Is it too hard or too easy?

If he is unemployed, for how long has he been unemployed? What is he doing to get employment? Is he discouraged?

If possible, find out what his weekly wages are. This must be handled carefully.

SCORING

Points   *Factors*

   5.—Has a profession and a steady income; reflects economic security.

   4.—Has a successful business or clerical occupation; seldom unemployed. Fair status.

   3.—Is a skilled laborer, out of work part time. Conditions of employment only fair.

   2.—Is a semiskilled laborer, not well pleased with his work; wishes for something better. Out of work about half the time.

   1.—Unskilled; ineffective; generally out of work; there is not much initiative in seeking employment.

If he is irregular in his profession, score one or two steps lower.

If he is very regular and successful at unskilled labor, score one or two steps higher.

49. ECONOMIC STATUS [1]

Children—Does your father own your home? If the house is rented, how much rent does he pay? How much does he earn a week? Use care with last question.

Parents—Do you own your home? How much rent do you pay? About how much do you earn a week?

ADDITIONAL QUESTIONS AND OBSERVATIONS

If the parents own the home, is it paid for or are they still paying for it? What are the chances of completing the payments? Did they pay too much in comparison with their income?

Is the rent too high? Is the family living in quarters which are too good or too poor for its general status?

How many rooms are there? Are they crowded, homelike, attractive, or undesirable?

Is the income sufficient for a bare or a comfortable living? Is it a constant source of worry and home trouble?

Is the family on welfare or other relief? To what extent? How long has it required assistance? What are the chances of independent support later?

How much is spent for shows, vacations, parties, smoke and drink, and other forms of recreation?

Does the family own a car, a radio, a refrigerator, a sewing machine, a washing machine, or a phonograph, piano, or other instruments?

Are there any other investments? Are they good or poor ones? How many debts are there and what are they? What are the chances of paying them?

[1] See page 279.

Points   *Factors*

5.—Own comfortable home; in fair circumstances.

4.—Sudden wealth; false standards.

3.—Paying for average home; renting a good one; live on fairly close economy.

2.—Rent fair quarters; often close to want; income irregular.

1.—Rent very poor quarters; chronic charity case; take no responsibility.

50. HOME LANGUAGE [1]

Children—Do all of you speak English at home? If not, what language is spoken? By whom?

Parents—Does everyone speak English at home all the time? If not, what language is spoken and by whom?

ADDITIONAL QUESTIONS AND OBSERVATIONS

Find out the extent of the foreign tongue used, if it is used at all —whether it is all foreign, all foreign except among the children talking to one another, all foreign except among the children talking to one another and to their parents, all English except when the parents talk to each other, or all English except when the parents talk to the children.

What language is spoken? How well is it mastered in the home? Do children use it in playing or in parochial school?

Do the children feel an advantage in knowing English better than their parents?

If the language is foreign, why have the parents not learned English? Was there no opportunity, especially for the mother, or are they generally slow in language ability in any tongue?

Have the parents attempted to assimilate American customs or

[1] See page 281.

are they still characteristically foreign? If the latter, why? Do they associate only with people of their own nationality?

Do they intend remaining in the United States or returning to their home country? Who encouraged them to come here? Have they been satisfied?

Points   *Factors*

5.—All speak English all the time.

4.—Children speak English; parents generally speak foreign tongue but can speak English. A good adjustment.

3.—Children speak English; parents know or speak very little English; not much home co-operation and understanding.

2.—Children know English fairly well but speak foreign language at home and hear foreign language only.

1.—All speak foreign language all the time at home and at play.

51. OTHER ADULTS IN HOME [1]

Children—Does anyone else live with you besides your brothers and sisters and your father and mother? Who? Are there any roomers or boarders? What do you do with them?

Parents—Who else lives in your home besides the immediate family? Do any of them have much to do with the subject?

ADDITIONAL QUESTIONS AND OBSERVATIONS

Get details as to who besides the family lives there, as immediate relatives, grandparents, uncles, or aunts.

[1] See page 284.

How do they fit into the family picture? Do they pay board and are they unemployed, welcome, or unwelcome? Is there friction? If so, what is its nature?

Do they try to dominate the children? How do the children like them? Do they give them too much money or favors or spoil them for their parents? Do they take the children to the movies too much?

Are there roomers or boarders who are not members of the family? Who are they and how do they happen to be there? Are they good or poor influences on the children? In what ways? Do they sleep with them or tell them dirty stories?

What has been done to offset the undesirable effects of the relatives or boarders and roomers? Why is it not possible to get rid of them? Can they be shown the effects they have on the children?

SCORING

Points   *Factors*

5.—None or desirable ones with good influence.

4.—One other relative, with fair attitude.

3.—Old or elderly relative, ill; expects too much quiet and waiting upon by children.

2.—One or more roomers; tend to interfere with children. Probably good or fair intentions.

1.—Several roomers or relatives; constant friction; are unscrupulous in influence upon children.

52. NUMBER OF AND POSITION IN SIBLINGS [1]

Children—How many brothers and sisters have you? Name them. Where do you come among them? Are any of them married?

Parents—How many children have you? Where does this one come among them?

[1] See page 286.

Make a list of all the children, including foster siblings, with the ages, schooling, and occupation. Include the married ones.

Are any of them sick or crippled or did they have any serious accidents? Is there any heart or lung trouble, epilepsy, insanity, or feeble-mindedness?

Which ones got along best in school? Which one is smartest? Which one is dullest? What special abilities have any of them, such as being unusually good in music or baseball?

In case of two children only, are they nearly the same age? How much difference is there? If there are several, are they fairly close in age or are there many years between them?

Where does this one come in the number? Is he a favorite of any of the others? Which ones are most liked by the father and mother?

Do the married ones get along well with their husbands and wives and have they children? Are they still much attached to the old home?

SCORING

Points   *Factors*

5.—One other child; subject usually the older of two.

4.—Two or three others; subject is oldest but there is not much difference in the ages.

3.—Four to six others; subject much older than others.

2.—Seven to nine inclusive; among the youngest but others not much older.

1.—Only child; one of ten or more; youngest and much younger than all others.

53. ADJUSTMENTS TO SIBLINGS [1]

Children—How do you get along with your brothers and sisters? Which one do you like best? Which one the least? Why?

[1] See page 290.

Parents—How does he get along with his brothers and sisters? Which ones does he like best? Least? What do you do about it?

ADDITIONAL QUESTIONS AND OBSERVATIONS

If he is the only child, score this point with respect to how he gets along with his best playmate.

If he is the older of two, is he jealous of the younger one. This is a common situation, not recognized by parents. What causes him to be jealous?

If the younger, does he strive to do the same things that the older ones do and worry about not being so successful? What does he do to make compensation?

Relate some experiences that show that they do not get along well together. Who was apparently at fault? Do the parents try to settle disagreements by argument or reasoning or by parental authority?

Is there respect of ownership by the different children or constant argument? Is it true of clothes?

Is one child favored above others—for being better in school, better to help at home, better in minding, and so on? What effect does this have upon the others?

Do the older children boss the younger ones and make them wait on them or is there a good feeling among them?

SCORING

Points   *Factors*

5.—Have wholesome respect for and good attitudes toward one another.

4.—Generally good but occasional difficulties not involving the particular child.

3.—Child has only a fair attitude; gets along only because others are tolerant.

2.—Child has a poor attitude; jealous; others are only fair; gets along by wise parental supervision.

1.—Children constantly quarreling; always in turmoil; parents can do nothing; take no interest. Fits of temper; destruction of property of other siblings.

54. LEGAL STATUS [1]

Children—Do you live with your own father and mother? Where were you born? Is your father a citizen of the United States? Have you a stepfather or stepmother?

Parents—Is he your own child or adopted? Is there a stepfather or stepmother? Does he know it? Where was he born? Have you a birth certificate?

ADDITIONAL QUESTIONS AND OBSERVATIONS

Establish whether or not these are his own parents—with caution if he does not know.

Is there one foster parent? Which one? What happened? Is there a foster parent because of death, separation, or divorce?

Are there two foster parents? Is the child legally adopted? What became of his own parents? Are the foster parents related to him? What is the relationship?

If the child is adopted, why did the foster parents want him? Was it because they had no children of their own, because they had a strong desire for children of their own, or because there was some obligation to a relative?

What was the age of the child at the time of the separation of the parents, the death of one of them, or his adoption? How did he accept it then? How does he now?

If he is boarded out in various homes by child-placing agencies, what success or failure has attended? If he is adopted and does not know it, why was he not told? When will he be? How will he accept it?

[1] See page 293.

Who cares more about him, his father or his mother? If he is a
foster child and the parents have children of their own, are
they more favored?

Points   *Factors*

5.—Lives with own parents; good or fair adjustment.
4.—Lives with own parents; but they are indifferent, considering separation. Adopted but well adjusted.
3.—Adopted, but this fact is unknown to child, although
strongly suspected by him; lives in some uncertainty.
2.—Adoption, known or unknown, but adjustment very poor;
foster parents indifferent or too exacting.
1.—Boarded about temporarily; does not adjust anywhere;
tries to take advantage quickly.

55. BROKEN HOME [1]

Children—Was either of your parents ever married before?
Which one? What happened—death, separation, or
divorce? With which one do you live?

Parents—Were you married before? Was your husband (or wife)
married before? What happened if you would not
mind telling us?

ADDITIONAL QUESTIONS AND OBSERVATIONS

With which parent does the child live if the parents are separated? Does he prefer that one? Did he have any choice in
the matter? Why not?

What are the specific reasons for the separation? Did the man
drink, gamble, or go with a bad crowd? Did either of the
parents keep company with someone else before the separation? Who? What influence did it have?

[1] See page 296.

Was there open quarreling or cruelty known to the children? What effect did it have upon the children? Was there complaint of poor adjustment in school?

Has the separation caused happiness or sorrow? Were the differences trivial or fundamental, such as temperaments, general tastes, culture, or attitude toward going to church?

Does the man pay alimony regularly? Was there court trouble? What other means of support are there? Is there financial want?

Is one of the parents considering marriage again? Who is the new person? Is he or she accepted by the children? Why is it thought that the new arrangement will be more successful?

Does the real father (or mother) see the children? How often? How does it affect them?

SCORING

Points   *Factors*

5.—Not a broken home; good adjustment.

4.—Child living with one parent but has fair adjustment. Home not broken but conditions not ideal.

3.—Child lives with one parent but not well satisfied; more or less disturbed by the other one.

2.—Child goes from one parent to the other; usually has his own way with both; fair adjustment on the child's part.

1.—Goes from one parent to the other; each jealous and trying to disparage the other; child takes advantage; does about as he pleases.

56.   GENERAL HOME ATMOSPHERE [1]

Children—Do you like to stay around home or do you prefer to go out to other places? Is it always pleasant at home or how is it?

[1] See page 298. See also Items 38-47, 59, 61, and 62.

Parents—Where do the members of the household prefer to spend their time? Is home a happy and agreeable place or do the children feel somewhat rejected?

ADDITIONAL QUESTIONS AND OBSERVATIONS

Is the atmosphere of the home free and cordial or restricted? Why does it seem to be limited?

Is there much confusion—in arrangement of furniture, in having things lying around, and in general planning of the housework?

Do the parents read quietly with the children or is there no chance to get together on common projects? Why?

Is there culture and educational stimulation? How many books does the family have? What kind are they? Do they enjoy good music?

Is there a lack of culture? Does the home offset and neutralize the cultural effects of the school? Do the children seek good atmosphere in church, with the Scouts, or in play groups?

Does the father take any part in trying to develop a good atmosphere at home or is he indifferent? What does he do with his spare time?

SCORING

Points   *Factors*

5.—Well regulated; fine type of feeling and relationship among all members of family.

4.—Home fairly well controlled and organized but atmosphere appears to be somewhat unnatural and strained.

3.—Atmosphere fair or neutral; not much done or planned for good home relationships. Children neutral.

2.—More or less confusion; poor organization; little or no time for quiet or reading; children seek other places to play and for recreation.

1.—Family always in chronic state of disorganization; confusion; no control; no one has any interest in the home as a unit.

57. IDEALS OF HOME [1]

Children—Do you get a strong desire to do right from what your parents do? If not, what do they make you feel like doing? Do they make you feel like lying or stealing?

Parents—Are your children stimulated to do right by you? Do they ever suspect you of deceit? Do they seem to see or hear more than you think they do of things you do not want them to? What?

ADDITIONAL QUESTIONS AND OBSERVATIONS

Does there seem to be a high moral standard in the home or is it only fair or possibly lax?

If it is high, is it at all artificial? Do the children get much real stimulation from it?

Is it preached to the children or merely put before them by suggestion? How do the children seem to take to it?

If the ideals are extremely low, what seems to be the cause? Is a member of the household serving sentence? For what? Do children know?

Is there open boasting or cheating by the parents, such as short changing at the store, paying no car fare, or getting advantage in any "shady" transaction? Do children hear about it? What is the effect? Have the children done similar things?

Do the children hold undesirable parents in contempt and maintain a better ideal? How do they seem to do it?

Do the parents try to hold the children up to higher ideals than they keep themselves? Are the parents really desirous of having the children succeed?

[1] See page 301.

Points   *Factors*

5.—High ideals, quietly and effectively practiced and admired by all.

4.—Ideals generally fair but too much imposed upon the children; lax in a few respects.

3.—Have ideals for children but do not observe them themselves; artificial conformity.

2.—Have few ideals and make little effort to practice them; do not encourage children to look for them outside of home.

1.—Complete lack of moral code; no desirable stimulation.

58. RELIGION [1]

Children—Do you go to church? What church? How often do you go? Do other members of your family go with you? Do you go to Sunday school?

Parents—Does he go to church or Sunday school? Which one? Do you go with him?

ADDITIONAL QUESTIONS AND OBSERVATIONS

How regularly does he go to church? How long has he been going? How many times each Sunday does he go?

Does he go to Sunday school? Does he go every Sunday? Is he a class officer or general officer of the Sunday school?

Does he really like to go or does he go from force of habit? Does he go because his parents make him? Does he have to go when they do not?

Does he seem to have a vivid and strong belief in religion or is he neutral or antagonistic? Does he practice a rigid moral code on account of strong religion?

[1] See page 304.

If he seems entirely aloof from religion, is his attitude reflected in a poor code of behavior? Cite examples of the two points suggested

Is there family worship at home? Is grace said at the table? Do all the family take part? Does the subject believe in God? What does he think God is like?

Is the religious influence so great that cards are not played and dancing is not allowed? Is there no pleasure on Sunday? What specific limitations are there?

Does he get much comfort and happiness out of his religion? Does he get too much excitement and feeling from revival meetings if they take place in his church?

SCORING

Points   *Factors*

5.—Parents use religious worship sincerely and wisely in developing ideals.

4.—Family attends church regularly but makes little application of principles to affairs of daily living.

3.—Family claims nominal church membership; seldom attends; children sent to church but parents do not go.

2.—Parents have no religion and have contempt for it; they cite the examples of scapegoats who attend.

1.—Religious and overemotional; life in high pitch of excitement from revival meetings; no intelligent application of principles.

59. FAMILY RECREATION [1]

Children—How often do you go out with your parents and brothers and sisters? Where do you go? What do you do? Do you go to the movies, to shows, on picnics, or camping?

[1] See page 307. See also Items 24, 25, and 34.

Parents—Do you take him along on recreation trips? What kind? How often? What do you all do together at home for recreation?

ADDITIONAL QUESTIONS AND OBSERVATIONS

What kinds of games are played at home? Who plays? Does the father play with the children? Do they run or play checkers or ball? Was there general play for the children when they were small? Was it shared by the parents?

If the parents do not share recreation, why is this so? Are they too busy? Do they not care to try? Do they know how? Are they too tired? Do not the children want it? Do they prefer to play with other children?

Are the parents tolerant of the play and confusion of their children? Do they insist upon quiet and order? Is there a formal, depressing, and severe spirit in the home?

Does the father take the child to a movie with him? Does he take the child to any other recreation? Do they play golf together or other games? Is there a good spirit between them?

Does the family go to a lake or other resort for week-ends? What happens there? Do they swim, play games, canoe and sail, row, chop wood, or raise a garden together?

If there is a touring trip, do they find recreation along the way or is there hurry, fatigue, and a series of strained relationships?

Do the parents always work and have no time for recreation? Do the children think they are hopelessly old and do not understand them?

SCORING

Points   *Factors*

5.—A liberal amount of time for and variety in family recreation; shared and enjoyed by all.

4.—Fairly good but varies greatly; may be concentrated in a week-end or occur occasionally.

3.—Generally very little; is merely tolerated by parents; there may be one automobile trip a year.

2.—Parents have little or no recreation; children go to the movies alone.

1.—No recreation; parents and children always work; no spirit of play.

60. PARENTS' SOCIAL ADJUSTMENT [1]

Children—Does your father seem happy and contented? Your mother? Do they have other grown-ups in for dinner? Do they go to other people's houses for dinner or parties?

Parents—Are you happy? Is your husband (wife)? Do you have many friends? Do they visit you and do you go to their homes?

ADDITIONAL QUESTIONS AND OBSERVATIONS

Form your own estimate of the amount of social poise possessed by each parent as he or she confers with you. Do they seem at ease or are they not used to talking with anyone?

If there is considerable time for social affairs, who makes the arrangements? Is there friction over it? Is too much time given to social engagements to the neglect of the children?

In social engagements who takes the initiative, the parents or other persons? Do they really owe engagements which they never pay? Do they take too much initiative and invite people who never repay?

Is there any marked difference in the social point of view of the two parents? Is the difference a source of argument and is it known to the children?

Are the parents soured and discouraged with lack of employment and with general financial stringency? Is it reflected in their general attitudes?

[1] See page 309. See also Items 27, 46, and 47.

Does one parent do more in social contacts for the children than the other and does this tend to divide the family?

Does the father find it difficult to get work on account of a lack of social initiative? Does he drink much, smoke to excess, swear, or become generally abusive? How do the parents get along with the neighbors?

SCORING

Points   *Factors*

5.—Are well adjusted and happy; good influence on children.

4.—Adjustment fairly satisfactory; have trouble on one or two issues.

3.—Rather easily upset; easily slighted; try to overdo social contacts; a neutral influence on children.

2.—One parent fairly well adjusted; other not; source of conflict; very little favorable stimulation.

1.—Socially inadequate; soured and disappointed; a poor example and stimulation to children.

61. DISCIPLINE [1]

Children—Are you punished very often? For what? How do your parents do it? Do they whip you, scold you, or put you to bed? Do you think they are too severe or too easy?

Parents—Do you punish him very often? For what? How do you do it? What effect does your punishment have?

ADDITIONAL QUESTIONS AND OBSERVATIONS

How often is any punishment used—every day or only once in a while? What kind is it? Do the parents resort to whipping even with the older children?

[1] See page 312.

For what is the child punished? Are there just reasons? Is the
   punishment very frequent, so that its effects easily wear off?
Is there continual scolding? Does it have any effect or does the
   child ignore it? Does he seem unhappy on account of it?
Is there a complete lack of control of the child? How does he
   show it? Why did control get in such a condition? What do
   the parents think they can do about it?
Is authority divided? Is one severe, the other lenient? Which
   one? Cite instances. Do they openly disagree before the child?
Is the discipline variable, now lenient and then severe? What
   are the reasons for discipline? Does the child feel that it is
   unjust?
Are there any effective punishments, are they necessary, and
   what is the effect upon the child's attitude toward home?

SCORING

Points   *Factors*

5.—No particular problems arise; child seems to respect par-
      ents' judgment.
4.—Discipline is generally fair, but occasionally there is some
      upset.
3.—Parents do not agree; children take advantage; there is a
      great amount of scolding that is ineffective.
2.—Child left to own resources; uncontrolled, wild, and poorly
      managed. Punished for incidental things.
1.—Child uncontrolled; no discipline effective; parents have
      tried everything. Discipline inconsistent; child openly
      defiant.

62. ATTITUDE TOWARD CHILD [1]

Children—Do your parents do too much or too little for you at
         home? Do they stand up for you or do they turn
         you down when you want a little sympathy?

[1] See page 316.

Parents—Does he feel that you have a friendly or neutral feeling toward him? Does he come to you for pity?

ADDITIONAL QUESTIONS AND OBSERVATIONS

Judge from the several contacts with the parents whether they are too blindly attached to or too detached from the child. Do they disregard him, finding excuses like being too busy to give him attention? (1)

If they are too much attached to him, do they let emotional tone overrule reason in making requirements of him? Is he pampered and kept out of school for minor illnesses? Is this because of a severe illness early in life?

If the parents seem neutral or antagonistic, why are they? Is there wrong behavior, unfavorable appearance, or unpleasant personality? Does the child feel or sense it? What reaction does he have? Does he lie or steal? Does he stay away from home as much as possible?

Does he feel insecure or is there a feeling of injustice? Does he try to get revenge on his parents? In what specific ways? Has he thought of running away? Do the parents know it?

Is there a neutral or possibly antagonistic feeling of which he does not seem aware? What do the parents do to make him suspect it, such as wearing better clothes themselves?

Was he an unwanted child? (Perhaps the parents will confess.) Was he difficult to bring up? Did this fact make the parents care more or less about him?

SCORING

Points	Factors
5.—	Have a wholesome care for and attitude toward child.
4.—	Generally good attitude; sometimes loss of temper; too much sentiment instead of reason.
3.—	Live in rather neutral state; care more for physical than

emotional life of child; assume that he will appreciate that policy.

2.—Too solicitous; guard every action; defend him unduly from rough playmates; take his part at school.

1.—Neglect, almost hatred; child knows he is not welcome or wanted at home; older ones expected to work and support themselves beyond reason.

63. Children's Attitude Toward Home

Children—How do you really get along at home? Do you feel happy there? If not, how do you feel? What do you want to do? Do your parents know you feel that way?

Parents—Does he seem happy at home and does he feel really welcome? How does he show how he feels?

ADDITIONAL QUESTIONS AND OBSERVATIONS

Make an estimate after you have met him more than once unless he quickly volunteers. He may tell you about his attitude later.

Is he obviously unadjusted or very happy? Avoid raising any distrust in his mind.

If he is unhappy, what is the cause of his unhappiness? Is it discipline, neglect, or poor school work or is he less favored than his brothers and sisters? Get his story if he will talk.

If he is very happy, what elements or factors make him so? Does he sympathize with and get sympathy from some playmates? Do they try to set him off against the home?

Is he sullen about doing chores or going places with his parents? Do they scold him for his defiance or do they ignore it?

Has he ever really faced the problem and analyzed it? Are the facts about his parents as he sees them?

Was he always in difficulty from early childhood or has the diffi-

1 See page 318.

culty developed in adolescence? How are the parents meeting this problem? (1)

Points   *Factors*

5.—Well adjusted, happy, wholesomely obedient.

4.—Rather easy to handle; obeys in most situations; seems fairly happy.

3.—Is obedient but always inclined to argue; a little sullen and stubborn.

2.—Seems to obey but has his own way much of the time; exploits his parents for his own ends.

1.—Antagonistic; defiant; hates his home; runs with a bad gang; there is no home control; parents not qualified or able to command his respect.

64. SCHOOL ATTENDANCE [1]

Children—Do you stay out of school very much? Why? Do you really want to go to school? Why? Who keeps you out? Where do you go?

Parents—Does he stay out of school very much? Where does he go? With whom? What does he do? What do you do about it?

ADDITIONAL QUESTIONS AND OBSERVATIONS

From school records or his report cards, get a detailed statement of his school attendance by semesters, terms, or years.

If he has been out much, has sickness been the cause?

Has he deliberately skipped school? For how many years has he done so? Where does he go? What is his motive?

Who encouraged him to be a truant? Does he belong to a gang?

[1] See page 321. See also Items 1 through 5.

If so, what do they do? How long was it before these facts were discovered?

Does he complain about teachers that he does not like? What have they done to him? Does he feel unjustly punished?

Are there school studies which he did not like? Which ones? What happened to him when he failed in lessons? Did he stay after school? Did he do the work over? Was he unable to grasp the point after much effort?

What has the home done to correct his truancy? Has he been kept out much to tend to ill people, to help with work, or to stay with younger children?

Is he willing to accept responsibility for attendance? Has he had a court record for truancy? Has he been on probation?

SCORING

Points   *Factors*

5.—Always regular and punctual; takes responsibility gladly.

4.—Is quite regular; is absent sometimes on account of illness; is sometimes tardy.

3.—Absent about as often as he can find any kind of excuse; parents try to have him at school.

2.—Absent at irregular periods; parents are lax about attendance; keep him out on slight excuses.

1.—Absent or truant most of the time; no home co-operation; runs with a bad gang; lawless; probation has been of little help.

65. SCHOLARSHIP [1]

Children—Are your school marks good, fair, or poor? What subjects are your best? Your poorest? Have your school marks always been about the same as lately? Why?

[1] See page 324.

Parents—What kind of record for school marks has he had during most of his life in school—good, fair, or poor? In what subjects? How does he feel about it?

If scholarship has been a source of trouble, try to get a fairly complete record of his school life.

Is there any one school subject in which he has been chronically poor, such as reading? How bad has it been? Why could he not succeed in it?

In what school subjects has he been best? Is he trying to major or specialize in something in which he is most successful? What is it?

Has he had difficulties with teachers on account of not being able to succeed, as in spelling? Specify the subjects and what happened.

Is his school record fairly uniform, with good or poor marks in all subjects, or is it extremely variable? Get a full description of details.

Are his educational aspirations much beyond realization, judged by his present status? Is he conscious of or does he accept this condition?

Get a complete statement of his educational age on standard achievement tests.

SCORING

Points   *Factors*

5.—Has good or excellent marks in all subjects.

4.—Does pretty good work in all but one subject; succeeds and is able to pass in the face of this special difficulty.

3.—Has fair work in most subjects; very poor in one or two; occasionally receives a good mark.

2.—Quite poor; fair work in one subject only; neutral or unenthusiastic in attitude.

1.—Failing in practically all subjects; indifferent; no help or stimulation at home; dislikes school.

66. CHILD'S ATTITUDE TOWARD SCHOOL [1]

Children—Do you really like school? If not, why not? Would you still go to school if your parents did not make you? If not, what would you do?

Parents—How does he like school? How does he like his teachers? Would he go to school if you did not make him? What do you do to improve his attitude?

ADDITIONAL QUESTIONS AND OBSERVATIONS

If his attitude is uniformly good, what has made it so? Has he found school a happy escape from a bad home environment.

Is his attitude bad? Why? What is the distance to school?

Does he dislike any of his teachers? Which ones? What is his attitude toward the principal? Why?

Is he often disciplined by the school? For what? What methods are used in discipline? Are they effective or ineffective?

What attitude do the parents have? Is it sympathetic to the child or to the school? What effect does that have upon the child?

Does he get along if handled very carefully or pampered by the teachers? How long has this practice continued? What can be done about it? What has been done?

SCORING

Points   *Factors*

5.—Never in any trouble; attitude commendable and desirable; a model to others.

4.—Does fairly well; occasionally has some minor difficulty; must be handled with care by the teachers.

[1] See page 326. See also Item 65.

3.—Has trouble often with two or three teachers; leads others in poor behavior; more of a constant source of minor difficulty than of anything serious.

2.—At best gets along fairly well with only one teacher; has always been in more or less trouble; tries to blame school and places self on the defensive.

1.—Always in serious trouble; leads others to difficulty; disliked by other pupils; known as a chronic "bad boy."

BIBLIOGRAPHY

1. FITZ-SIMONS, MARIAN J.—*Some Parent-child Relationships*. New York: Bureau of Publications, Teachers College, Columbia University, 1935. 162 pp.
2. TERMAN, LEWIS M., and ALMACK, JOHN C.—*The Hygiene of the School Child* (Revised and Enlarged Edition). Boston: Houghton Mifflin Co., 1929. 505 pp.

PART III

INTERPRETATION OF THE SIXTY-SIX FACTORS

CHAPTER VI

HEALTH AND PHYSICAL FACTORS

For convenience in interpretation the sixty-six items have been divided into five sections, with chapters to correspond. A short discussion will be presented for each item, usually including a description or definition of terms, some causes, and suggested remedies or preventions. In some instances short reports of cases or problems are presented to illustrate avenues of approach to conditions connected with the various factors. An attempt has also been made to describe cases, serious or extreme, with respect to feelings or emotional responses precipitated by the factor of deficiency.

In the present chapter there is considerable description of physical and sensory defects to give some familiarity with them, but in no sense is it a complete guide to detailed diagnosis of exact physiological status. Parents, teachers, and workers are always urged to consult competent medical authorities for final diagnosis and treatment. At best these paragraphs may stimulate an interest in better health and in the cure of defects and may show their possible psychological significance.

These chapters should be studied constantly in connection with the detailed questions, methods of diagnosis, and plan of scoring which are offered in Chapter V. For example, if a behavior case discloses serious difficulty with three items, such as Items 10, 26, and 54, it is recommended that the worker peruse these three particular sections of Part III on interpretation.

In Table XII (page 350) of Chapter XII there is a list of all sixty-six items with respect to their ability to distinguish between behavior and non-behavior groups. It was noted that certain types of items make a more definite distinction than others. For some reason health and the physical factors, as discussed in that chapter, show comparatively little difference between the two groups. The sixty-six factors have been grouped according to the five chapters of Part III, and a rank order of the factors in each chapter has been determined. The results are shown in Table VII. At this point it is recommended that the worker refer to these later tables and chapters for aid in interpretation. See list of tables, page xiii.

TABLE VII.   RANK OF DIFFERENCES BETWEEN BEHAVIOR AND NON-BEHAVIOR CHILDREN BY GROUPS OF FACTORS

RANK	GROUP OF FACTORS	ITEM NUMBERS	MEDIAN DIFFERENCE
1	Personality and social factors	27–37	1.63
2	Home atmosphere and school factors	56–66	1.52
3	Personal habits and recreational factors	14–26	1.10
4	Parental and physical factors	38–55	.52
5	Health and physical factors	1–13	.44

There is probably an indirect effect of health and the physical factors on the personality and on social factors, so that the lesser importance of the physical is not actually as marked as the table indicates.

The discussion of all these factors assumes that workers who wish to use the Detroit Scale in evaluating behavior problems have had some training and background in social adjustments or are about to undertake such training. For the experienced worker this compilation of discussions should prove definite and useful for specific diagnosis and treatment.

1.   CHILD'S EARLY HEALTH [1]

It is necessary in taking a history of behavior problems to go back into the developmental conditions: the mother's condition at conception and during her pregnancy, details of the labor and birth, and the first few months of the child's life.

[1] See page 40.

Physicians generally believe that a child's future bodily resistance and constitutional type depend upon his early health. Some even declare that all personality traits have their roots in as early a time as the intrauterine period. Drunkenness at the time of conception, for instance, has been known to cause feeblemindedness and instability. The system of a mother who is unhappy and nervous or sickly during her pregnancy contains poisons which may affect the system of the embryo. When the child of such a mother is born, he is apt to be delicate, sensitive, and nervous. Thousands of case histories of nervous, unstable, delicate children show this correlation. The mothers confessed that they were depressed, or upset, or in poor health in the carrying period.

Many cases of feeble-mindedness can be traced to no other apparent cause than that the mother had such poor health that she was unable to nourish her child properly. Another important factor in feeble-mindedness is premature birth. It is believed that where hereditary predisposition exists, the child who is prematurely born will have less chance of good mental development than the one who goes to full term.

Long labor and difficult birth must be very painful to the child and possibly leave a lifelong stamp upon him, even when there is no birth injury. Injury to the child's head at birth, or while still within the uterus, or in the early months of life is the frequent cause of mental defect; it may produce brain lesions which may later cause epilepsy or some type of insanity.

When the breast-fed baby does not get sufficient nourishment from the mother's milk, he may develop rickets. Doctors believe, however, that in most cases the mother's own milk is the best formula for the baby, and that he will thrive upon it. Moreover, the breast-fed baby is a happier and better satisfied baby. The bottle-fed, early weaned child often craves more love and security. He frequently sucks his thumb for comfort. Certain later personality peculiarities or behavior patterns can apparently be traced to the lack of satisfaction during the nursing period.

In obtaining the developmental history of a child, inquiry

should be made regarding his walking, his continence, and his disposition. The emotional experience of the first twelve months may determine his reactions toward later experiences. For example, the child who is trained in toilet habits by an overanxious mother may later be the type of person who is exacting, systematic, and too orderly—all his plans must be prearranged. His affairs must always be in proper order or he is emotionally upset and confused. Mothers say that they can tell what kind of disposition their baby is going to have when he grows up by the amount of crying or laughing he does when he is an infant.

Spinal meningitis, infantile paralysis, and encephalitis are the most dreaded of all diseases. Their mortality is high and their after-effects most vicious. These diseases will be discussed in later chapters. Rachitis, or rickets, is a general disorder of nutrition which affects the growing organism and is chiefly characterized by changes in the bones, ligaments, and muscles in conjunction with nervous symptoms. It is most frequently found among children of parents who themselves have suffered from nutritional trouble or who have been the subjects of alcoholism or tuberculosis. The enfeebled offspring of such parents are particularly liable to rickets when they are improperly fed and live in badly ventilated, sunless quarters. Rickets, moreover, can be the cause or the accompaniment of mental deficiency.

The foregoing facts may be useful to social workers who are endeavoring to understand the background of a child referred to them for attention. It must be remembered that just as important as the ailments themselves are the attitudes and the emotional associations of the parent and child during periods of sickness. Many parents volunteer the statement that "he is bad now because we spoiled him when he was sick as a baby." The baby ruled the house because his parents were afraid that discipline might aggravate his physical weakness; and he grew up expecting to rule his family, his companions, and his teachers in the same way.

To recondition a child spoiled in babyhood is not easy. He must go through a long process of resocialization. He cannot rule but must yield to ruling. He must not receive attention for self-neglected body conditions or for misbehavior; he must receive attention only for good actions. Obviously he requires the most skillful and sympathetic handling. The parents are too often a problem for the worker. They may continue to spoil the child and protect him against the school or rough children; yet when they are angry with him themselves, they may browbeat or punish him severely. The child is torn between these two types of treatment, and in his confusion he becomes ugly and resistive. A third person, an outsider, can often deal with the situation better than school or home.

When it is believed that the child's present peculiarities have their sources in his infancy, it is a practical method to take him back into that period to relive his experiences. Through a process like catharsis he thinks about and forms again the events that once distressed him but which he has since forgotten. Often when they become clear to him once more, he can face his own problem and help solve it.

It should not be implied from this discussion that all children who have had poor health in infancy are maladjusted from the standpoint of behavior. Many are not. But some are, and the cause is probably poor health plus some instability in personal or social characteristics. One of the best safeguards against later malbehavior is good health in infancy. If poor health has led to undesirable habits, attitudes, and behavior, a thorough mental and emotional analysis, with an honest facing of the facts, will surely assist in bringing a better point of view. Much has been said and written about the physical aspects of health, but there could be greater stress on its psychological and emotional aspects.

2. CHILD'S PRESENT HEALTH [1]

An investigation into a child's present health is of primary importance in diagnosing his behavior difficulties. The results may indicate, first, how his illnesses affect his physical and personality

[1] See page 41.

growth and, second, how the attention he receives during his periods of illness influences his emotional attitudes. In taking a family history, particularly of behavior problems in which a great many sensitive points must be mentioned, the best rapport is established by first dwelling upon the health of the child and his parents. Parents are sensitive about their intelligence, morals, and social and economic standing. The child's poor behavior, or peculiarities, or backwardness is a reflection on them, and they often resent much reference to it; but if the subject can be introduced by convincing them that their own failings have a physical basis, they feel better about the matter.

The condition of the body has a great deal to do with the state of the emotions and consequently with the mode of behavior. Few people can function efficiently, either in school or in an occupation, if they are feeling definitely uncomfortable or if they lack physical energy. Children need robust health to face life's problems. Their bodies are growing and their resistance is often low. Muscles as well as minds need nourishment if the children are to progress normally in school and to play actively and happily. Parents and teachers are quick to punish a child who is failing in school, who is inattentive, or who is cross and pugnacious or stubborn; but few of them consider first whether he is really feeling well.

A child who has chronic colds, sore throats, or toothaches is not apt to be bright and pleasant. Anemic, underweight, and undernourished children are almost always listless, dull, and whining. Constipation at any age makes a person irritable and heavyheaded. Some children complain of frequent headaches. Many have digestive trouble. A weak stomach, acidosis, weak bladder, or congested kidneys may be the cause. Unrecognized cases of appendicitis bring acute distress. Many girls suffer great pain or depression during the menstrual period. Hernias keep boys from playing actively and often make them ill-tempered. Practically all of such disorders can be cured or lessened in severity; if they are unchecked indefinitely, a change in personality and the attitude toward life can be expected to take place in the individual.

A child with heart trouble is greatly handicapped, particularly in his social relations. Someone is always at him to rest oftener and to play less boisterously for fear that he will die or become worse. He misses much fun because he cannot take gymnasium work or swimming in school or run about on the playground. At home he is inadvertently pampered because he cannot be allowed to do much work around the house, or fight his own battles lustily, or receive very severe punishments. As a consequence he may become overbearing, egotistic, selfish, or lazy. Hot temper and mean disposition may be either the actual result of heart trouble or the reaction to the treatment received from oversympathetic persons or from the unsympathetic who are contemptuous of the weak.

Public health departments are doing splendid work in checking the spread of tuberculosis among children. Neglected children or those exposed to the dirt of cities are easily infected. If a child is exposed or infected, his health should be the primary consideration with parents, workers, and teachers. Those most susceptible to it are usually the tall, thin-chested ones who are growing too fast. The common cold should not be overlooked in this type of child, nor should such children be deprived of food and rest. These children do not have any unusual personality manifestations, especially in the earlier stages of the disease, although they may develop them later.

A small number of school children are born with or catch venereal disease. Public-health physicians state that there is a greater number of cases among high-school students now than formerly. The modern laxity of morals and the tearing down of taboos and inhibitions seem to be increasing sex relations among adolescents. The worry, shame, and bitter resentment in those who become infected are difficult to combat. It may be well to note at this point that frequently younger children accused of masturbation prove to be victims of some venereal disease which irritates the pubic region.

The child's glandular system, which is discussed further under Item 12 on size, may also be considered under this topic of health. The overaction or underaction of glands may affect health and consequently personality and behavior. For instance, a hyperthyroid person is apt to be nervous, irascible, high-strung, unreasonable, erratic, and a bustling but not always an efficient worker. The hypothyroid, on the other hand, is sluggish, slow, often dull mentally, and phlegmatic in personality. Exophthalmic goiter, due to an abnormal increase in the growth and activity of the lobes of the thyroid gland, also causes personality changes. It is rare in early life but occurs about the time of puberty, especially in girls of the neurotic type. The child is apt to be irritable, easily excited, and depressed if left without companions. Diagnoses and treatment by gland specialists bring most gland cases back to, or closer to, normality, at least in behavior.

Chorea, or St. Vitus's dance, is a neurotic affection characterized by purposeless movements of various parts of the body. Rheumatism and tonsillitis are antecedent causes. Hypertrophied tonsils and valvular disease are sometimes associated with it. Girls are more often affected than boys. It appears most frequently from the fifth to the twelfth years of life. It may develop as a result of fright, excessive school duties, intestinal autointoxications, or imitations of other choreic children. The offspring of neurotic parents are especially predisposed. The symptoms usually come on insidiously. The child is chided for carelessness, awkwardness in dropping articles, or for unnecessary fidgeting. Nervousness and irritability of temper are noticeable. Upon little or no provocation the child begins to cry. The muscles in various parts of the body begin to twist and contract and there are ludicrous facial grimaces. After a severe fright or chastisement, chorea suddenly develops with well-marked symptoms. Removing the child from school and giving him long physical rest in a well-ventilated, quiet room are the most important measures in treating him. Uncomplicated cases tend to recover in from one to seven months. Ignorant or cruel parents and thoughtless teachers may cause a relatively mild case to develop into a serious and complex one.

Chronic ill-health creates in the individual a need for some kind of compensation or a defense mechanism. The latter may be evidenced by pugnacious or mean behavior and unsocial acts whereby he tries to punish society. On the other hand, many famous people of history and of present times have suffered from great ill-health but have compensated for it by making a tremendous effort to succeed in some vocation.

Imaginary illnesses constitute a phase of health. A complete physical examination may reveal that the patient is in reasonably good health, but for certain reasons he believes or has been made to believe that he has ailments. All his faults and failures he lays to his "poor health" and makes no effort to overcome them. Ordinary school and home duties are neglected on the grounds that his health will not permit him to do them. For the same reason he feels that he should be exempt from punishments and be given special privileges by adults and other children. Not only does he become self-centered, selfish, and unsocial; but he also gets so much satisfaction and gratification out of the attention paid his health that he goes out of his way to refuse to co-operate in improving it.

Overprotective parents are often responsible for such a situation. They make a great fuss every time their child sneezes, looks a little pale, cannot eat all his good food, or oversleeps. They are always sure he is coming down with something or has some disorder which no doctor has been clever enough to diagnose. The child of course plays up to this parental attitude, taking advantage of it every chance he gets. Unfortunately he carries it over into school and expects to take advantage of his teachers in the same way. Imaginary illness is often an escape mechanism whereby the individual avoids difficulties. He may actually show all the physical signs of sickness. A little girl of eight who was sent to a clinic for analysis used to have vomiting spells whenever she was requested to do any work at home or school. By paying no attention to her gagging and by providing work in which she could succeed easily, her symptoms were eliminated. In extreme cases imaginary illnesses are symptoms of hysteria and other forms of insanity.

In all health problems the mother and nurse must be warned not to give the matter too much obvious attention, lest the child crave the same attention after he is well. A system of corrective habits must be arranged and consistently practiced. If there are other children in the home, each should have some similar routine so that the ailing child is not made to feel that he is different. If the sickness necessitates long absence from school, the nurse or mother should try to keep up a contact with the classroom. The child should devote certain hours during the day to doing a few lessons. News from school and progress in the textbooks should be reported frequently so that his interests may be kept alive.

Much could be said of the many emotional problems which arise as a direct result of illness. If parents could recognize the destructiveness of their overanxiety, if it were possible to measure just what the constant worry and persistent fussing over him does to the child's emotional values, or if one could see immediately the detrimental results of prolonged coddling during convalescence, more effort would be made by parents and nurses to preserve the emotional as well as the physical integrity of the child.

It is important to remember that bodily conditions alone do not cause behavior problems, except possibly in epilepsy, encephalitis, and insanities, which will be mentioned later. But they supplement the various other factors which may be militating against the child's proper development. If teachers and parents would work with the medical profession, the solving of many of our children's problems would be easier. For those parents who cannot afford a private physician, a liberal system of health clinics has been provided and in smaller communities, the county doctor. There is no need to neglect health either in its physical or its mental aspects. If parents really understood that more is involved than just the inconvenience of having to care for a sick person, part of the problem would be solved.

3. Children's Diseases [1]

As pointed out in the preceding topic on health, a child's sicknesses are of interest to a psychologist for only two main reasons: their effect on his physical growth and their effect on his personality development. Children's diseases are so common that their consequences are often overlooked.

Measles is one of the most frequent of children's diseases and is regarded as relatively unimportant by the majority of people. It is not, however, always mild; its complications can be really serious. Bronchopneumonia and other inflammatory conditions are often accompaniments of measles. Cerebrospinal meningitis is occasionally encountered, particularly in the pneumonia cases. Osteomyelitis and superation of the joints have been noticed, although they are rare. Ear trouble may follow the disease—otitis media or mastoiditis. Conjunctivitis is the most frequent complication in measles. Keratitis and iritis may result and do permanent damage to the eyes. Confinement in a well-ventilated room where the light is thoroughly subdued is imperative. Eye baths and catharsis through calomel or enemas are the hygienic measures generally prescribed by the medical profession for the average case of measles.

Whooping cough, like measles, is dangerous because of its complications. Bronchopneumonia may accompany it, and tuberculosis not infrequently follows. Severe attacks of vomiting reduce the general nutrition and predispose the patient to more important complications. Convulsions result from congestion of the brain or from minute capillary hemorrhages which may occur during the paroxysm. Hemiplegia sometimes follows a severe paroxysm. Hemorrhages into the conjunctiva and hernias in various parts of the body also result from the severe strain imposed by the paroxysms. This disease is treated by drugs and vaccine, diet, and fresh air.

The disease of mumps is accompanied by fever, but it has less severe complications. Deafness, inflammatory eye diseases, and,

[1] See page 42.

rarely, nephritis may occur. In boys at or near the age of puberty, the testicles sometimes cease their development.

Chicken pox is a milder contagious disease which seldom has serious complications. Otitis, pneumonia, and nephritis are rare accompaniments. The worst result of the disease is the pockmarks left after the child has scratched and infected the scabs.

Tonsillitis, quinsy, and jaundice are other diseases of childhood which usually need the services of a physician. Boils, pinkeye, and impetigo can be treated by hygienic methods. Mastoiditis and ear infections are often serious and require professional attention.

Personality traits, habits, and emotional attitudes of an undesirable nature can be the indirect results of a child's having had a number of these diseases. Retardation in the development of self-reliance and maturity are the outcome of the unusual attention the child receives during frequent illnesses. His period of babyhood is apt to be prolonged through the constant attendance of mother or nurse. Their services become so pleasurable to him that he is unwilling to relinquish them. He may resort to various little tricks—attention-getting mechanisms—to obtain them. Even scolding may be more gratifying to him than no attention at all.

At school this child wishes his teacher to act as a mother substitute and expects privileges and spoiling from her. Instead of concentrating on his lessons, he spends his time creating silly disturbances which focus the attention of the children and teacher upon him. Truancy is not uncommonly a sequel to long absences due to sicknesses. The child has been out of school so much that he has fallen behind the class and finds it difficult to make up the work. He may therefore skip school to avoid putting forth extra effort, or his enforced vacations may have been so pleasant that he dreads getting down to a routine.

School and home should maintain contacts during a child's sicknesses. His interest in the progress of the class should be stimulated. A special attempt should be made by teachers and pupils to help the child catch up with the others on his return.

Since he is likely to feel a loss of importance as a part of the group because of his long absence, they should assure him that they have missed him and are glad to have him back.

An outside worker may have to be called in to help the mother readjust the child in the home. She must cease waiting on him and babying him. Instead, she should give him certain responsibilities which will bring him privileges and satisfying attention to replace those given him during his period of debility.

4. Serious Infectious Diseases [1]

While the serious infectious diseases are well known by name and are common to every class of people, a short description of the chief characteristics of a few such diseases may be useful to those interested in the physical and social welfare of children.

Tuberculosis may attack any organ or part of the body; the bacilli easily invade meninges, bones, joints, and lungs. They are believed by some physicians to remain latent in early life and to develop later into the pulmonary form. In childhood there is little resistance to the disease. A child with poor muscular development, with flat and narrow chest and small abdomen, and with defects of the nose and mouth is especially prone to it. Children of weak and unhealthy parents, living in unsanitary surroundings, are susceptible. Common sources of infection are human sputum, food objects, dust, milk of tubercular cows, urine, feces, or soiled clothing and beds of infected people, and handling and kissing by such people.

Diphtheria is an acute infectious disease which usually occurs in widespread epidemics, especially in the more thickly populated cities. It is more prevalent in winter and fall than in the summer months. It is contracted directly or indirectly from other cases or from carriers and even from contaminated food. The most common early symptoms are sore throat, with a gray-colored membrane, and swollen and painful glands. The heart must be carefully watched in diphtheria, or it is left permanently weak. The

[1] See page 43.

patient must be kept quiet and in a recumbent position until complete recovery takes place. Otherwise sudden death may easily ensue, even during convalescence. Immunization with antitoxin, which assumes the first place in prophylactic treatment, has saved many lives.

Scarlet fever is an acute infectious and contagious disease, characterized by a sudden onset, vomiting, and a generalized scarlet rash accompanied by high fever. The mortality averages about 3 per cent. Nephritis, deafness, arthritis, and occasionally a paralysis are frequently sequences of the disease.

Smallpox is an acute contagious disease characterized by eruptions of pustules on the body. The mortality is very high, especially with children under ten years of age. Convulsions are often among the complications, while pneumonia and arthritis sometimes follow the disease. Permanent injury to the eyes may result from inflammation. Deafness, chronic boils, and acne are possible consequences. Vaccination is a measure which, if thoroughly carried out, would eradicate the disease.

Typhoid fever is an infectious disease contracted from infected drinking water or milk and from contact with carriers of the germs. Dishes, thermometers, and flies may carry the infective agent. Forty-six per cent of the cases occur between five and fifteen years of age. A controlled diet, rest, and fresh air are of primary importance in treatment.

Bronchopneumonia is perhaps the most common disease of infancy. Bronchitis and the infectious diseases, especially measles, influenza, diphtheria, and scarlet fever, are predisposing causes. Children with rickets, malnutrition, syphilis, and kidney and intestinal troubles, particularly if they live in unhygienic surroundings, have their resistance lowered and are consequently susceptible. The ear, heart, brain, and speech centers may be involved. The mortality is high.

Cerebrospinal meningitis is essentially a disease of the young, with the second year of life claiming the greatest number of victims. It occurs most frequently in the spring, after prolonged confinement in ill-ventilated and superheated apartments. Children with lowered resistance and depleted vitality are the most susceptible. The onset is usually sudden and abrupt. In the epidemic type headache, vertigo, vomiting, and high fever are soon followed by coma and death. Complications are in the forms of eye, ear, brain, and joint afflictions.

Encephalitis seems to follow epidemics of influenza, although the specific causes of this disease are still to be discovered. There are, however, dreaded consequences. A marked personality change is almost always seen. The child becomes antisocial, mean, unreasonable, ill-tempered, and cruel. Retraining of such children has as yet been relatively unsuccessful except in a few instances (2). A minority have been stabilized by removing them from their homes and placing them in private institutions whose setup was especially designed for their treatments.

Rheumatic fever, a febrile disease of the joints, is believed to have an infectious origin, the nature of which is still in dispute. The mouth, tonsils, and teeth are regarded as the portal of entry of the infecting organism, with exposure, cold, and damp apartments as predisposing factors. Heredity also seems to play a part. It is not common before the fifth year. Rheumatic fever is dreaded because of its cardiac complications. Warmth and rest in bed are of great importance.

All these serious infectious diseases demand the services of a physician. It is imperative that his orders be followed in all matters of diet, drugs, rest, disinfecting, and quarantine. When parent and child are lax about carrying out these orders, complications may set in which are more malignant than the disease itself. Since the diseases are so serious and need the constant attendance of nurse or mother, the afflicted child finds himself in a position of some importance, especially during convalescence, when he is more aware of the situation and strong enough to enjoy it. The danger is that he will try to maintain this position after his recovery. Many a mother has claimed that the child who is now giving so much trouble had perfect behavior until after he had had one of these major diseases. She attributes his change of behavior to some mysterious change in his brain caused by the disease.

There are only a few diseases which of themselves actually produce a marked change in a child's nature, *e.g.*, encephalitis, epilepsy, chorea, sometimes cerebrospinal meningitis, and diseases affecting the heart and ductless glands. The main cause of change is the unusual attention received by the child, which so satisfies him that he expects and demands it thereafter. When he does not succeed in obtaining it, he creates mechanisms which will force attention of some kind upon him.

Many parents and teachers, realizing that the child was spoiled during sickness, try to correct the situation by strictness and entire withdrawal of attention. A better policy is to diminish gradually the attentions and services given him, placing upon him the responsibility for his care and recovery. If he himself keeps a chart or graph of his daily habits during convalescence, he is likely to continue taking an active interest in the care of his health after recovery instead of leaving such matters solely to his parents. Their praise of his charts will encourage his keeping them. A small child, unable to read, will have an interest in a chart if his mother makes one of gold stars and lets him paste them on. The teacher should show an interest in the home charts and make suggestions about his keeping one of his progress in making up work at school.

5. ACCIDENTS [1]

In spite of excellent instructions by teachers, police, and parents on the prevention of accidents, fatalities and injuries to school children still exist in great numbers. Forty-four per cent of blindness or defective vision is caused by accidents, explosives, firearms, or blows. About 4 per cent of the orthopedic defects come from accidents. Head injuries are particularly dangerous. Severe blows on the head may cause amnesia or aphasia, epilepsy, insanity, or mental deficiency.

[1] See page 44.

When a child has had one or more serious accidents, the solicitous attentions of his worried parents and relatives can produce the same undesirable effects on his personality as those mentioned in connection with the preceding topics. The child gets an inflated idea of his own importance. He may be deliberately careless thereafter and apparently not try to avoid accidents, because subconsciously he would like to be laid up again with the accompanying pleasurable attention. Several mothers have reported that their children have been injured by cars two or three times and still run out into streets without looking in any direction, entirely fearless and unconcerned about danger.

In most cases of accidents, however, the reverse is true. The children are left with morbid fears. They are afraid of another accident not only from the same cause but also from various other causes. They develop a fear of the dark, of animals, of strangers, of loud noises, and of thunderstorms. They want to remain at home near their parents instead of playing with their companions. Some of them will not go to school unless accompanied by a parent or an older child. These fears might have been avoided had the parents helped them to re-establish their independence after convalescence and to develop caution mixed with courage.

Parents too often are responsible for the development of these emotional associations. Many of them are insecure persons who feel excessively a need of their children. The thought of losing them fills them with panic. On the opposite side are the parents who did not want children. They have a subconscious desire to be rid of them and therefore, through their feelings of guilt, tend to overprotect them. Since most fears are acquired, children would probably remember few of their experiences if they were not reminded of them by their parents. They imitate their parents' attitudes. If a parent is afraid of accidents, the child becomes afraid of having them, too, and he remembers his former ones with horror.

When a worker or teacher wishes to help a child recover from the fears which he develops after his accident, he will find that usually the greatest problem is with the parents. He must go to the parents and help them analyze their fears. If the parents can lose their own, then the child will very likely lose his, too; or if the parents cannot overcome theirs, at least they can be told how the child is imitating them and what the bad effects of this imitation are on his general behavior.

A typical example of this tendency is in the following case: A fine little boy was reported because of his failing in school work and his poor attendance. He was the only child of a mother who had been deserted by her husband. The mother of course was very much attached to this son and gave him the love she would have given the father. The boy had been hit by a car on two different occasions, though with no serious injury. However, the mother became so afraid he would be hit again that she would not let him cross any streets alone or go to school without her. The boy had not yet become infected with her fear but was growing more apprehensive the longer the situation went on. The treatment consisted of analyzing the mother's own personal problem with her. Fortunately she was able to face it squarely and to co-operate in reorienting herself. She was more willing to do this when she was made to realize the harm she might do her child by tying him too closely to her and by not letting him learn how to take care of himself when away from home as other children do.

Fear of accidents may prey on children's minds so that they cannot concentrate on their school work. They sit and daydream and thus bring some reminder or reprimand from the teacher. They look up in bewilderment and inwardly rebel at the teacher's unjust accusation. When fears are unusually severe, the child may take on the pathological behavior of lying, stealing, or running away. Healy's discussion of these types was mentioned in Chapter II.

A six-year-old boy from a wealthy family came to the Detroit clinic for stealing pennies in spite of the fact that he had a liberal allowance. Investigation showed that he had recently witnessed his father being hit in a so-called safety zone, while he himself had escaped accident there. He was dreaming nights of large wheels looming up to crush him. As a cure for this condition, his father took the child for walks and showed him different degrees of danger from cars. Gradually he became less fearful and his stealing disappeared.

The results of shock from accidents seem so far fetched that parents usually do not recognize them—a real impediment to curative treatment, for their attitude tends to disparage the worker's suggestions on other issues which are less subtle. Newspapers and magazines carry on a constant campaign as to the physical dangers of traffic hazards, but very little is said about the more important mental and emotional effects.

6. DEGREE OF SPEECH DEFECT [1]

A speech defect, from the child's point of view, may be a greater handicap than an orthopedic, a visual, or an auditory difficulty. Certainly it can be more embarrassing, and it receives less sympathy. As the child's principal mode of expression is through speech, such an impediment is a source of constant frustration. His feeling of being thwarted and his consciousness of being different increase as he grows older. He reaches adulthood with a deep-set belief in his inadequacy and inferiority. As a result he either loses his normal initiative and withdraws into himself or he develops mechanisms through which he becomes overly aggressive. The fact that there were in one year 5890 children in Detroit's speech classes shows how large a per cent of the population must suffer from this defect.

Other children are seldom kind to the child with the speech defect. Few can resist teasing and mimicking him. Even teachers lose patience with his unintelligible recitations. If he is not fortunate enough to have talent in the motor or artistic fields, he is decidedly a social misfit. Wendell Johnson (4) gives a fine description of this problem in his own case.

Speech is superimposed on organs already used for more funda-

[1] See page 45.

mental purposes. The child begins by a crying which has melody and rhythm. He makes certain repetitions of sounds which soon take on a meaningful character. In the babble stage he perfects the vowel sounds and soon begins to articulate. It is with the articulation of consonants that some speech defects first appear. The child, finding some sounds difficult to pronounce, makes substitutions, such as "thupper" for "supper," "dwink" for "drink," or "piwow" for "pillow."

There are many causes of speech defects. In the field of stammering alone, fifty-one causes have been distinguished. These causes seem to be either anatomical abnormalities or mental and emotional strain. When seeking the cause of a speech impediment, the possibility of birth injury must be considered first. If the injury is serious, there is not much hope; but if only a small area of cells has been injured, a near-by set of cells can be trained to take over the work of the affected part. Organic malformations in the oral organs, such as a high arch, cleft palate, crowded or wide-spaced teeth, or disproportionate tongue and tonsils interfere with normal speech.

A child cannot of course inherit a speech defect, but he may receive a mechanism which is predisposed toward certain types of troubles. The fact that during the World War many shell-shocked men reacted with speech defects indicates that certain families have a tendency toward a weak speech mechanism. Moreover, since the child learns to talk by imitation, he is apt to copy the speech defect of another member of his family and to exaggerate his own speech tendencies or at any rate to distort his own natural speech through the conflict between correct and incorrect speech. In the same family a mother may talk too fast, one child may lisp, and another may stutter or talk baby talk.

Weakened bodily conditions through disease, malnutrition, anemia, or toxic poisoning—from bad teeth or tonsils—can cause speech impediments. Many speech defects, particularly stuttering, have been considered to be possible glandular cases. In hypothyroid persons there seems to be either too loose or too tight activity in the oral organs.

One psychologist claims that 50 per cent of all cases of stuttering develop from forcing naturally left-handed persons to use their right hands. Retraining the use of the left hand has helped many. Ambidexterity may impede speech, for in such cases neither side of the brain is dominant and a block may follow.

When the cause of a speech defect is not an obviously anatomical one, it is probably some mental and emotional strain. A great fear coming at the time when speech is beginning may cause stammering. There have been cases of children who lived in homes with drunken, abusive fathers or who were in terrible fires or wrecks who developed this defect later, although they had forgotten the traumatic experience. Family relationships can effect a young child's speech mechanism. The youngest is particularly prone to speech defect because of pampering or being looked upon as the family "goat." Nagging, unjust punishments, and broken promises, as well as disorderliness, poverty, and worry, can disturb the speech mechanism.

A child may want to do one thing and be forced to do another. He may stutter or lisp when he lies, though he may do so at no other time—just as some people blush when lying. Shame over some "secret sin" has resulted in emotional conflicts evincing themselves through speech defects. Adolescence, with its unaccustomed feelings, new strains, and new demands, makes good ground for the stammering habit, especially if the child never stuttered before. Children of foreign parentage who have a partial knowledge of two languages, so that they think in one language but must translate their thoughts into English when in school, may develop speech conflicts. Then there are children who, though they talk relatively fluently at home, are not eager to express themselves upon entering school. It takes them some time to gain control of their school situations. They want to express their impressions before they are ready, or an emotional blocking may take place which results in stuttering. The fact that 25 per cent of the pupils do not begin to stutter until after they enter school shows the effect that the excitement and fear of their first few days in school may have upon them. Teasing, shaming, and harshness can make a child with a weak speech mechanism begin to stutter. Some children may think so quickly that the oral organs are not able to respond properly, or the oral organs may work so fast that stuttering is the consequence.

It seems wise to note, before leaving the subject of the emotional causes of stuttering, that emotional complexes are not always the *cause* of the trouble; sometimes they are the *result*. Stuttering may be just as much a part of one's personality as is ordinary expression for a normal person; the individual may be quite unconscious of the stuttering. It is only after he has been laughed at or imitated that he begins to have any emotional association with it.

Treatment for speech defects begins with the removal or repair of any anatomical defect and improvement of the general physical condition of the body as a whole. Practice in speech correction follows. Teachers of the subject are of course trained in the special techniques for changing the various types of impediments. In general they try to make the child happy and comfortable, using every chance to relieve his embarrassment. They create an atmosphere of ease and relaxation in the classroom. They do not hurry him or scold him. By sympathy, kindness, and encouragement they win the child's trust and cooperation. Then, having relieved his strain, they begin to retrain him.

7. Degree of Vision Defect [1]

There are in this country, about 100,000 people who are totally blind, and estimates show that 60 per cent of the educated Americans have impaired vision. From 10 to 30 per cent of all school pupils have sufficiently defective vision to demand medical attention.

Doctors claim that over 50 per cent of the blindness is preventable, since it is self-made by neglect and careless use of the most intricate mechanism we possess, the human eye. The in-

[1] See page 46.

dividual himself is seldom aware that he does not see well until his sight has deteriorated beyond hope of adequate treatment. Parents do not always realize that the large, deep eyes of their child cannot see all that the largeness implies.

The dearest hope of every prospective mother is that she may bear a child well equipped with healthy organs and a mind with which to compete on an equal basis with his fellows. Great is the distress if he is physically weak or crippled; large amounts of money are spent to correct his defect. If the child is born totally blind, everything possible is done for him. Few parents realize the importance of the protection and correction of vision in the early years, for they have not considered the possible effect of poor vision on character development or how poor vision jeopardizes the chances of success in a competing world.

Who stops to puzzle over the fact that the bookworm, popular with his teachers and family because of his fine classroom powers, is often unpopular on the playground or in athletics? This type of person may be *myopic*. If he is, the eyeball is too long, so that rays of light in distant vision focus in front of the retina and thus produce a blurred image. This defect makes it easy for the child to read and do close work but difficult to hit a golf or tennis ball or locate the hoop accurately in a basketball game. Walks outdoors are not very pleasurable to him because the beauties of nature are dim to the myopic eye. He wins at bridge or checkers, is a good speaker in clubs or at intellectual gatherings, or, lacking opportunities to excel at these activities, may get his pleasure vicariously from books and magazines. Because of little exercise outdoors, he is likely to be pale, sluggish, phlegmatic, or irritable with pent-up physical energy. While he makes his family and pedagogues happy and can usually win success in the world, he is not always happy himself, being deprived of the chance which everyone wants to be a good sport and to play like other people in group recreations. Boys, more than girls, are apt to suffer from effects of myopia. In the milder form of myopia the length of the eyeball does not continue to increase, and the individual is able to enjoy good vision with the aid of glasses. But in the malignant form the lengthening of the eyeball keeps on increasing until the retina of one or both eyes is damaged. In this disease strict hygienic measures must be employed and sedentary occupations avoided. There should be a minimum of reading, much good food, fresh air, good posture, and good elimination. The possibility of complete or industrial blindness must be borne in mind.

Hyperopia is caused by too short an eyeball. In hyperopia the retina intercepts rays of light before they are brought to normal focus. The eye is under great strain from incessant demands made on the ciliary muscle. The nervousness which often accompanies hyperopia may result in chorea or vomiting. The child with this handicap is sometimes inattentive, dull, and lazy in school. His eyes wander from his books to the fields outside the window. He is disliked by his teachers and nagged at by parents for his poor school achievement; but he is a great fellow on the playground and at games. He is skillful in the use of tools, especially large ones. His eye easily detects a bird's nest in a tree or an animal under a distant bush, and he reads a signboard which others cannot see. A girl with hyperopia is inclined to be a tomboy. She is interested in muscular activity, she is an outdoor girl, or she is clever at mechanics. Application to close work causes strain and fatigue to hyperopic eyes. Every teacher or parent with children unable to concentrate should take them for an eye examination. Glasses can easily correct hyperopia. Since they need be worn only for reading, the antipathy against them is less when they can be left in the school and put on only during school hours. Continued use of the eyes without proper glasses will seldom impair the vision permanently; but the continued strain, if unrelieved, may make a nervous wreck of the child.

Astigmatism is produced by an uneven radius of curvature, usually of the cornea. Thus the eye is double-focused; it is impossible to focus an image clearly in both meridians at once. Letters and lines blur before the eyes, making reading difficult. Sixty per cent of all headaches are said to be traceable to astigmatism. This defect often accompanies myopia and may vary in the two eyes. It should invariably be diagnosed and treated by a good oculist.

The psychological effect of cross-eye on a child is far-reaching. Such epithets as "cock-eyed" soon make him conscious and ashamed of his defect. He gradually shuns contact with other children, prefers to play alone, and loses the influence of comradeship which is natural to the normal child. As he grows older, an inferiority complex develops, which gathers momentum as he approaches adolescence. He may develop defense mechanisms of meanness and bullying to compensate. Because his vision is thus impaired, he is excluded from many vocations in which he would be otherwise well qualified.

Strabismus is the result of the failure to develop the habit of fusion or the habit of using the two eyes together. Each eye sees singly, but the two images ordinarily become blended or fused. This fault may begin with weakness at birth, when strabismus may set in. In several instances it has been caused by forcing a naturally left-handed person to become right-handed. It may be caused by an illness or accident. In most cases the vision is better in one eye than in the other, and the eye with the better sight will fix while the weak eye will tend to turn in. The child then ignores the image of the turned-in eye. Vision fails rapidly in the eye which turns in.

Doctors assure parents that many crossed eyes can be corrected. The several steps necessary to put the cross-eyed child on an equal footing with normal children are these: testing of vision, fitting of glasses, preventing lessening of vision in the weak eye, awakening fusion faculty, and finally, when necessary, operation. Contrary to the common belief that the child outgrows his affliction, treatment, to give perfect results, should begin in the formative years, before the age of seven. If glasses are worn as early as first or second year, nothing else may need to be done for the child. Postponing the fitting of glasses until later may save the vision in the weak eye but it will not straighten the eyes. On the other hand, operation will straighten the eyes, but it may not correct the loss of vision in the weak eye. The important point is to fit the cross-eyed child with glasses at the earliest possible age.

In some individuals there exists an imbalance or asymmetry of eye movement which is known as heterophoria, which is a more latent tendency toward asymmetry than actual strabismus, or heterotropia. Esophoria is a tendency to see parallel lines as if they were converging toward one another. Exophoria is seeing them tending outward or away from one another. In hyperphoria there is a tendency for one line to seem to be above the other. When lines seem to go in oblique directions there is hyperesophoria or hyperexophoria. These tendencies are concealed in the ordinary use of the eyes on account of the strong desire for binocular vision, but they feature deleteriously in the reading processes. Many reading problems could be diagnosed as having for their basic difficulty no other handicap than one of these tendencies. The pupil therefore has trouble distinguishing between similar letters: n is m or u or v or even w; c is e; and t is l or f. Heterophoria in the vertical plane can be helped with glasses. In the lateral field, glasses are not very effective. Exercises or prisms can be tried here. This peculiarity is often caused by an infection in the ethmoid sinus. Therefore building up the general health and the general muscle tone may assist in correcting the defect.

Until recent years there has been a great deal of foolish reticence about speaking openly and truthfully about venereal diseases and their hideous effects upon the human system. Among their ravages is that of blindness. From 10 to 20 per cent of blindness is caused by the gonococci, or germs, of gonorrhea, which enter the eyes of a new-born babe from its infected mother. Drops of silver nitrate put into the eyes of the child at birth prevent such blindness. Good physicians use this prophylactic measure as a matter of course; but there is ample evidence to prove that many midwives or careless doctors still fail to perform this duty, which is required by law.

Another treacherous and preventable disease responsible for

blindness is syphilis, especially the congenital type called lues. Careless parents who neglect having treatment before bearing children cause the latter to pay dearly for their neglect and folly. Apparently healthy children, usually rosy-cheeked and playful, become suddenly blinded, while their eyes are salmon red and teary. They are the victims of congenital syphilis, which produces atrophy of the optic nerve, cataracts, and interstitial keratitis. The last named can be checked and treated by medicine if it is met in time; if not, it ends in blindness. Interstitial keratitis, it should be noted, can also arise from rheumatism, a tubercular condition of the eye, a run-down system, and various toxins.

Trachoma is an infectious disease which, if not treated in time, causes blindness. It is manifested by infection of the conjunctiva and granulated lids. Glaucoma is another vicious eye disease which causes blindness. It is a hardening of the eyeball, a pressure within the ball, and an increase in ocular tension accompanied by severe pain. Unfortunately it is rarely cured. It is caused by toxins, injuries, and anything which causes hardening of the arteries.

Cataracts usually appear after the age of fifty, but they may be congenital, traumatic, or the companion of another disease. In some cases they do not progress to the point of destroying sight, but in most cases they do. However, operation has been successful in eliminating them and restoring vision.

There are many other serious eye diseases which end in defective vision or blindness; here we have mentioned only the most prominent ones, those met with most frequently in school children.

Good eyes can be endangered from five main causes: accident, contagion, poor general health, wrong eye habits, and neglect of minor visual ills. Except for accidents these causes can usually be avoided and vision protected.

Contagious diseases like measles and scarlet fever may have serious aftereffects on eyes. Reading should be forbidden during and immediately after these diseases; eye baths should be given, and lighting should be kept subdued. "Babies' sore eyes" should not be mistaken for colds; neglect or poor treatment with home remedies may jeopardize eyesight for all time. Bad teeth and tonsils may generate poisons which inflame the eyes, making them muddy and painful. Anemia deteriorates the visual efficiency just as it affects general body efficiency.

Wrong eye habits are largely responsible for eyestrain. Reading in poor lighting, such as poorly diffused or insufficient light, or with a glare on the page or in the eyes causes a fatigue reaction. The pupil of the eye is kept small by constant overaction of its constrictor muscle, and the visual purple is so rapidly used that the retina of the eye becomes fatigued. Woodwork and furniture should have a dull finish. Movable desks should have tops capable of being tilted at an angle to avoid progressive nearsightedness. More or less diffused light should come over the shoulder on to the page. A northeast exposure is the most favorable condition. Dark glasses should be worn outdoors if one is to be long in bright sunlight.

Eclipse of sight and snow blindness come from different types of exposure. One should not look directly at the sun without using a well-smoked glass, lest the fovea (center of vision) be destroyed. Care should be taken to protect infants' eyes from direct glare and from burning of the lids by the sun. We have often seen crowds of children watching welders on the street, staring with their young eyes straight into the crackling blue sparks which the workmen themselves never look at unless their eyes are protected by dark glasses. Teachers and parents should warn children not to gaze at this fascinating fire without such glasses.

So that teachers and parents may be on the alert to diagnose eyestrain we offer a summary of the symptoms: crossed eyes, peculiar head posture, frowning, holding books too near the eyes, difficulty in reading from the blackboard, red or sore eyes, sties, granulated lids, sensitiveness to light, headaches, fatigue, nervousness, nausea and indigestion, poor school work, calling words wrong, blurred or double vision, scars on the cornea, and seeing colors or movements of letters or lines. Children with any of these symptoms should be taken for an examination by an eye specialist. Pupils who cannot see 20/70 with one eye alone should also receive an examination.[1]

For children who have very defective vision but are not wholly blind, good glasses must be obtained from a specialist. If the family cannot pay for them, a city charity organization or the board of health will usually take care of the matter through sums put aside to cover such charges for indigent school children. These youngsters should be segregated in sight-saving classes, where every effort is made to conserve what vision is left them. Should no such class be provided in the town, teachers or nurses must try to furnish the children with books set with 24- to 36-point print.[2]

The totally blind should be given instruction in the Braille or raised-point letter system for reading, and should have courses in typing and special handicrafts. Most large cities have at least one class for instructing the blind, but far too many have none.[3]

We have shown how various eye defects and diseases can affect visual efficiency and learning ability; but there are many hundreds of cases where other, more subtle peculiarities of vision hinder the child from learning to spell, read, and write as well as other children of his mental age. Considerable research by psychologists (Walter Dearborn of Harvard University and others) has led to the discovery of certain visual and motor conditions which characterize many cases of reading disability (3).

Although the great majority of individuals learn to read material which is written or printed in the traditional ways, among those who do not learn to read readily there is a high proportion of ambidextrous people and of those who have been changed from left- to right-handedness in a more or less arbitrary and forcible manner. Those who are definitely left-handed and re-

[1] Cards for testing vision may be obtained from C. H. Stoelting Company, Chicago.

[2] These can be obtained from the Clear Type Publishing Company, 36 Elston Road, Montclair, New Jersey.

[3] Teachers or parents can obtain information and material on the Braille system from the National Committee for Prevention of Blindness, 50 West Fiftieth Street, New York City.

main so and those who are definitely right-handed seem to encounter little difficulty although they may even also learn to read with facility certain languages which are printed from right to left as well as from left to right.

Dearborn noted that among poor readers there was an unusual proportion of left-handed and especially ambidextrous persons. Then the surprising observation followed that what the sportsman speaks of as the "sighting" eye, the eye which takes aim in shooting or the eye with which a scientist looks into the microscope—in other words, the dominant eye—was often on the opposite side from the dominant hand. That is, many were left-handed but right-eyed or right-handed and left-eyed, and many were ambidextrous as to both eye and hand, shifting from one to the other. Among such children the most common errors are the reversals of the forms of individual letters, as reading *dig* for *big* or *pig*, and reversal of the order or sequence of letters, as reading *saw* for *was*, *on* for *no*, *tog* for *got*, *form* for *from*, or *stop* for *spot*. Dearborn also observed that, when children read words by the flash method, they tend to tackle words from the wrong end. A similarly back-handed or back-eyed tendency was also noted from his photographic records of the eye movements of some children when reading. It appears, then, that in order to avoid difficulties in reading and writing one should be either left-eyed and left-handed or right-eyed and right-handed, preferably the latter.

The reason for this situation is that in reading and writing the Aryan languages the hand and eye move in a dextral way, *i.e.*, in a sequence from left to right. It is natural for the right-eyed and right-handed person to make movements going from the center of the body out to his right, and he consequently does not have the trouble in reading as has the left-eyed and left-handed person, who wants to move from the center out to the left. The person who is ambidextrous or mixed in dominance does not know which way to go and so may try both ways uncertainly and in great confusion.

One other peculiarity of vision which ought to be mentioned

here is that of color blindness. The individual so affected may be able to see only black and white combinations or only black and white and blue and yellow, but not red and green. The handicap is usually compensated for by a special ability in discerning shades which indicate differences in a color. How serious such a handicap can be in traffic where "go" and "stop" lights are green and red is easily imagined. The handicap interferes with learning to read in the first grade, where the picture-story method gives such directions as, "Color the boy red, the cat yellow, and the tree green." Nothing can be done to remedy this defect, but it must be recognized before a vocation is chosen.

This discussion of vision has been necessarily lengthened because of its close and important relationship with personality and social types, with learning achievement, and with vocational choice. The various kinds of visual defects and diseases have been mentioned to acquaint teachers, nurses, social workers, and parents with their nature and effects so that they may be able to identify them tentatively and to seek immediate correction wherever possible. The facts given in each case can be used by the worker in convincing an indifferent, ignorant, or unwilling parent of the necessity of co-operating in the matter of correction and prevention. Poor vision results in nervous and mental strain and inability to sit still in school. Children become irritable and school work lags. The problem has many social implications beyond the mere inconvenience of not being able to see well.

8. Degree of Hearing Defect [1]

It has been shown that poor health, disease, injury, and visual defects can affect general efficiency in school and in occupation, warp or change personality, and interfere with the individual's happiness. Equally important is another physical factor, the sense of hearing. The deaf form a definitely handicapped and isolated group. They suffer intensely from being misunderstood and underestimated. Their personality and mental progress are

[1] See page 47.

often completely stunted by neglect, derision, or callousness on the part of their more fortunate fellows. Because of public indifference toward them in the past, of failure of teachers, parents, and associates to recognize the defect and of inefficient methods of curing and teaching them, much good material, intellectual and physical, has gone to waste.

The deleterious effects of deafness on the individual and his chances for more nearly normal development depend upon the degree of impairment and upon the length of time he has suffered from it. There exist varying degrees of deafness, ranging from slight and temporary impairment of hearing due to colds to the stage of absolute and permanent silence. The deaf may best be divided into these five classes:

1. Totally deaf
2. Practically deaf, hearing only intense and continuous sounds
3. Possessing a degree of hearing power; that is, hearing loud sounds but not understanding vocal speech
4. Deaf for ordinary school conditions; that is, hearing but needing special training in articulation
5. Hearing only words spoken loudly and close to the ear

Obviously these degrees of deafness present different problems from the standpoint of personality and of social and educational adjustments. Studies show that 90.6 per cent of all deafness occurs before the age of twenty, 75 per cent under the age of five, and 52.4 per cent under the age of two, while 33 per cent of these people are born deaf.

Nearly two thirds of the cases of deafness are caused by accident or disease. The disease may be of the auditory organ or a consequence of disease or infections elsewhere. In either case it occurs usually in infancy or childhood and attacks either the middle or the internal ear. Seventy-two per cent of the cases are of the suppurative or abscess type, and 28 per cent are non-suppurative or catarrhal in character. The chief causes are these:

Cause	Per Cent	Cause	Per Cent
Scarlet fever	11.1	Measles	2.5
Meningitis	9.6	Typhoid fever	2.4
Brain fever	4.7	Colds	1.6
Catarrh	3.6	Malarial fever	1.2
Disease of the middle ear	3.6	Influenza	.7

There are smaller causal proportions for diphtheria, pneumonia, and whooping cough. Still other causes are foreign bodies in the outer ear, teething, convulsions, abscesses, tonsillitis, falls, paralysis, and diseases of the ear and throat. In general it is suggested that treatment for adenoids will stop incipient cases, that careful medical aid be given during and immediately following any one of the diseases mentioned, and that infectious diseases be prevented from spreading. In any event a doctor's advice should be sought and followed to alleviate or check this affliction.

Congenital deafness is usually discovered by the parents when the baby is still under a year old; no loud noise startles him, the usual mother cooing brings no response, and he makes few little practice vocalizations himself beyond crying or hollow laughter and perhaps other shallow sounds. The child develops physically, learns to walk, and plays about. But he cannot play with others nor understand any language; in fact, he appears to be just a dull, subnormal person. Parents and brothers and sisters may lose interest in him, beyond feeling sorry for him. He takes little part in the household life unless given certain menial tasks to perform. Many parents do not realize that, even though a doctor may pronounce their child's affliction incapable of cure, there are modern educational methods which will teach this dull, even imbecile-looking child to understand and speak their tongue. Overwhelming is the joy when, after some months of schooling, he can read words on the lips of his family and answer intelligently, if at first only in a flat, peculiar voice. Many, too, have been known to learn to speak in a wholly normal voice after considerable training. Soon he is playing with normal-hearing children who forget he is different from them. If he is natively bright enough, he can go on through school and college. The choice of a vocation is limited, but many interesting and remunerative occupations are open to him. How different from neglecting the congenitally deaf child and leaving him to vegetate—a foolish dependent or at best a struggling, unhappy, unsocial laborer!

Defective hearing, like defective vision, may exist in a serious degree and yet pass unnoticed by the child, the teacher, his parents, or his friends. The best description of the effects of this situation on the deaf child may be in the story of a child named Lena. She was a big girl who sat in the back seat in school. She saw the teacher talking to the other children but thought she was just addressing her favored few, and that all the rest had to guess at what she said to them just as Lena herself did. Always she hoped it would soon be her turn to come up and hear the interesting remarks that made the other children smile and raise their hands. When the teacher said something directly to Lena, she only smiled back as the others had done. After this happened a few times, the teacher considered her silly, inattentive, and stubborn. This treatment persisted more or less throughout her school career. She was put back or failed because she could not keep up with the group. Her mates pointed to her as the biggest and dullest pupil in their group. She was punished at home for her poor school marks, because she did not come when called, and because she did not follow directions properly. Not unnaturally she became bitter, hateful, and unsocial. It was not until long after she had left school at fourteen years of age that she discovered she was deaf.

Not only does the deaf child seem inattentive, lazy, phlegmatic, and stupid, but he also appears unattractive. In his efforts to hear he develops odd bodily postures; he holds his head on one side, thrusts his neck forward, or hunches up his shoulders. Since facial expressions usually are accompaniments of, or reactions to, speech, his face is usually blank and expressionless. Even when the child and his associates are aware of the defect, he still suffers. He learns to know he is different, and he often broods over his unpopularity or lack of normal accomplishment. He sees the annoyed, impatient look on the faces of people who have to keep repeating what they say to him. Many children, however, do not give up easily but develop an active hostility toward society and try to punish it by all sorts of nonconforming behavior. Seashore, with an audiometer, found that in a Chicago school for backward and troublesome boys the percentage of partial deafness was greater than that among boys of the same age in other schools. The mental growth as well as the personality development of the deaf child is stunted. In Chicago Seashore also examined 5706 pupils and found that pupils below grade have at every age more cases of deafness than those at and above grade. Other examinations here and abroad show that from 65 to 75 per cent of pupils regarded by teachers as mentally backward had defective hearing. It is obviously impossible for a deaf child to keep up with the large group of the regular school, in which much of the scholastic progress depends upon responding to oral direction and giving oral recitation.

The medical profession can do wonderful things in clearing up or improving certain types of ear defect, though it is still unable to help the majority of cases. Education, on the other hand, has a great deal to offer these afflicted ones in their struggle to adjust themselves to normal society. Investigations show that from 10 to 20 per cent of our school children do not have normal hearing and that from 2 to 5 per cent have their hearing seriously impaired. In view of these facts, every school should test the hearing of its children once or twice a year. Towns or cities vary in their facilities for training their deaf children. Most of the largest have a lip-reading class in several or all regular public schools where the child with a slight hearing defect can go for a part of or the whole day to fortify himself through this method of understanding the speech of others. Those with a greater impairment may go to the central day school for the deaf, where many other methods for expressing and understanding speech are taught the children. Practically every state now has one or two state-supported institutions which take the most serious cases. They also accept children from towns providing no special instruction for the deaf.

Where there are no special schools or classes and the defect is not deemed serious enough to send the child to the state school, the teacher must seat him as near her desk as possible, give him clear directions, perhaps written on the blackboard if he has learned to read, and afford him every chance to learn with the rest of the group. At an early age he can be instructed to watch the lips of speakers. Young deaf children easily pick up the trick of lip reading, especially if the speaker articulates properly and takes the time to get the child's eyes focused on his face. The other children in the class must be cautioned to be kind and considerate without making him feel markedly different from them. They can do this by moving their lips plainly while looking directly at him and always including him in their play. It is very useful for the teacher to know the mental level of the deaf child, for it is otherwise difficult to determine whether his failures are due to lack of hearing or of native intelligence. Unfortunately the deaf child does not receive a fair chance in the average group intelligence test, nor even on an individual test, because the directions are administered orally. However, on a non-language performance test he can utilize all his ability. Pintner has devised and standardized two very good group tests with directions which can be given through pantomime or written on the blackboard.[1]

There are many instances where mothers have taught their deaf children to read lips. It is a task which takes a great deal of loving patience but which is not impossible. The children long to learn and are usually ready pupils. It is another matter, however, to make the deaf child vocalize, especially if he is very deaf. His voice is found to be flat and hollow, and he will speak as little as possible. Teaching him to articulate in front of a mirror and encouraging him to express himself on all occasions will help him. It would be of interest to teachers and students to observe some of the modern methods of teaching the deaf. The instructor,

[1] *New Pintner Primary Non-language Mental Test* and *Pintner Non-language Mental Test*, published by the Bureau of Publications, Teachers College, Columbia University.

realizing that this child must set up a pattern of speech in a different way from the normal child, who develops it in babyhood from listening to his parents, gives him a familiar object, such as a ball, and lets him play with it. Then, pointing to it, she says, "Ball." As she speaks the words, she holds the child's hand so that with his fingers he feels the movements of her jaw and face muscles and, in his palm, the force of her breath. So great is a child's tendency to imitate that he will soon try to produce with his own mouth the same movements she makes with hers, while placing his hand on his cheek to make the same muscle movements and his palm on his lips to get the same force of breath. With thousands of trials and exaggerated movements he can learn remarkably fast. A few schools have electrical devices for training pupils who have a vestige of hearing left. A child puts to his ear what looks like a telephone operator's headpiece, and through a microphone a teacher talks to him. By means of this instrument he can hear his own high-pitched, monotonous voice and compare it with the pleasanter tones of the teacher. In this way he overcomes those characteristics of vocalization which make the voice of the deaf person sound different from the voices of other people.

The number of cases of malbehavior caused by slight deafness will probably never be known. They are far too many, and active steps are now being taken in schools and by mental clinics to reduce them to a minimum.

9. DEGREE OF ORTHOPEDIC DEFECT [1]

It is not our purpose in discussing this topic to give a detailed anatomical discussion of the various diseases and injuries which leave orthopedic defects but rather to present their psychological implications. However, in order to make these clear, it seems wise to give a brief description of the chief types of orthopedic defects and their causes and effects.

Persons whose muscular movements are restricted by disease,

[1] See page 48.

accident, or congenital deformity are considered cripples. They number about two per thousand of the general population. Surveys indicate that the principal causes of crippled conditions are as follows:

Cause	Per Cent
Infantile paralysis	29.29
Surgical tuberculosis	18.00
Congenital deformities (at or before birth)	11.42
Rachitic deformities and malnutrition	9.10
Traumatic deformities	4.04
Osteomyelitis	3.67
Other causes	24.48

"Other causes" includes arthritis, rheumatism, muscular dystrophy (for which no cause or permanent cure is known), and diseases which affect the central nervous system and result in paralysis and palsy.

Orthopedic defects fall into two main classes: the paralyses and palsies and the bone deformities. Several different diseases and types of injury can cause the same defect.

Paralyses and palsies of various parts of the body may result from birth injuries, hemorrhages, or tumors and abscesses in the brain in later infancy or early childhood. They may follow such diseases as diphtheria, typhoid fever, meningitis, tetany, encephalitis, syphilis, scurvy, and sometimes measles. An inflammation of the peripheral nerves may cause paralysis, and the muscular contractions accompanying the inflammation may leave deformities. Nerve and muscle paralysis frequently follow fractures, dislocations, or diseases of the joints, bones, or tendons.

Poliomyelitis is responsible for almost one third of the paralysis of crippled children. Fully half of the cases are attacked before the age of three, boys more often than girls. As yet not a great deal is known about the sources of the disease. It progresses rapidly; paralysis often sets in within twenty-four hours after the initial symptoms occur. There is a complete paralysis of various groups of voluntary muscles followed by a rapid wasting of these muscles. Full recovery is exceedingly rare, but the disease is seldom fatal. For all paralyses exercises and massage and sometimes bran baths and passive movements by the use of pulleys are needed in attempts to restore function.

Deformities of the skeletal frame are caused by rickets, syphilis, tuberculosis of the bones, birth and later injuries, bones that have been improperly set, and inflammation of bones and joints, as in arthritis and rheumatism. Of these causes tuberculosis of the bones and joints is the most common; and it in turn is most frequently precipitated by the infectious diseases, especially measles and scarlet fever, although traumatism may also lead to tuberculosis of bone and joint. More than half of the cases occur under six years of age. The treatment involves the use of apparatus to rest the part affected. Bone grafting and excisions are performed in severe cases.

There are but few diseases on which prophylaxis can accomplish as much for the child as in tuberculosis. It is largely a problem of sociology and preventive medicine. Laws prohibiting the sale of tuberculous milk and meat, tenement inspection, health-board notifications, and educational exhibits all tend to decrease the spread of this disease.

All school children with any kind of deformity should be examined by an orthopedic specialist. Those who suffer from fatigue or who need correction should be segregated in special classes or schools where rest rooms, therapeutic materials, and industrial art supplies are provided. There are still far too few of these schools and classes in the country. If crippled children are to be assisted physically and trained for useful work, more such schools and classes must be established.

Teachers of crippled children find that the latter are often spoiled before coming to school. Of all handicapped children, cripples receive most sympathy from society—usually of a maudlin sort which is destructive to their mature growth. Entertainments, parties, presents, and free trips to the circus are given them; yet nothing is asked of them in return. The result is that the children begin to think that "the world owes them a living."

A child whose orthopedic defect has been improved sufficiently to allow him to return to the regular classroom or to qualify him to compete normally among the average children is often quite unprepared emotionally to do so. After having been the center of attention for so long because of his defect, he finds himself suddenly considered just an ordinary child. In his desire to regain his former prominence he returns to the old childish level in his actions, thereby making himself ridiculous in the eyes of the children and a nuisance in the classroom. In fact, not a few of them are incorrigible problems.

As was pointed out in the discussions of health, disease, vision, and hearing, any defect which makes one physically different from his fellows necessarily also makes his behavior and attitudes somewhat different. The sensitive, crippled child feels a stamp of inadequacy in his handicap, although he may hide this knowledge under a cloak of superiority. He may be over-bearing and demanding or he may be cringing, according to the kind of treatment he receives from parents, nurses, and teachers. In rare cases crippled children have been handled so skillfully that they have developed enough security and independence to meet well the competitive relationships of school and later life.

10. Size for Age [1]

Children of all ages show a great range of size, just as do persons of adult stature. Such variations produce psychological and emotional effects which should be given more time and study than they have usually received. The child who is small for his age probably lives in the hope that he will catch up at least in adulthood. Some adults who are small gradually become used to their condition, while for others it acts as a powerful drive for compensation in various kinds of intellectual or other achievement. Generally the child who is large may have feelings of superiority; but when his size is coupled with a too rapid rate of growth, the effects are painful physically and certain feelings of awkwardness and clumsiness may result. When adults reach

[1] See page 49.

extreme size, particularly of height, they become uncomfortable and try to lessen the effect by slouching or bending over. It seems to be a rather common desire among women to have husbands who are somewhat taller although in actual practice this wish does not seem to have been very well fulfilled.

In interpreting the size, particularly the height, of growing children of school age, general intelligence of the child also plays an important rôle. The following four cases will serve as illustrations:

Child	Age	Size Age	Mental Age
A	8 years	10 years	10 years
B	8 years	6 years	10 years
C	8 years	6 years	6 years
D	8 years	10 years	6 years

All four are of the same actual or chronological age, but they differ in size age and in mental age as shown in the table.

Child A offers little in the way of a special problem for his size; his mental maturity permits him to advance rapidly in school, and in his social contacts he can probably select children of his size and mental age. He acts the part of the ten-year-old and has no difficulty in doing so.

Child B is somewhat more handicapped. He is small physically but tall mentally. He finds it difficult to get double promotions in school, and it is not easy to get older children to accept him in their circle. He has to show unusual achievement in non-physical lines, but he is more resourceful in doing so by virtue of his mental ability.

Child C is fairly well adjusted. His mental slowness tends to hold him back in school with children of his size; in play he can select playmates among the younger children; and he thinks and acts as they do.

Child D is the most serious problem of all. His size tends to move him ahead in school and in play, but at the same time his mental immaturity makes some painful adjustments necessary. At home he is often chided for not doing better, for his size rather than his mental age is taken into consideration. At school he seems to be the largest and should be the most mature in his class, but actually he cannot measure up to that standard. Everywhere he is continually pushed and stimulated beyond his ability. This practice results in setting up in his mind a vague feeling of injustice which he does not understand. He cannot concentrate upon his studies; he becomes negative and resistive; his spirit of childish play is snuffed out; and he seeks the comradeship and sympathy of older children, who praise him for his size and often use him as a ready and suggestible tool in minor delinquencies. In the writers' personal observations of maladjusted children many are similar to type D. Their cases are very commonly pathetic.

There are several types of causes of variations in growth and in adult size. The most obvious cause is that of heredity; parents of small stature tend to have small children and large parents to have large children. No case should be judged until the background is known. Another somewhat more obvious but little understood cause is normal biological variation. If a large number of children are born of parents of average size, most of them will be of average size but one or two may be very small or very large. These deviations are constantly occurring in the fields of plant and animal life and should be expected to happen in the human family. This phenomenon may apply to the children of parents of average size as readily as to one theoretical family in which the members are impossibly large.

Cases of abnormal smallness of stature may be caused by a glandular condition known as cretinism. In cretinism there is a deficiency in the thyroid gland, with resulting mental retardation and reduced bodily stature. Accurate diagnosis and treatment under the care of a competent endocrinologist at an early age offer some hope for a certain improvement of this condition.

In another type of thyroid deficiency, which produces particularly marked overweight, the child develops into a heavy-set type about twice the normal weight for his age. For example, boys of twelve who should weigh about seventy-five pounds have been known to weigh one hundred fifty pounds. They have keen appetites; they are lazy, awkward, cowardly in playing with other children, and generally out of social and emotional adjustment. Treatment has been known to produce remarkable effects on the physical growth.

In a second type of oversize, known as gigantism, the child often attains an unusual height but not overweight for height. The cause is an oversufficiency of the pituitary gland, compensated for by a possible lack of the thyroid secretion. If children with this affliction grow quickly to adult heights without detection and treatment, it is very difficult to benefit them; treatment cannot take away from their height. The case of a nine-year-old girl who had suddenly reached mature height reminded one of some hothouse flower, with the childish face perched at the top of a long and slender stem of a body. At the age of fourteen she underwent further glandular change and also became very obese, weighing more than two hundred pounds. The irony of this case was that the parents noticed nothing unusual until it was too late; they felt only that her rapid growth was a tribute to their skill and care in rearing her.

In the cases in which there is glandular disturbance prevention is suggested through the early detection and treatment of endocrine disorders. Regarding the outcomes of treatment specialists have generally taken a much less radical view than some press agents would lead us to believe. In the types of cases already mentioned where there are hereditary tendencies toward unusual growth little can be done about the physical condition, but more attention can be given to the emotional and social patterns which tend to develop. In cases like type D teachers and parents must work against their tendency to expect too much of the large, slow child. He should not be scolded and chided for his erratic actions; he should be encouraged to play like younger children and treated in many ways as they are treated. If the pressure for responsibility is somewhat relieved by this treatment, he is more likely to be happy and to attempt mental concentration on his school work. Up to the present, disorders and variations in the growth and physical development of children have been considered matters of fate about which little or nothing could be done. In the future the emphasis will be placed upon regulating as far as possible extreme physical variations and in developing and applying better principles of psychology in the treatment of all such cases.

11. Motor Control and Muscular Co-ordination [1]

Motor co-ordination is a factor of general intelligence. Usually it is in direct proportion to the other factors considered in these chapters. When it exists in a lesser or greater degree, the individual is said to have an ability or a disability in motor skill. Moreover, there is said to be no general factor of motor ability; that is, an individual need not necessarily be apt in all phases of motor control but may be better in one type than in any other. These facts may seem remote from the discussion of behavior problems, at least at first glance. It can be shown, however, that motor control is related to personality, to social type, and to intelligence, and that these in turn are related to behavior problems.

Individuals have sometimes been described as "not smart in their heads, but smart with their hands." A little child may be slow in learning to talk or understand language; yet he may walk early, maintain a steady balance on his feet, and seldom fall or hurt himself when playing with tools or toys. He may grow up to be a poor verbalist, slow in those academic studies which involve oral recitation or theme writing; but his art work, manual-training work, handwriting, and skill in athletic games may be always above average.

This type of person is not always happily adjusted, particularly in school. He does not recite or learn to read easily. Even the usual intelligence tests do not show him to be very bright, because they are somewhat dependent on verbal directions and re-

[1] See page 49.

quire an adequate speaking vocabulary. High achievement in academic subjects is the aim of most pupils and the ambition of their parents and teachers. In fact, such subjects as reading, spelling, literature, history, and arithmetic are too often deemed the most important school subjects, while manual training, handwriting, and gymnasium work are thought to be of minor importance. Therefore the nonverbal child, superior in motor control, does not receive credit equal to that of the child who is superior in other mental abilities. The consequence is that he may develop feelings of inferiority about his defects. Not being able easily to express himself in words anyway, he closes himself up all the more. Naturally he soon begins to dislike school.

Nonlanguage performance tests and vocational tests have shown that many school rebels and truants have the motor type of mind. Their reading and spelling scores are below the average for grade and age. In fact, even the general-intelligence rating is below average. They find themselves baffled, as it were, in school—at a point where they can get no farther. They are urged by parents and teachers to work harder until they become completely discouraged. Their records, however, show that they have been good in manual training and athletics. Their interests outside of school have been in the motor field. Their vocational ambitions are chiefly those of the mechanic, aviator, engineer, carpenter, decorator, machine operator, or automobile driver. Rearranging the school curriculum so that it gives them more shop work and more gymnasium has rekindled in many of them a liking for school. Moreover, it has given them direct training and practical experience in the direction of their chosen vocations.

The nonlanguage performance tests have revealed interesting facts about children unable to read. Many of them seem to be of the nonverbal type. In the performance tests their ratings are in many cases much higher than their ratings in the other types of intelligence tests. This knowledge is of importance to teachers. They need not despair that the motor-minded child is unable to read; they must, rather, devise methods for teaching him which are based on his special ability. He should be given blocks in the form of letters which he can learn to know through the sense of touch. He can build words with them. When he learns new words, he will remember them better if he prints them or traces them time and time again.

There may not be such a thing as a *general motor ability;* rather, one should speak of *motor abilities.* That is, strength does not always go with skill nor speed with accuracy. Success in the use of the fine muscles does not necessarily mean success in the use of the larger ones. For vocational guidance purposes each specific combination of movements in any occupation will require specific motor-ability tests for measurement.

The defective motor control of some children may be hereditary; or it may be the result of a disease which attacked the nervous system, leaving the child with a generally delicate, feeble constitution. Sometimes it is due to lack of training and exercise, especially in the earlier years. Also, variations in motor skill have been traced to emotional upheavals which have left the child nervous, tense, and unable to control himself.

Emotional states caused by fear, anxiety, shame, anger, and thwarted love may block the smooth running of all bodily functions. They interfere not only with efficient mental activity but also with motor activity. Handwriting shows clearly the effects of fatigue and worry. Athletes try to avoid conflicts and emotional strain before a contest, lest they fail to co-ordinate mind and body perfectly. When manual-training teachers find a boy clumsy or careless in his shop work, they want to know what he was doing the night before. Emotional states cause temporary deviations in motor skill. Furthermore, if a child has grown up in an atmosphere of conflict where his emotions were constantly played upon, it is possible that he has developed inhibitions on the motor side which may keep him from ever becoming as skillful as he otherwise would be.

Clumsiness in movements and lack of motor skill can cause a child to have feelings of inferiority, particularly in social groups. He is unpopular in games, is not chosen for teams, and is pushed aside on the playground. He is always falling, stubbing his toe, or dropping things—for which he is roundly scolded at home. Some children are good in control of the large muscles and therefore excel in the gymnasium but are poor in the use of the small muscles in shop work, art, or handwriting.

Whether a person is to be left- or right-handed is determined before birth. The handedness, however, does not show itself clearly until many months after birth, usually between the ages of one and three. The baby uses either hand at first, but sooner or later one hand becomes dominant. Often a left-handed person accidentally becomes right-handed through imitation or suggestion when a child. He sees his brother or sister pick up a spoon or pencil with his right hand; so he does likewise. Parents often think it proper to teach a left-handed child to be right-handed. Whenever he picks up something with his left hand, they tell him to use his right.

The change from left- to right-handedness may cause later difficulties. Speech defects, especially stuttering, have been traced to it. The speech and certain other motor centers occupy closely related areas in the brain. When the left-to-right change is made, it seems to produce a confusion of motor and speech tracts. Retraining the child to use his left hand can sometimes eliminate the speech defect which has arisen from this source.

Reading difficulties are sometimes caused by confusion in handedness. (Part of this problem was discussed in connection with the consideration of vision.) The right-handed person *naturally* reads from left to right. The left-handed person must *learn* to move in that direction. The person who is confused in handedness is confused in his directions in reading. He interchanges the positions of letters in a word or the words in a phrase. *H-o-w* may be read as *w-h-o*, *b-r-e-a-d* as *b-a-r-e-d*, *t-h-r-e-e* as *t-h-e-r-e*, or *s-p-i-t* as *t-i-p-s*. He gets little sense out of a passage when he has a tendency to read a phrase backwards. "A man at the door" reads "door at the man"; "a school house" is "house a school."

A few children can read words more easily by seeing them in

the mirror; that is, the writing is legible only if reflected in a glass. These sinistral, or left-handed, tendencies, evidenced by disabilities in academic subjects, cause children afflicted with them much unhappiness in school. One little girl in the first grade had violent temper tantrums and crying spells in class, especially during the reading period. She pummeled the children and fought the teacher. As she did mirror writing and was unable to read, the other children called her crazy and the teacher thought she was subnormal or abnormal. The psychologists found that, though she was apparently right-handed, she had many left-handed tendencies. Her parents admitted that she used to try to use her left when a baby, but that they had made her use her right instead. Retraining her to use her left hand and emphasizing left-to-right directions eliminated the mirror writing and helped her catch up with her reading. Baker and Leland (1) describe a few such cases in their book *In Behalf of Non-Readers*.

A teacher may often have more success with her pupils if she takes note of the type of thing they seem to do best. If the child appears to be more apt with his hands than in his understanding of language, his teacher should devise ways of utilizing his motor ability in teaching him. Copying and tracing words and drawing the appropriate picture by the word help to imprint the words upon his memory. Moreover, providing him with opportunities to show off his motor talent will give him a keener enjoyment of school. Especially in the lowest elementary grades should the teachers try to find out whether each child is natively right- or left-handed in order to avoid the possible confusions mentioned in the preceding paragraphs. Give him a bat or a stick to see over which shoulder he holds it. Throw him a ball suddenly and observe with which hand he catches it. Have him write a new word, first with one hand and then the other; after he has had a little practice, notice which hand made the most improvement. Thus in many cases the child's motor skill can be made the basis of pedagogical methods.

12. CONVULSIONS, SEIZURES [1]

Convulsions and epilepsy have a pronounced influence on personality, mental growth, and general behavior. A convulsion is a symptom. It is the result of cerebral irritations which produce temporary unconsciousness attended by irregular muscular contractions. An apparently trivial cause, such as psychic or sensory impressions resulting from unusual excitement in a child with an inherited unstable equilibrium, may produce a typical seizure. Foreign bodies in the nose, ear, or intestines, improper or indigestible foods, poisons, and toxemias preceding or following certain diseases are possible causes. The organic sources are hemorrhages at birth, brain tumors, cerebral abscesses, or hydrocephalus.

Convulsions are dangerous when they occur in earliest infancy or even in advanced childhood if they are unduly prolonged and recur often. If they usher in a disease, they are said to be of less prognostic importance than when they occur in the course of the disease, except when they precede cerebrospinal meningitis. In arresting the attacks the cause must be determined and treated by a physician. Emergency palliative measures are mustard baths, warm soap and water enemas, an ice pack on the head in case of fever, or a few drops of chloroform given for inhalation if the attack persists.

The child who has had a few convulsions in babyhood may not have any recurrences of them later or any abnormal personality or mental manifestations. However, in taking the developmental histories of thousands of mentally backward children, it was noted that a great number of them had no feeble-mindedness in their heredity and no trauma that might have caused the condition other than a series of hard convulsions in babyhood.

When convulsions occur periodically, the disease is called epilepsy. It is characterized by seizures which vary in their intensity and body area. In the milder seizures, which are called *petit mal,* the patient may have only momentary lapses of con-

[1] See page 51.

sciousness, fainting attacks, or moments of staring vacantly into space. In the *grand mal* type, however, there are, among other things, a marked convulsion, frothing at the mouth, and longer periods of unconsciousness.

A great deal of study has been made and is being made regarding the cause of and remedies for this malady, a few of which will be mentioned here. A significant percentage of children of neurotic parents (those afflicted with epilepsy, hysteria, chorea, or similar nervous diseases) fall victims to this disease, as well as the children of parents suffering from syphilis or alcoholism. Traumatism during or after birth, tumors, and brain lesions may lead to seizures. Among the *exciting* causes are intestinal toxemias, visual defects, obstructive growths, falls, accidents, and even great scares or excitement.

The gravity of epilepsy is determined to a great extent by the age of the patient. The earlier the seizures appear, the poorer the prognosis. Frequent recurrences of well-marked attacks may result in feeble-mindedness. Uncertainties and controversies exist among scientists regarding treatment. All agree on rest and a quiet life, preferably in a rural district, gentle exercise in the fresh air and a simple, controlled diet. The latter varies according to the patient. A diet high in fats and low in starches helps some cases. Others profit by glandular therapy. Operations for brain tumors and lesions relieve certain patients. The drug luminal (a nerve sedative) reduces the number of attacks but is only palliative.

A review of hundreds of cases of epilepsy reveals that almost without exception they suffer some peculiarity of personality or behavior. "Unstable emotionally" is the chief phrase used to describe them. They exhibit many marked and definite antisocial traits. Viciousness, destructiveness, and temper tantrums are frequent. They torture animals and children, throw things, bite, scratch, and hit parents and teachers. They tear paper into bits, tear their clothes, break dishes, make fires, and pull things apart. Minor incidents will provoke them into fits of temper in which they storm about or act like mad people. Mild punishments drive them into wild hysteria or, indeed, into a seizure—as will any kind of overexcitement. Among the mental phenomena of epileptics may be noted delirium, anxiety, religiosity, sensitivity, egocentricity, paranoid trends, tantrums, hallucinations, sadism, superstitiousness, and often sexual and murderous assaults. The change in those afflicted consists of irritability, memory disturbances, failure of ordinary stimuli to elicit proper responses, lack of interest in personal appearance and surroundings, and finally loss of irritability with a gradual decline to the lowest level of existence.

The characteristics just mentioned may be typical of the patient afflicted with actual epilepsy. They are also often typical of cases of incipient epilepsy. Children may have had no actual seizures other than a few convulsions in childhood, but later in life they may develop the traditional seizures after some illness or slight accident or, indeed, from no obvious cause at all. When, therefore, teachers and workers encounter children who have a number of the traits listed and generally unstable behavior which cannot be traced to any great environmental influence or emotional disturbance, they must search carefully into the family heredity and the child's developmental health history for possible signs of incipient epilepsy.

The epileptic child is a misfit at home and in school. Because of the distressing nature of his seizures, he cannot be kept in the classroom, where other children through the power of suggestion sometimes imitate his contortions or acquire nervous tics or other imitative habits. At home the unfortunate one is a burden to his family. He cannot play for long with companions but has to sit around the house, where he is of little use at household tasks. He seldom, if ever, can get or hold a job. Mothers become weary of cleaning up after those who have the worst type of grand mal. Near relatives are the only ones, however, who have much sympathy for children afflicted with this disease. Others feel only horror regarding them. Because of their tendency to possess those antisocial and unstable traits described earlier, they are hated and feared by those who come in contact with them.

In spite of his peculiarities the child with actual epilepsy has a more comfortable life than the incipient epileptic. The latter evinces the same unsocial tendencies but is not understood to be just as sick as the former. A person with incipient epilepsy is said to have an epileptiform personality. There has not been enough follow-up work on bad-behavior cases—juvenile delinquents and criminals—to determine how many of them later actually develop seizures; but there have been enough cases to indicate that a small percentage of them have epileptiform personalities.

If everyone could feel that these bad-behavior problems are really just sick children rather than mean, hateful, "ornery" savages, a great deal more could be done to adjust them. Parents and teachers should control their own tempers at the antics, tantrums, or stupidity of these children and should not depend upon scoldings and physical punishments. Their classmates must be taught to be considerate of them and to understand that they are not bad, but ill. Seeing that the afflicted children are busy at occupations congenial to them will keep them out of trouble. Praise for self-control, lessons in relaxation, and helping them to face their own conduct and to work out ways of improving it are helpful methods. It is not always possible to diagnose incipient epileptics; but workers will not be making a mistake if they apply the foregoing suggestions in treating bad-behavior problems.

13. NERVOUSNESS [1]

Nervousness is an ambiguous word. Its strictest definition denotes a pathology of the nervous system—a malfunctioning or an organic disease. Laymen let it cover any more or less slight agitation of body or mind. If they cannot eat or sleep properly, their "nerves" are bad. If they are irritable and jumpy, they say they

[1] See page 52.

are "nervous," without considering the cause or degree of their condition. In taking the family case history, it is obvious that even the most unintelligent person, English-speaking or foreign, knows the general meaning of nervous. To ask, "Is the child nervous?" will start a stream of information about the child very likely otherwise unattainable. In excusing him on the grounds of his nervousness, the parent will admit all sorts of characteristics—anger, revenge, meanness, disobedience, whining, crying, laziness, lack of effort and concentration, truancy and lying, sometimes sex offenses, and even stealing.

Nervousness is a symptom of other trouble. It is manifested by restlessness, irritability, ill temper, depression, excessive laughter or tears, susceptibility to shock or other disquieting stimuli, poor appetite, disturbed sleep, indigestion, intestinal trouble, heart irregularities, and various forms of physical or mental agitation such as sweating, nail biting, and tics. In more abnormal cases it takes pathological forms like delusions, hallucinations, and complete lack of physical and emotional control.

Nervousness has two principal sources: physical and emotional. The two are of course interrelated. Physical covers the constitutional basis, the effects of disease, and the type of living habits. Emotional covers all situations which arouse emotional reactions in the individual.

There are certain diseases which make a more or less direct attack upon the nervous system: chorea, epilepsy, encephalitis, infections causing neuritis, paralysis, and palsy. Any severe sickness lowers the general resistance of the body, including the nerves. Under any of these circumstances an individual is made quite susceptible to the unsettling effects of poor living habits or emotional strain.

It is a common observation that whenever a parent has been weakened by disease or malnutrition, is chronically alcoholic, or is suffering from venereal disease, at least one of the children is predisposed to nervousness and lowered vitality. Studies of heredity disclose that nervous diseases as well as outright insanity run predominantly in certain families, although not necessarily affecting all members of such families. There are other instances of instability in children which are frequently ascribed to the worried and nervous condition of the mother during pregnancy. Naturally it is difficult to establish and prove conclusively that there is a direct hereditary or environmental relationship in such instances, but enough cases exist to warrant an inference of such relationships and also a challenge for further proof for verification.

Poor physical habits can undermine the health of an individual and predispose him to nervousness. These, combined with an hereditary predilection or a system already weakened by disease, are strong factors in nervousness. Insufficient and constantly disturbed sleep and irregular meals of a poor caliber are prominent in nervous cases. Constipation has ruined the disposition of many a child.

The need of circumcision may cause the small boy considerable discomfort. He may be displaying too great interest in sex matters or practicing masturbation; often it will be found that he would not have done so had he not felt a constant irritation in his genital region which centered his attention there. Tight and rough clothing may also cause it. A circumcision is a simple and inexpensive operation and should certainly be performed if the physician thinks it advisable. There is a similar condition in little girls which often causes them nervousness. Certain parts of their genitalia are overgrown and need cutting. Modern baby specialists recommend this for the high-strung baby girl.

Emotional tension can harass the most healthy person. It has of course a much more poignant effect on children whose health background is not propitious. It is an unusual home that is entirely free from emotional strain, but the homes which produce problem children have more of it than others. The baby shows signs of reacting to the emotional coloring of his home soon after he is born. He is tied so closely to his mother that he feels her changes of mood and the strength or weakness of her love for him. The oversolicitude of one parent may put a weight upon the child which becomes evident in his nervousness. Jealousy between children or between parents may breed an atmosphere of nervous tension.

A child who was an habitual thumb-sucker was brought to a clinic by his worried parents. They had tried to "cure" him of the habit by putting red pepper on his thumb, but they found that the child replaced this habit by masturbation. When he had been spanked out of the latter habit, he began to roll his head back and forth against a chair or a pillow and his parents thought he was going insane. The psychologist who examined him found that he was a lonesome, unwanted child, who turned to these elementary pleasure sources for solace. Both parents were insecure people, who were unwilling to undertake the rearing of a child and needed parental guidance. When the worker acted as a parent substitute and helped the parents solve their own emotional problems, they were led to a better understanding of the needs of their child. As soon as the youngster felt loved and wanted, he had no need to comfort himself and his nervous habits fell away by themselves.

Nervous tics in older children are signs of their feelings of inferiority. They occur oftenest with unattractive people, those with a physical defect or peculiarity, or those who have suffered frequent failures and humiliations. Shy children, unaccustomed to social gatherings, often develop tics through self-consciousness. They lick their lips constantly, open and shut their mouths, or keep twitching one side of the face, blinking their eyes, wrinkling their noses, shrugging their shoulders, or jerking their heads.

A teacher or outside worker can help a child overcome these defense-mechanism tics by helping him to acquire self-confidence. Emphasizing his abilities and good points, while minimizing his failures and faults, makes him believe that someone has confidence in him. Advice on recreations and occupations may place him in activities in which he can excel. Friends should be chosen who will not overshadow him. Once he is befriended and esteemed and has gained strength and capacity and especially when he has once succeeded in some activity, the tics are likely to die away without the need of any reference to them.

Bed-wetting, or enuresis, is more than a lazy habit. Parents attribute it to the child's nervousness. But like other nervous manifestations it is a symptom. Occasionally it has a purely physical basis; but usually it arises from an emotional condition: fear, rejection, a sense of failure, or a desire to remain on an infantile level. Palliative methods of trying to break the habit are seldom successful. The emotional source must be sought before palliative methods can be used. Jealousy of a younger child in the family is a frequent cause of enuresis; the older child wishes to put himself on the level of the younger to gain the attentions of the mother. Rejected and unwanted children resort to this habit. Perhaps they feel that by it they can hold their parents' attention longer.

In dealing with all problems concerning the child, it is necessary to combat those forces in his environment which are militating against his full development. As most of his time is spent in his home, where he learns his chief attitudes and ideas, the worker must start there in undertaking to help the child solve his problems. Children are suggestible and tend to imitate the attitudes and actions of those about them. A nervous person in the home may affect them. The nervous mother may make her child seem extremely nervous.

When the worker encounters such a situation, the best course is to agree with the mother that the child's actions are upsetting her, and that for her sake arrangements should be made for him to stay elsewhere for a short period. With sympathy for her overwrought condition and with great tact the worker may suggest ways for her to overcome it: advise her to rest when she feels an irritable streak coming on and teach her how to relax even when resting and to watch her health habits. With a responsive and intelligent woman one may point out how she is hindering the development of her child, and she may then without further assistance change her attitude and adjust her dealings with those about her. Changes in disposition will not come about suddenly. Positive suggestion must be used by the worker at every meeting. Assure the mother each time that she looks much healthier and calmer. It is of great importance to analyze her background for the cause which brings about her nervousness and treat her from that viewpoint. If it is not her health or an hereditary taint, it may be unpleasant relations with her husband, friction with a relative or neighbor, or worries over finances. It may be a conflict in her sex life or a conflict hanging over from her early life in her own family. Get her to talk it all over and relieve herself about the matter. Lighten her feelings of guilt about herself and her past actions. Make her see that she is really no different from other women, and that her lot is indeed better than that of many others. Give her confidence in herself. Let her find security in your faith and affection. Have a talk with her husband. Learn his side of the story. Try to wipe out as much antagonism between them as possible by convincing each of the other's love and admiration or to explain shortcomings as if they were illnesses, so that each will be tolerant, tender, and responsive in giving help and understanding.

When a case of nervousness is presented to a worker, the first step in procedure is a complete physical examination of the child, with treatment and correction for any physical defects. The second step is a check of his eating and sleeping habits. The child with nervous symptoms needs more and longer rest periods than the average child. His diet should contain a minimum of rich, acid food and should consist of nutritious elements like milk, eggs, fruits, and green vegetables. A short vacation at a friend's or relative's is often beneficial, for it relieves the strain felt by the child and his parents and makes a change to an improved home routine easier on his return. The chief point with which the worker must be concerned is the emotional basis of the problem. The palliative methods just mentioned are of course helpful, but their effect is of short duration if the center of the difficulty is not found and treated. In cases where the symptoms seem to be of abnormal degree and where none of the usual methods of diagnosis and treatment are effective, there should be examination by a neurologist and psychiatrist.

BIBLIOGRAPHY

1. BAKER, HARRY J., and LELAND, BERNICE—*In Behalf of Non-Readers.* Bloomington, Ill.: Public School Publishing Co., 1934. 39 pp.
2. BOND, EARL D., and APPEL, K. E.—*Treatment of Behavior Disorders Following Encephalitis.* New York: Commonwealth Fund, 1931. 163 pp.
3. DEARBORN, WALTER F.—"Difficulties in Learning," *Radio Lecture No. 22 of the Psychology Series.* Chicago: University of Chicago Press, 1932.
4. JOHNSON, WENDELL—*Because I Stutter.* New York: D. Appleton-Century Co., 1930. 126 pp.

CHAPTER VII

PERSONAL HABITS AND RECREATIONAL FACTORS

Items 14-26, inclusive, comprise the group of factors which deal with personal habits and recreational factors. These factors differ slightly from the health and developmental factors of Chapter VI in that the child himself tends to have more control over them; still to a large extent they are governed by the environment in which he finds himself placed.

14. PERSONAL HYGIENE AND CLOTHING [1]

On the whole the subject of personal hygiene and clothing is closely related to economic status. In schools to which the parents of the wealthier or middle classes send their children there are few dirty or ragged youngsters. Not only do the children receive good care at home, but also each child follows the fashion of the majority. In these schools the child who is dirty and untidy is likely to be ridiculed or ostracized by teachers and children. This social urge may cause him to dun his parents for new clothes or for mending old ones; he will see that his shirts are clean, his hair combed, and his face and hands washed. A few children, however, resent criticisms from others and become negativistic about the matter, making it a point to look even more dirty and untidy.

Not all poor families neglect their children's personal habits of hygiene and dress. The children may not have first-rate clothes, but those that they have may be clean and well cared for and

[1] See page 53.

the children themselves may be thoroughly washed. Many parents, however, are too busy or too slothful to take an interest in the appearance of their children. They use their poverty as an excuse for their slovenliness.

This topic is important from the standpoint of sanitation and health. It is necessary of course that children wash before meals and keep their hands, face, and teeth reasonably clean. For the sake of those who sit near them they must take baths and wash their underwear often enough to avoid unpleasant odors.

Psychologists are interested in hygiene and clothing because of their relation to the self-feelings. Every adult knows that unpleasant feeling of self-consciousness or lack of self-confidence when he is wearing a garb that he knows is unbecoming, out of style, or untidy. Children react in the same way. Teachers notice a change in their behavior or in their classroom responses when they are dressed in some new apparel. Clothes can mean more to children than their parents realize. Even boys have cravings for certain types of clothing, although it is true that they do not always take good care of them after they get them. A boy is in his glory if he possesses a pair of rubber boots, or "high-tops." Most of them want bright neckties, sheepskin coats, and colorful slipovers. Truant children who have been given pleasing clothes by friends or organizations are often quite willing to re-enter school and take a normal part in its functions.

Parents are too often unsympathetic with these longings of childhood, feeling that the children will have plenty of time to dress up when they are older. Children are often embittered by this lack of sympathy, and, being denied something that means a great deal to them, they put up various defenses at home and among their playmates. Letting them work around the house or for a neighbor to help buy a piece of the desired clothing will not break the parent's purse and will do much to establish feelings of love and comradeship between parent and child.

The question of personal care usually solves itself as the child grows older. It is hard to do much with boys in the early elementary grades because their minds are on so many subjects other than their own cleanliness. In time, when they approach the adolescent age, they themselves begin to take an interest in washing and dressing. Then they judge their friends by their appearance and make life uncomfortable for anyone who does not take baths or dress according to reasonable standards. In the adolescent period children are very much aware of their appearance. Clothes are of vital importance to them. The lack of acceptable clothes often figures in cases of stealing or truancy. The child may already have feelings of inferiority or resentment against society. His immediate need of finery may bring such feelings to a head and incite him to steal. In cases of truancy the child may have feelings of inferiority which his poor clothes tend to accentuate. He is truant from school because he cannot bear to compare himself with better-dressed children. A derisive remark from one of them may cause him great suffering. Indeed, their derision is often imagined.

A great deal of clothes consciousness in children is due to the emphasis adults put upon clothes. Parents frequently satisfy their own ego by overdressing children for school. Some of the blame may belong also to the teacher who overcompliments a child on the new clothes he is wearing. A clever teacher can swing the interest to the side of cleanliness. Her praise may influence some boys to go home each night and wash and iron their own shirts.

Dealing with parents about clothes is a delicate matter. Many of them are unwashed and ragged themselves. They are ignorant of good buying values or are unskillful in mending. Their personal vanity is easily affronted. Many mothers, when approached by school or nurse on the subject of their children's poor appearance, become unfriendly and hostile; they think and say that it is nobody else's business. Occasionally such a mother can be convinced of what a good appearance does to a child's self-confidence and success in school. Sometimes appeal can be made to her pride by having her visit the school, where she can see how her child looks in contrast with the others. Practical suggestions on methods of buying or mending or making over old things are often gratefully received. The most satisfactory method, however, is to appeal to the child himself. He does not have to be very old to learn to darn, to sew on buttons, to wash, and to iron. A system of rewards, *e.g.*, using gold stars on a chart, often stimulates children to establish habits of good personal care.

It must be remembered, however, that a child's appearance is not so important that he should be nagged and his existence made miserable on account of it. If any stand is taken on the subject, it should be only a positive one. Praise and encouragement for tidiness will do more to win the child than punishment and nagging for untidiness.

15. Looks or Appearance [1]

Scientific tests have proved that there is little basis for the contentions of either phrenology or character reading from faces; but people go about in everyday life judging others by their looks. Magazine illustrations, plays, and the movies encourage the identification of certain bodily characteristics with special walks of life. There are standardized types of virile heroes, demure heroines, angular old maids, jolly fat men, and slick gamblers. Many harsh judgments are thus made. As a matter of fact, in institutions for the mentally handicapped there are often beautiful countenances, high foreheads, and bright, clear eyes. A real criminal usually looks no different from a baseball player or a shoe clerk. Some geniuses seem to be hideous, vapid-looking creatures with no apparent brains or sensitivity.

Little can be judged of true character from exterior features beyond the fact that the individual is healthy, happy, active, or forceful or sickly, sullen, sad, phlegmatic, timid, or self-conscious. Even after deciding about such traits one is often amazed to see changes in a person after he is known better. The phlegmatic man may on acquaintance prove to be very gay and dynamic; the healthy, happy-appearing man may be high-strung and easily aroused.

[1] See page 55.

In taking notes on a person's appearance, among the points to be observed are facial features and facial expressions, body structure, carriage, clothing, neatness, use of cosmetics, and a summary of the general impression made on the observer. Any odd characteristic which may later stand out to identify him should be recorded—scars, deformities, unusual gestures, left- or right-handedness.

There are successful people in public life, even on the stage, who are excessively homely, yet others never seem to notice it. They make their personalities raise them above their looks. Many of them have struggled hard to do so. They realized early that their appearance was a drawback, and that they must depend on brains, talent, or will power to reach their goals. There are other people who grow up oblivious of the fact that they are not so handsome as are others. These very likely have had wise parents, who began early to make their ugly ducklings believe that they were just as important and capable as any other children. They helped them to develop defenses against teasing, or they avoided that subject altogether, concentrating on their attractive qualities.

Many children seem unattractive because of ill-health. They are underweight, anemic, or undernourished. Their cheeks are pale, their eyes dull, and their shoulders droop. They need more and better food, more sleep, outdoor exercise, or in many cases the direct care of a physician. Bad teeth may need to be pulled or straightened. Adenoids, which may be causing mouth breathing, need to be removed. Gland treatment may be necessary.

Teachers and workers must analyze their feelings for pupils and patients so as to avoid overestimating the attractive person and underestimating the ugly. It is the ugly person who is most in need of love and understanding; most people may be hard on him. Often such persons suffer untold agonies because of their looks. The tragedy is that little can actually be done to improve them. A great deal, however, can be done in establishing a reasonable attitude toward one's appearance. Mother and teacher should be especially kind to homely children, should persuade them that they are not hopelessly ugly, and should find ways for them to succeed in life other than through the force of appearance. They can help them to dress neatly and becomingly, to carry themselves well, and to look strong and healthy. Voice cultivation, a wide knowledge of literature, and a lively interest in current events and allied activities are excellent means of helping the child to overcome his natural diffidence and play his part in society.

If the homely child finds himself rejected at home or at school on account of his appearance, he may seek recognition, favorable or unfavorable, through various channels of behavior. He may take to disturbing the classroom in school, or he may become saucy and disrespectful to his parents. Although he may usually be punished in some manner for his acts, he obtains a certain delight and satisfaction which is not understood by anyone except himself. Such a child senses the real mechanism of course in only a vague way.

Sometimes the physical appearance itself invites antisocial situations. A ten-year-old boy was reported for fighting and being disagreeable with other boys of his age. The cause in his case was a protruding lower chin which, seeming to extend a sneering invitation to be hit, had been hit frequently. As a matter of fact, he was quite a mild-tempered boy from a good home, with no innate pugilistic tendencies; but he had changed his attitude in response to the many blows on the offending chin. Another similar case was that of the boy who had been much pestered through being pinched continually by other children. His last name was Pinches; so some of the pupils had decided to pinch him. In his case the seriousness of the problem was explained to his father, and a change in the family name was suggested. But Mr. Pinches declared that it was an old and honorable English name, and that in England no one would stoop to making fun of a family name.

Extremely good-looking children display certain evidences of maladjustment which originate in their looks. Others are inclined to favor them and pamper them, and naturally they become spoiled. It is commonly said of them that "they get by on their looks." Once they have discovered the secret of their power, they continue to use it more or less successfully as a mechanism to gain favors and to compensate for inadequacies of action and thought. Handsome boys gain certain advantages although they are not so likely as girls to be aware of their good looks. Pretty girls find their looks a natural part of their stock in trade.

These hypotheses of looks or appearance as a motivation for behavior suggest certain ulterior advantages of being near the average of the population in looks or appearance. If there were an absolute uniformity in this respect so that we all looked like identical twins, some of the problems of looks would tend to disappear; but the uniformity would be so deadly monotonous that human beings would probably fall heir to some other maladjustment growing out of uniformity. Lack of uniformity tends to make for individualism and variety and to motivate our evaluations of all individuals in the social order.

16 and 17. Early and Present Self-Care [1]

Early self-care is an issue in the problems of certain types of children. It concerns those who are lazy in school and at home; those who are too dependent on mother and teacher; those who are lacking in self-reliance, in aggressiveness, and in co-operation; and those who are "spoiled"—unmanageable, selfish, demanding, or disobedient. Present care also is linked with these traits. Two items are made of self-care on the diagnostic history blank because the child's early and present care may not be identical.

A biological law of nature is that the young break away from their parents as soon as they are able to care for their elemental needs. Some species are equipped to do so at birth. Birds guard their young only until they are able to fly. Most mammals keep their offspring until the latter can digest solid food and are strong enough to fight for their own wants. Few animal parents are inter-

[1] See page 56.

ested in their young after the nursing period is over. But human babies have much more to learn than animals.

At an early age the normal child shows signs of wanting to help himself. When about one year old he will begin to walk and talk; he may refuse to eat unless he can wield the spoon himself. He seems ashamed if he wets his clothes or his bed, and he is proud of continence. He slows up the dressing process by insisting upon putting on his own shoes and trying to lace them. The bath gives him a splendid chance to wash himself and to scrub the tub and everything else on which he can use a rag and soap. At about three years of age he usually can dress himself entirely, button his clothes, lace or buckle his shoes, wash his hands, face, and teeth, and brush his hair. He worries his mother by dashing out into the street and trying to cross through traffic alone. He worries her by fighting with other children, grabbing their toys, and being very possessive about his own. At five years he can go to and from school alone; he is ashamed to have his mother take him. He shows a preference for certain apparel and is often particular about his appearance; he asks permission to buy certain pieces of clothing for himself.

Most mothers do not have much trouble in teaching their children lessons in self-care, though each child may have difficulty in acquiring a few habits. Bed-wetting is the hardest difficulty to overcome. The mother herself may have been lax in establishing habits of self-care; perhaps she does not take the child up at night regularly or forbid him to drink just before bedtime, or she may assume a hopeless attitude, shame him, or punish him too much.

Breaking the sucking habit also presents difficulties. It is among the first pleasures in life and it continues to give pleasure until death. The baby sucks his thumb for comfort and happiness, the old man sucks his pipe. Weaning the baby from the breast or the bottle is no easy task. To do this abruptly may end in his sucking his fingers. To prolong breast or bottle feeding sets up a habit, so that the child refuses to take milk in any other way than by the sucking process.

A low score in early self-care usually indicates that the child was weak, sickly, and not physically able to begin caring for himself early. Probably his parents felt so sorry for him that they did not make the same effort to teach him that they made with their other children. The child has grown up with a double handicap: he is physically weak and he is more immature socially than his contemporaries. He may therefore always seem inferior to them in aggression and self-reliance.

Sometimes the mother has been weak. In one case the baby was slow or unwilling to learn; the mother found it easier to do things for him than to force him to care for himself. This attitude was carried through his other training, so that the child developed along unsocial lines, aware that his parents gave in to his resistance. When he grew older, he would not obey any order at home or at school. The parents, not having established his habits of obedience earlier, could not now control him. Life became one long struggle. The child continued to wet the bed. He would not dress himself or wash for school on time. After nagging or punishment, the mother would end the fracas by taking care of him herself. He was fussy about his meals and would not eat the proper food unless someone stood over him. He was careless about his playthings. He would not fight his own battles but ran home crying to his mother. He lagged on the way to school until someone had to accompany him every day. Obviously the mother was to blame for being weak and ineffective.

There have been many cases where the mother was at fault in other ways. Certain women have a craving for mothering. They want to protect someone; accordingly they lavish too much love on their children and derive too much pleasure from waiting on them. The result is that the children suffer.

There is the case of the twelve-year-old boy who was called a "sissy" by other boys and picked on and scorned by them. In the classroom he could not keep up with the others even though his mentality was average; he gave up easily, complained about and resented the teachers' orders and criticisms, and went home crying to his mother every other day. She obviously had the "mother complex." Her own mother had died early, and she had lived with her father and a younger sister. She had adored this sister with all the love of her starved heart and was sick with grief when the sister died. Her marriage was successful until her baby came, when she devoted her full attention to him. Her husband naturally felt slighted and expressed his skepticism as to the necessity of so much time and worry spent on a healthy baby. This angered her; she felt that he was unsympathetic and unfeeling. As the child grew, she anticipated his every desire so that he actually never talked until he was four years old, never having had the need to do so. She kept him so closely by her side that he never learned to mix with others. In consequence he made a wretched adjustment at school. There was an unpleasant scene whenever the father tried to interfere. Finally the man left home temporarily.

At last the boy gave so much trouble at school that he was expelled. This was quite a shock to both boy and mother. As she could not afford to send him to a private school, she found it necessary to listen to the advice of the school authorities and was wise enough to follow the suggestion offered. Although he was not really a bad boy in any way, the child was transferred to an ungraded school (for incorrigible or otherwise unconforming boys) some distance away. The lad was quite contrite and willing to co-operate in solving his problem. The long trip to school every morning did a great deal to develop him. He was in a small group where the teachers had time to study him. Every possible chance was used to praise him for manliness and trustworthy traits. He built things for his mother in the workshop. He took charge of a class of younger children. He washed dishes in the lunchroom. In a quarrel he was too far from home to run to his mother; he had to fight it out until the teacher thought that he had had enough. The mother at first worried herself constantly at his "harsh" treatment; but her tears before long made the child angry, and he would not tolerate being treated like a baby at home any longer. At this point the father stepped in and took him to ball games, to the movies, and on educational trips. The treatment required two years; but by the end of that time both son and mother were completely and satisfactorily readjusted.

18. Home Duties [1]

Social workers and teachers find that children who have never been trained to work at home are much more immature than the average child. They lack ingenuity, persistence, and concentration. They hesitate to attack problems without assistance. They lack motor adeptness and the ability to organize their time. Moreover, they usually resent instruction; they disregard orders or they are too slow to grasp them.

Because of such ineptitudes, these children have difficulty in adapting themselves to school and to industry. Parents and teachers complain that such children are interested only in play and that they hate work. Children exert themselves at various kinds of play, yet resent anything labeled work. Therefore work itself is an attitude of mind. Most successful business and professional men consider their work their play. It is often argued that work is play if one can work at one's hobby; but if this were always true, much of the world's labor would never be performed, for it is inconceivable that many would choose menial tasks as hobbies. However, if one early develops the philosophy that all must work to live, that any honest labor which brings in a livelihood is respectable, and that any job well done gives satisfaction to the ego, there is less likelihood of misfit in life. Such a philosophy or attitude should be developed early in childhood and should be one of the precepts on which all other thinking is based.

A child can perform motor feats before he understands reasons for them. Therefore, to develop in the child a well-adjusted attitude toward work, set him at it early so that it seems to him only a natural part of his life. Praising a task well done will bring him enough satisfaction to compensate for the loss of other immediate pleasures. It is no hardship for a one-year-

[1] See page 58.

old child who can walk to pick up his own clothes and toys or for the two- or three-year-old to dust certain chairs every day. If the little task is performed regularly at the same hour daily, it is no more unusual than the fact that he must bathe or eat regularly. A habit is established.

Any habit, if deeply set, gives pleasurable sensations when performed. Many pleasure-bringing habits are undesirable, like thumb-sucking. Breaking any habit is painful and often disagreeable. A man accustomed to sitting in the same easy chair every day is much annoyed if he finds someone else in it. Performing regular home duties can bring pleasurable satisfaction and failure to perform them can bring uneasiness. There are girls who cannot rest after a meal until their kitchen work is finished, and there are boys who need no alarm clock to get them up to build the morning fires. Therefore allot the child home duties early, and the habit of performing them regularly will be a pleasure.

Not only do home duties teach habits of work, ability to carry out directions, motor co-ordination, and the power to plan, attack, and persist at tasks to their finish, but they also teach responsibility, co-operation, and regularity. These qualities are necessary for socializing the individual and fitting him to take a post in society and to work as a reliable and efficient citizen. Some geniuses, who work only when the spirit moves them, accomplish great deeds without well-established habits. But few are in this class; they do not succeed without the above mentioned training.

Application to home tasks develops self-reliance and self-confidence, particularly when family and friends give the child plenty of praise so that he feels important and not just a drudge. It also gives a chance for the child to use his own creative ability, especially if the parents use patience and forebearance and do not demand that he work in their way.

Home duties carry over into school tasks. The child who has certain specific work habits at home usually succeeds at school within the limits of his mental ability. The child who has poor habits of home work or of self-care often shows no initiative in his school work. He waits for someone to tell him what to do or expects tasks to be done for him. But he does not succeed without his own individual effort, he does not learn, and the teacher believes that he is either lazy or mentally backward. A psychological examination does infinite good in disclosing the actual mental status in such cases. A more thorough investigation thereafter by a child-guidance clinic is needed to analyze the underlying factors and interpret their true significance to school and home.

To bring about improvement, various duties should be assigned, if necessary with daily charts to be checked and possibly some system of awards, such as bird, flower, or animal stickers for young children. The effects of these awards, rather than any general rules which might be laid down, should decide their use in each individual case.

The following is a case where prescribing home duties in the treatment of an unmanageable school child helped solve his problem. He was a colored boy of ten years, very mischievous, silly, noisy, disturbing, and irresponsible in school. He upset the entire classroom and was making no progress in the academic curriculum. Not all the material on the case is given here because it is not pertinent to the principle being illustrated, but among other facts he was found to be the older of a fraternity of two. The mother was a fussy, overmeticulous housekeeper who did not want the boy messing around underfoot; the husband was a social person but a poor father. He seemed to dislike his older son, never was a companion to him, and gave him little attention except to spank him. Obviously the boy did not feel very much wanted and derived little satisfaction from his home. To compensate, he was making every play for attention at school and getting great satisfaction out of any he attained, whether it was complimentary or not.

In the course of the treatment there were discussed with each parent alone ways for making the child take a more important part in his home in order that he might feel more happy and secure there and receive satisfaction for good deeds instead of having to go outside the home for reassurance. One of the suggestions was to have him help his father as an equal. They would work together fixing and cleaning the car; as a reward the boy would be taken for rides alone with him. Then, since it was spring, he could plant a garden. When vegetables grew up he would be paid for giving them to his mother. Also he was to be given an allowance for doing other work in the home. This was introduced to him by telling him that his father worked for his wages, and that his mother worked for the money her husband gave her. Just so he could work for his allowance. The child accepted these suggestions without opposition. The parents were told the probable cause of his trouble and advised to show him considerable love, kindness, and friendliness, and not to stint their praise and encouragement.

It is true that the social worker was called upon from time to time to smooth out conflicts at home and at school and to inspire the persons concerned to continue their improvement. Gradually the troubles at school disappeared as the boy began to become more and more absorbed in his home and as he felt more loved and wanted there. Concomitantly as his conduct improved, so did the attitude of his parents and teacher change toward him.

19.   Conditions of Eating [1]

Since all bodily growth and energy are dependent upon the intake of food, of vital importance are the kinds and combinations of foods, the regularity of meals, and other conditions which influence digestion. Furthermore since bodily states and emotional reactions mutually affect each other, a study of eating conditions is necessary in understanding personality manifestations.

Regularity of food habits and eating are closely related to digestion. The organs function most rhythmically and efficiently if given their respective activities at regular hours. It is disap-

[1] See page 59.

pointing to be hungry at mealtime and find no food prepared. Children who come home from school or play ready to eat become irritable if meals are delayed. They may develop headaches or lose their appetites. Anger at being frustrated interferes with their digestive processes.

There are many mothers who have no regularity in their homes. Sometimes they are hard workers but poor planners. Too frequently they are irresponsible. Often both parents are employed, and the children must prepare the meals. The result is that they may eat only canned food, standing up in a disorderly kitchen. Good cooking and attractive serving are essential for digestion. Many mothers apparently cannot learn to cook without burning and spoiling the food. Their children do not approach the table with their digestive systems in a good anticipatory state. There is no reason to believe that such children are as cheerful, stable, and optimistic as the children whose mothers understand the culinary art.

Food variety depends somewhat upon economic status and upon nationality. Polish boys complain of endless meals consisting of soup as the sole dish; they have been known to leave home for that reason alone. Italian boys complain of spaghetti in the same way, and many other children complain of the ubiquitous potato or of pork and beans. Perhaps still worse is the table where diets unsuited to children's needs are served: Meat and potatoes three times a day; bread, cheese, and coffee, or cake and coffee, as the only foods at each meal; diets with too much starch; or meals with rich, indigestible foods. These meals, which the children may enjoy, are certainly not giving proper sustenance for their brain and muscle growth. As a result they develop digestive disorders which put them in chronic ill temper or they do not have sufficient physical energy for normal work and play.

The most unfavorable condition of all is the home where quarreling exists. Parents quarrel before the children; children quarrel with one another. Mealtime, the hour when all are together, gives them the best opportunity to air their grievances. Experiments show that the emotions of anger and fear are stronger than hunger, and that during anger and fear the glandular secretions sent into the blood directly interfere with digestion. Children might better not eat at all than try to eat when emotionally upset. During economic depression, when incomes are reduced or wiped out, strife and conflict increase. The father, worried and unhappy, is irritable and overcritical, "picking on" the children for poor table manners, for slight offenses, or for eating too much food. There may not be enough food to go around, and all quarrel over it. Each child feels that another gets more or needs less than he himself does. Father and mother, not seeing each other during the rest of the day, discuss their troubles or blame each other for them. The arguing may even end in screaming, crying, abusing, and fighting. The teacher seldom suspects that the ugly, sullen, irritable, or inattentive child with whom she is having so much difficulty has just arisen from this kind of table.

Finally, there is the nagging overanxious mother who stands over her child constantly, expostulating with him to eat more and thereby getting him into an emotional state where he cannot or will not eat at all. This occurs most frequently with little children. Physicians now believe that a child's needs normally tell him how much he should eat, and that adults have no right to demand that he eat all that is given him. Children differ in the amount of food they need. A child may be overwhelmed with helpings that are too large, or he may feel insecure and unwelcome with helpings that are too small. Mothers also are much annoyed because their children take dislikes to certain foods— usually vegetables and cereals. Frequently the mothers themselves are to blame because they do not vary the selections of their foods or present them in an attractive, tasteful way.

In dealing with the subject of eating conditions the teacher or social worker finds it rather hard to get reliable information without being present at a meal. Mothers are not apt to admit their shortcomings without considerable questioning, and children either cannot express their desires well or, because they have no basis for comparison, are relatively unaware of conditions. A great deal of information can be gathered by a surprise visit at luncheon time. Following it, a tactful discussion with the mother can be opened to point out that the history of gastronomy reveals the importance of good food and happy mealtimes, and that the digestive process is directly influenced by emotional states. Lists of desirable foods and their prices can be given, together with suggestions for cooking and serving. Perhaps there is a cooking school in a community center or in connection with a newspaper or gas company to which the mother may be persuaded to go for lessons and ideas. Most charity organizations and the board of health have pamphlets containing food budgets or suggested menus at low prices. The newspapers of large cities often have fine household departments whose editors are glad to send on request pamphlets with suggestions on cookery.

20. Eating Habits [1]

If a child's appetite is poor, it is probably a symptom of trouble which arises either from a physical cause, an emotional upset, or poor home training. The child refuses to eat or wants only special foods. He whines and cries at his meals and is cross and sulky all day. From lack of proper nourishment he has little energy to play actively with other children or to apply himself attentively in school. His parents are worried over his condition and try to force him to eat, thereby making the situation worse. There is a scene every time he comes to the table. This emotional behavior is carried over into other reactions in the home and at school.

It is not subject to question that people should eat temperately of a good variety of foods in order to keep up strength and avoid fatigue. To overeating may be attributed many discomforts arising from a clogged system, the toxic effect of rich foods, unbalanced diets, and general digestive disorders. It is generally true that during times of economic depression there is relatively

[1] See page 60.

less sickness simply because people cannot afford to overeat or buy as rich foods as they did. Children, however, suffer less often from the results of overeating than from an appetite that is too small or too fussy.

A temporary loss of appetite usually means that there is an undesirable physical condition present or incipient. Diseased tonsils may need to be removed. During the teething period there is often a loss of appetite. Constipation is another prominent cause. Common colds, measles, whooping cough, mumps, and other children's diseases are preceded by loss of appetite. A physician can find the cause of the trouble and prescribe a remedy which will remove the source. Lack of fresh air and exercise take away the normal need or desire for food at any age. Vigorous play out of doors is the best prescription to sharpen appetite.

More insidious is the loss of appetite arising from worry, shock, and general emotional conflict. It works in a malicious circle— the less one eats, the larger seem his troubles. Sometimes the mother, sensing that things are wrong, prepares a favorite dish and serves it in an attractive way. She tempts the child to eat in spite of his worries; he is surprised to find that, when his stomach is full of good food, his troubles diminish. But when the favorite foods fail to stimulate, the emotional upset may be considered serious in its effects. Mother or worker must try to find the cause. Perhaps the child has failed or fears failing at school, or he perhaps has had difficulties with his teacher and was sent to the principal's office. Often other children are annoying him and hurting his feelings by reference to some sensitive issues which he hides from his family. Perhaps a gang is trying to persuade him to follow evil ways, or perhaps it has already initiated him and his conscience is troubling him. It may be that there is a conflict at home. With adolescents, love—usually unrequited love—is a cause. Both boys and girls at this period are too shy or ashamed to confide in their parents. They mope in silence, harassed by the unaccustomed feelings of affection, jealousy, and longing.

The best rôle of a worker in these situations is that of sympathetic confidant. Talking things over with a mature friend who understands and does not chide but gives only kindly advice and consolation relieves the oppressed child of the burden of his worry. The home and school can co-operate to settle matters arising in classroom or playground. Church, community center, and home should strive to provide new and higher interests to divert the worried child.

Frequently the mother is responsible for the poor eating habits of her child. She may have forced the baby to take more of his bottle than he wished, thus associating with the feeding time unpleasant impressions which he carries along with him as he grows older. Children in large families have more chance of developing normal eating habits than those in a small family where an overanxious mother sits with a medical book in her hand, reading weight and height charts and worrying for fear her child is going to be underweight or undernourished. Such a mother is apt to nag her child to eat his spinach or so many spoonfuls of cereal without any question as to whether he may be hungry or not. She scolds or bribes him until he reacts by refusing altogether, thereby receiving further punishment, or by creating a disturbance just for attention. At any rate he develops emotional associations with food which kill his appetite and prejudice him against many foods for all time.

Doctors distinguish between lateral and linear types of children and therefore say that there is no dogmatic weight for any one age. One type of child may be able to assimilate a great quantity of food, while the same amount would give another child serious indigestion. The child's immediate physical needs dictate the amount of food he should eat each day. Therefore the mother should give him a minimum portion and let him ask for more. Incidentally this aids appetite. If a child refuses to eat after a little urging, his food should be removed. He will not starve before the next meal, and he is more likely to realize that, if he does not satisfy himself when he has the chance, he may be uncomfortably hungry later. Such things as a small table and chair and miniature dishes have interested children in food and made them feel more independent about eating. It throws the responsibility of choice and serving upon themselves.

New foods or unpopular foods should be introduced at the beginning of the meal, when the child's appetite is sharpest, and in small amounts—about a teaspoonful at a time. These can be disguised by being put in soups or combined with preferred foods; but they should not be forced on a child or served too often. This does not mean that, when a child takes a dislike to certain types of necessary foods such as milk or vegetables or cereals, he should not have to eat them. It is, rather, a task for the ingenuity of the mother to present them in such ways as to help him like them.

Eating between meals, especially sweets, will spoil any healthy person's appetite. Often the mother is weak about this habit. To end a child's whining or to silence him on some other score, she gives him candy. However, an apple, a sandwich, or a glass of milk given at a certain hour regularly between meals is harmless and often necessary for a growing child. It is a poor practice to give children much solid food just before bedtime, for the digestive organs are too inactive to assimilate it properly. Bad dreams, stomach-aches, and bad temper generally follow.

Since this material is meant primarily to reach workers and students rather than parents, giving further remedial measures for eating habits is unnecessary. Should social workers and teachers wish to give parents instructions on helping children to improve their appetites and to eat the proper foods, they will find excellent material in pamphlets published by the National Committee for Mental Hygiene, 50 West Fiftieth Street, New York City, and by the Infant Welfare Society of Minneapolis, 404 South Eighth Street, Minneapolis, Minnesota.

21. TIME OF SLEEPING [1]

The growing child needs many regular hours of sleep. Experiments have shown that lack of sufficient sleep deprives a child of

[1] See page 61.

the energy necessary for performing mental tasks with normal speed and accuracy. Furthermore, some doctors say that loss of an hour or two from the regular amount of sleep will produce definite changes in personality—more noticeable of course among children than among adults. The report of the White House Conference on Child Health and Protection proposed the following schedule of sleep:

Age in Years	Number of Hours of Sleep
9–10	11½
11	11
12	10½
13	10
14–15	9½
16	9

The amount of sleep depends somewhat on the child. A good test is: Does the child awaken by himself in the morning refreshed and ready to meet the new day with a smile? There is a positive correlation between hours of sleep and Item 14. Adolescence is a period of important growth and demands more than the ordinary amount of sleep. But parents, not realizing this, let the older children stay up longer than the younger ones. The result is that children of fourteen, fifteen, or sixteen years of age come to school listless and irritable. High-school children need plenty of sleep to carry their busy schedules; when sleep is short, they may begin to think of leaving school; they may play truant to walk around outdoors where the fresh air and street excitement revive them.

Teachers often dread Monday morning because a good proportion of the children are tired-eyed, dull, and cross from staying up the night before. The family had company; there was a special radio program; or all went to the movies or to call on friends. These are the excuses given by the sleepy ones. But it is not only on Sunday night that children are kept up. The parents wish to go out on week nights and having no one with whom to leave the children, take them along. It is impossible for children to rest when other members of the family are sitting up talking, laughing, quarreling, or keeping the radio turned on. Some parents are too ignorant or neglectful to see that the children keep regular bed hours. Social worker, school nurse, and teacher must make it their business to inform parents of the benefits of sleep to school children. Successful appeal can be made to the youngsters themselves by pointing out to them how much more smoothly their day runs and how much brighter they are when they have slept long and soundly the night before. Certain teachers have kept charts or organized teams within the class to stimulate interest in the time and condition of sleep.

Some children are put to bed at an early hour but do not fall asleep for some time or are wakeful during the night. In addition to the possibility of physical distractions, such as noise, light, a poor bed, a stuffy room, too many or too few covers, there are likely to be certain other causes acting as destroyers of sleep; namely, emotional upsets or fears. The memory of quarrels with other children during the day rankles in the mind. The child turns them over and over, thinking how he might have won the battles. Failure in school, jealousy of the teacher's favorites, worry over coming examinations distress children, and they are kept awake especially when conflicts arise just before bedtime. A heated argument with a parent or a punishment or a threat stirs up the system so completely that sleep is impossible. Other sleep destroyers are fearful bedtime stories of ghosts, giants, dragons, robbers, and fire and brimstone. Episodic radio dramas, no matter how good they may be, are inappropriate for young ears, especially just before bedtime. Another great mistake is reading reports of murders, suicides, accidents, gangster activities, and kidnaping from the newspapers.

A girl of fourteen was reported for truancy and tardiness. It turned out that she overslept in the morning and could not be aroused by her mother. This was because she could not fall asleep until very late at night. Her bedroom was on the first floor, and she was obsessed by the fear of robbers entering and killing her. She would not allow the light to be turned off in her room and of course could not sleep with it on. Through lack of sleep, fear of robbers, worry over school, and dread of parents and truant officers, the girl was in an exceedingly nervous condition. Analyzing her fears with her and restoring her confidence in her home and in herself took many weeks. A successful accompaniment was a hygienic program including brisk exercise out of doors just after supper, relaxing in a warm bath for half an hour, and drinking a cup of warm fresh milk just before getting into bed.

Insomnia cannot be cured by drugs. Attempting it is almost fatal to young people. In addition to the few suggestions above on physical conditions, the best remedy is unloading worries, fears, and emotional conflicts onto the shoulders of a quietly sympathetic older person, preferably the mother.

22.   Sleeping Conditions [1]

The most favorable conditions for a child's sleep are a cool room for himself, with the windows open, and a good bed with warm, light covers. The next favorable condition is twin beds or a large bed shared with a child of the same sex. The benefits of sleep on the mental, physical, and emotional disposition of the person are closely related to the conditions under which he sleeps. Children from good homes of good social and economic status or in small families of fair status probably always have good sleeping conditions.

Teachers, social workers, and nurses who have been brought up in good homes seldom realize the conditions under which some of their young charges live. Workers who must enter other people's homes or who go into detail in taking a family history find amazing situations. Three children to a bed is a conservative arrangement compared to cases where four, five, and, impossible as it seems, six sleep together or where all the younger children sleep on coats on the floor. The beds in poor homes are often worse than none at all. They either sink in the middle, forcing the children to roll down on top of one another, or they are as

1 See page 62.

hard as the floor. Often they are malodorous or bug-infested. Old coats and ragged cotton blankets are coverings. Clean sheets or sheets of any kind are luxuries, as also are pillows. Perhaps one of the children wets the bed and those who are forced to sleep with him become soiled. For brothers and sisters of all ages to sleep together is not uncommon. Frequently the whole family sleeps in one room, particularly in apartment houses. And to have one or two children sleep in the same bed with the parents or several in the same room with them is not at all extraordinary.

There is the instance of a fifteen-year-old girl who slept with her married sister and husband, both young people. The girl was absent-minded in school, a poor student, a poor mixer, and obviously suffering from conflicts on sex matters. Then in a home of good social and economic status was a beautiful young girl of seventeen, bright, gifted, but "boy crazy." Her brother, aged eighteen, was also bright but "girl crazy" and termed a good-for-nothing. The family history revealed that they had had twin beds in the same room ever since childhood. Neither one would admit any unseemly relations, but there is no doubt that such close intimacy was overstimulating and put active suggestions into their minds.

Anyone who has awakened cranky and tired after a night on a bumpy bed in a hot room or with a restless bedfellow can surmise the influence such chronic conditions must have on children. And when they witness the intimacies to which many of them are exposed, it is a wonder they are as pure-minded and well balanced emotionally as they are.

It frequently occurs in good as well as poor homes that a baby or a very small child is allowed to sleep with a grandparent or with one of his own parents. The old saying used to be that this was inadvisable because the older person sapped the strength of the younger one. Indeed, there is some truth in that statement, though not necessarily in a physical sense. A child allowed to sleep indefinitely with an older person is likely to be hindered in developing independence and the maturity normal to his age. He is apt to maintain the baby state much too long.

The regretful fact is that little can be done to ameliorate the situation in most cases of poor sleeping conditions because so much of it is due to poverty. Parents have all they can do to feed and clothe their families adequately. Too many children in the homes make it a difficult problem to have good beds, the right types of covers, and separate or uncrowded bedrooms. Where families are dependent upon charity, charitable organizations do their best to remedy matters; but when most of their allotted funds are meant for food and clothing only, there is relatively little they can do. Many parents have the means to furnish less crowded sleeping quarters at least, yet through ignorance or thoughtlessness the younger children are permitted to sleep in their parents' room or brothers with sisters. Parents let them remain there year after year, forgetting that they are growing up. Workers who learn about these situations must instruct parents and suggest better arrangements. When mothers are made aware of the inadvisability of such conditions, they are usually willing to try to move to a larger home or, when the family already owns its home, to do something in the way of fitting up another room for a bedroom.

It cannot be proved that poor sleeping conditions and undesirable bedfellows cause *all* children to become maladjusted. Some children do not seem to be harmed. Those children who live under other unfavorable conditions, particularly unsatisfactory personality and social characteristics, are probably more susceptible to the suggestive influences of poor sleeping conditions.

23. DREAMS [1]

Dreams as an item for investigation have been included in the diagnostic history for two reasons. First, when the child or parent is unable to give satisfactory information on the affecting cause of the child's maladjustment, an inquiry into his dream content may reveal something significant. Second, when the affecting

[1] See page 63.

cause is known, it is sometimes possible to determine from the nature of the dreams to what extent the cause is disturbing his emotional life.

The dreams of children are more easily analyzed than those of adults. Their mental content is still simple and elemental. They have not yet absorbed the inhibitory influences of social and moral taboos which repress the feelings and desires of adults. As a child advances in years, his natural impulses and wishes are pushed into the background by the censorship of his conscious mind; but since these impulses and wishes still exist, they show themselves by appearing in dreams. Various associations among objects, feelings, and attitudes made by the person in his experiences cause many censored impulses and feelings to reappear disguised by symbols.

As there are several contradictory schools of thought on the subject of dreams and dream symbols, it is impossible to discuss them in detail here. Moreover, the interpretation of dreams can be a dangerous procedure unless it is done by experts.

Children are on the whole such sound sleepers that they do not remember many of their dreams. The one or two which they can recall, however, must be related to important states of their subconscious minds or they would not leave imprints upon the memory. The dreams of children and of average, normal people are generally obvious and devoid of any symbolic disfigurement. The presence of symbols in dreams, on the other hand, indicates a lack of freedom of expression due to some fear or repression. Such a dream might be of flying or making a wonderful speech.

A highly symbolical dream is often a pathological dream. It means that the subject does not, even in his dreams, visualize directly the things of which he is thinking.

The general sources of children's dreams fall into these three classes:

1. Desire for wish-fulfillment
2. Specific fears and general states of fear
3. Physical conditions of the body

In England Dr. C. W. Kimmins made a study of the written records of the dreams of five hundred children between the ages of eight and sixteen. It was apparent that the majority of these dreams of childhood were wish-fulfillment dreams in which conscious and unconscious desires were gratified. Dreams of eating, recreation, receiving presents, and living in comfort were common. In adolescence these children had dreams of grandeur—of being heroes and heroines—still dreams of wish-fulfillment. The boys' sexual dreams were more overt than those of the girls. The latter, repressing their erotic feelings, had dreams of fear in which amorous pleasure was obtained through symbols. The survey showed that fear dreams were common among children. Both sexes feared wild animals, reptiles, vermin, and old men who chased them.

Fear occasioned by hearing scary stories or seeing gangster and detective movies produces nightmares. Terrifying experiences influence dreams. Accidents, fires, explosions, or robberies which have happened to the child or to one of his acquaintances are lived over again and again during sleep.[1] Fear is a prominent cause of dreams among maladjusted children. Not only is their sleep disturbed by the usual fearsome situations; but they also have the fear dreams which arise from feelings of insecurity, failure, and guilt. Fear of failure in school, fear of detection and punishment after committing a misdemeanor, fear of the abuse of a parent or of losing the love of a parent, all these are manifested in dreams by the apprehensive, worried child.

A poor physical condition agitating the system may result in nightmares. An overrich or overheavy meal before bedtime, constipation, an irritated bladder, and chronic indigestion are possible causal factors. A poor bed, a restless sleeping companion, or a noisy room may disturb the slumbers. Dreams of animals gnawing at an organ may be related to an infection in that organ. One patient reported the recurring dream of a cat clawing at his throat. An examination revealed a toxic goiter. After an operation, the cat never reappeared. Patients with weak hearts often

[1] For further details see Forman's *Our Movie-Made Children*.

dream of trying to climb a hill and failing. When teeth occur in dreams, X-rays should be taken for possible pus pockets.

When a child is referred to a mental hygienist because of his night terrors, the first procedure is a thorough physical examination. Treatment for defects and illnesses has eliminated many nightmares. Next the living habits are investigated. When simple, regular eating habits are established and when the sleeping conditions are improved, sleep is more restful. The third step is to determine the emotional factor which is distressing the child. The usual method for diagnosing is used—gathering and weighing data on home and school relationships and attitudes, the temperament of the child, the influences which play upon him, and the equipment and ideals of the home. When the case seems completely enigmatic and the dreams are very symbolical, it is best to refer it to an expert psychoanalyst.

24 AND 25. EARLY AND LATER RECREATIONAL FACILITIES [1]

Educators used to look with a critical eye at children's play, believing it necessary but not really important. They feel now that experience with constructive and related materials and a variety of play situations tend to make the child an inquiring, experimenting person—which is the first step toward being educated. Some even think that play ought to lead directly into occupations of a more serious kind. If these beliefs are true, then the choice of toys should be given considerable thought.

Early and later recreational facilities fall into two separate items on the Diagnostic History Blank, because it is necessary to find out not only the child's recreations when his problem is presented to the worker, but also the type of play and recreation which influenced his early development.

Probably in no other country in the world are parents so indulgent and generous with their children as in the United States. On birthdays and Christmas youngsters are given not one or two toys, but several, often of considerable value. It is a common

[1] See pages 64 and 65.

joke that fathers take their sons' toys to play with them themselves. A father is inclined to buy for his children not so much what they need or want as what he wants or did want at some earlier age. One father on a moderate salary bought his only child on his first birthday a tricycle, a BB gun, and a large toy automobile. Mothers of course identify themselves with their daughters when they buy them enormous French dolls. Grandparents, aunts, and uncles often deluge the young ones with more playthings than they have time to enjoy.

The result of this excessive generosity is that the child may become satiated and bored with all toys or grow into a materialistic, grasping person, desiring everything that he sees but finding little real satisfaction in anything. Having so much given him for little or no asking, he does not learn the value of things. He plays with the baubles for a moment, then tosses them aside or destroys them. If he is indulged when very young, he grows up expecting parents and adults to keep on showering him with expensive gifts and becomes a burden to everyone; or he is bitterly disappointed when they can no longer afford to gratify him. Relatives do not seem to enjoy giving presents to older children so much as to little ones; they harshly term the former greedy when they demand presents, not realizing that they themselves developed these selfish traits in them. Furthermore, giving a child toys unsuitable for his age teaches him nothing and only gives him "toy indigestion." If he is not mentally or physically ready to use the toy when it is given, he will have no interest in it later when he might normally use it, for it has lost its novelty and charm. Children in the midst of unsuitable, though expensive and attractive toys can be inactive, discontented, and quarrelsome and may continually nag at adults to be entertained, inasmuch as they cannot learn how to amuse themselves with these materials without instruction.

On the opposite side of the picture is the small child who has few or no toys. His parents may be too poor to buy them or without sympathy for a child's play needs. Such a deprived child may find play values in any available object. Thus he may develop superior imagination, ingenuity, and initiative by making the best of what he can find. But the average dull child who is not natively equipped with imagination will not be so resourceful in inventing his own playthings. He will probably grow up a rather uninteresting, phlegmatic person, not so full of fun as he might otherwise have been.

Three factors determine the course of a child's pastimes:

1. Play materials must be furnished him—the tools of his craft, things with which he can follow out his play impulses.
2. The arrangement or disposal of them in the environment must make them available material—blocks on shelves or in cupboards accessible to the child, and personal belongings like crayons, paint, and paper in individual pigeonholes—so that he can easily find and keep them in order.
3. Adults must have an attitude of respect for play as the business of childhood and as a stimulus to physical and mental growth.

In his first play period the baby is exploring his surroundings and his body. He looks, listens, tastes, and handles. He is trying to disintegrate the great mass of sight and sound around him into the smaller components of which it is made. Then he begins to relate them to himself. He grasps a rattle, finds that it makes a noise, and learns that *he* can make a noise with it. He feels the shape of a round ball and probably compares its shape with the feel of some other object. Soon he reaches out to test the feel of other objects in his environment. If presents are to be bought him in the period from birth to one year, they should be limited to balls, balloons, bells, rattles, soft animals and dolls, water toys of rubber or celluloid, and large linen books containing pictures of familiar objects.

In the next period the child creeps, walks, and climbs. He uses everything he finds for a play purpose. Because he is clumsy and inquisitive, he breaks and tears things apart. His span of attention is short. At first he deals very little with real playthings. He is more interested in investigation and in acquiring a finer control of his body and hands. Many repetitive processes go on, almost like practice, as when the child takes blocks from one box and puts them in another over and over again. He has little aesthetic appreciation at this period. He needs large pieces of material to help his motor and sensory development. Such development is aided through the use of large blocks that fit together, nests of boxes, peg boards, form boards, rocking horses, low wheel toys to ride, chairs, a door swing, pens, slides, wooden screw toys and pyramids, animals, soft dolls, carriages, furniture or housekeeping toys, pails and shovels, and sandboxes.

During the years from four to six the child should be given constructive toys: blocks to build houses and garages, a hammer and big nails, blunt scissors, simple puzzles, clay to model, bubble pipes, a drum or a horn, a phonograph and records, trains and trucks, doll houses, paste, and crayons. As he becomes more robust, such devices as trapezes, slides, and bars may be added. Play is not merely taking on more life situations. Creative imagination begins to enter into it. The child recreates procedures to which he has been subjected. He dramatizes his own experiences.

During the period from seven to ten, the same toys that were used earlier are appropriate for physical exercise—roller skates, jumping ropes, and pedal toys; and also devices to teach social activities—banks, play money, costume outfits, and garden toys. Later there should be activities suitable for a group, as archery, basketball, and baseball, and there should also be construction sets, chemical sets, and typewriters.

The principle at each age is to provide stimulation for exercise and to provide also the materials with which the child can create his own play situations. For instance, instead of giving a girl a doll with a complete outfit of clothing, present her with a doll and strips of cloth, thread, needle, scissors, and even a little sewing machine. Instead of giving the boy a big playhouse or elaborate mechanical devices, give him slabs of wood and tools. If children are found scribbling on the walls, pounding good furniture, or taking apart the clocks, it is a certain sign that they have not the proper constructive toys with which to play. Each toy should be chosen with a definite purpose before it is bestowed in order that the child may develop motor and sensory capacities and imagination, acquire information and skill, and learn to play with toys in a social group.

Not only can these recreation facilities keep children from undesirable pastimes and direct their social educational development, but they can also serve as the means of teaching the significance of ownership and of sharing and caring for property. Possessing only communal toys is likely to lead to quarreling. A child should have at least one thing which he knows is his to play with and care for. Then he will learn to enjoy sharing it or exchanging it temporarily for that of another child and to have respect for others' property. A child should learn early to keep his belongings in their places and to guard them from theft or careless breakage. It is deplorable that many children leave their toys in the streets or yard or underfoot to deteriorate and fall to pieces. They have probably found that a few tears will persuade the parents to replace the loss. So they grow up wasteful, extravagant, destructive, and with a poor sense of values.

When a teacher or social worker undertakes to assist a parent in readjusting a wayward child, she must look into the subject of recreational facilities and with the parents plan equipment (within purse limits) which will develop the child along the proper social and mental lines. As yet the true value of recreational facilities has not been realized. In a later section, the recreation of the family, Item 59, will be discussed.

26. PLAYMATES OR COMPANIONS [1]

The need of companionship is so necessary and fundamental to the existence of human nature that gregariousness has been considered to be an innate trait of mankind. Children abandoned to their own resources find companionship in dolls, dogs, cats, and imaginary personalities. If a human being grew up knowing no other human beings, he would seem more or less like some

[1] See page 66.

weird vegetable or animal type rather than the type recognized as man. A child growing up without the society of children of his own age is an awkward and pitiful misfit. It is from his playmates that the young child learns most of his code of social conduct: greediness, selfishness or generosity, combativeness, a large part of his vernacular, games, evaluations of toys and children's property, and many of his attitudes towards adults, other children, and school.

An only child, deprived of the companionship of brothers and sisters, is unfortunate; so is the child who lives too far from others or who is forbidden playmates until he goes to school. He is a conspicuous figure in the kindergarten and early grades. He has no idea of how to play with his group; and the other children recognizing this fact avoid, taunt, or take advantage of him. The child, feeling that he is different, suffers keenly. He may strike out blindly to avenge himself, or he may withdraw completely within himself. Or he may become a weak tool in the hands of children among whom he thinks he is being popular. Another disadvantage in isolation from playmates is that the child is thrown too much with his parents or other adult relatives and is less apt to mature into a self-reliant, happy person.

A child's personality and social type depend partly on native traits, partly on his relationship with his parents and siblings, and certainly upon the influence of his various playmates. Parents can see marked differences in their children as they change schools and neighborhoods or even rooms in schools. One child, naturally shy, may be driven farther into himself because he happens to be thrown with a group of children generally aggressive and thoughtless, or he may be drawn out to express himself in happy ways by a group in which he can compete on the same level emotionally and mentally. Children normally happy and contented may suffer untold agonies because another school child teases them about their clothes, speech, failures, or homes, and nothing their parents can say or do will quite erase the shame.

Contemporaries have more influence over one another than

people of one generation on another generation. Parents may put forth every effort to train their offspring in proper conduct and to instill the best interests and character traits. They may spend large sums educating and outfitting them to the best advantage. They usually can make the children eat the proper foods and keep good hours. But sooner or later the children begin to rebel about certain points, saying, "Other children do not have to eat spinach," or "Other children do not have to go to bed so early." The phrase "other children" is dreaded by all parents. Its significance is one of the most insidious forces parents have to combat.

Children make definite impressions upon one another—impressions which are never forgotten. An experienced social worker told that as a child she had been kept free of superstition until a girl moved into her neighborhood who related hair-raising stories of ghosts and spooks, so that for many years after she was afraid of the dark. Children cannot express at the time the impressions other children are making upon them. But how often adults say, "I know I would have been a different person now had I not associated continually with this or that kind of child when I was young!"

When a child is in trouble and blames another child for leading him into it, adults are inclined to discredit the statement; but surveys made by psychologists, criminologists, and students of juvenile delinquency rate the influence of companions as being highly significant. There is usually one room in a school that has more behavior problems than the other rooms. There are more sex problems in certain schools. More juvenile crimes are committed in one district than in another. Of course there are other factors in such cases, but there is no doubt that the children are influencing one another.

Sex information is passed from child to child before parents think of imparting it. The majority of children would probably reach adolescence without much curiosity about sex if one child or a few children did not interest them in it by their salacious talk. Many later misapprehensions and conflicts regarding sex are due to the wrong interpretations put upon it by misinformed children.

Children can be influenced by a strong personality as easily as by group pressure. They come in contact with a new child in the neighborhood who, for some reason arising from one of the peculiarities in his own background, has certain definite undesirable traits. In the schoolroom his dirty mind may affect the whole room; his saucy impertinence may rouse otherwise mild-tempered, generally conforming children to emulate his rough manners. He may be unconscious of his power, but because he has the traits of leadership or a magnetic personality, the other children think anything he does is worth copying. On the other hand he may actually bully others into following him, or perhaps a group may be bound to him through such circumstances as fighting with another group against whom he defends them. Thus gangs are formed (2).

A juvenile gang is primarily a chance getting together of a group of boys (more rarely girls) of about the same age who have a common interest. That interest may be conflict with authority or with other groups, or it may be similar recreational tastes regarding ball teams, hikes, various games, rowdyism, or crime. The group is formed spontaneously and integrates best under opposition. A gang may become conventionalized and have a reputable standing in the community. In some instances its standards and aims are lofty. But usually the gang is a social menace, destructive in its effects upon its individual members, and, by encouraging stealing and truancy, dangerous to property and general peace.

The wise teacher in the regular school is sensitive to interplays of personality when two children clash or get along together smoothly. By subdividing her groups and considering her seating program, she can throw congenial friends together and separate the conflicting pupils. She can study the leaders to learn which lead for good and which for evil. She can watch the followers and guide them to follow the better leader. And she can work with the home, making suggestions to the parents as to the type of companions with whom they should allow their children to play.

The question of the advisability of segregating the delinquent is a much debated one. Those opposed to it say that it marks the delinquent definitely as a kind of social outcast. Sooner or later he must be returned to the average group, but his consciousness and shame over having had to be sent away may interfere with his normal adjustment. A few teachers, knowing that a child has just been released from a school or class for the unruly, expect him to repeat his misdemeanor and so do not give him a fair chance to settle down. On the positive side of the question it seems advisable to segregate the delinquent because in a special class or school he can have an individualized curriculum to suit his particular mental and personality needs. He is placed under the supervision of teachers especially trained to understand his type. Another positive factor is that, when a group of children of the same caliber are put together, no one of them is likely to feel odd or marked. Each realizes that he has a better chance for readjustment than when he was with the average group. Furthermore, one delinquent child often helps another to overcome his undesirable traits. The spirit of co-operation in some of these special schools is truly remarkable.

To break up the influences of gangs and delinquents, workers try to win the friendship of the leader. If he co-operates with them, his followers may be persuaded to end their unlawful activities. But the work does not stop there. Recreational or vocational facilities must be provided to absorb the energies of these young street gamins and direct them into more constructive channels. Churches, schools, social agencies, and city governments must co-ordinate to appropriate funds for community centers, summer camps, boys' and girls' clubs, Scout organizations, and playgrounds—all under the supervision of trained directors who understand the needs of children and who can keep their energies in the right courses.

The problem of sex information or of actual sex experience merits some discussion—most appropriately under the topic of companions. Sex experiences are very private matters. There is scarcely any individual with whom anyone wishes to discuss them. Children find this topic tabooed as if it were a shameful affair. Suppression merely tends to arouse their curiosity. Children are hushed when they honestly ask where babies come from. They recognize an obscure answer and set about trying to find actual facts. Unfortunately their quest throws them into contact with other ignorant, uninformed children. They consult together, distort facts, and put an evil light upon them. Discrepancies in facts regarding sex leave children abnormally curious. They ponder the subject much more than adults realize. Often their faith in their parents is completely destroyed because they are given false accounts by them.

It is just as normal for a child to have an interest in his reproducing organs as it is for him to be interested in his toes or thumbs. It is natural that he will have a curiosity about the organs of the opposite sex when he sees that they are different from his. But if he experiments or explores, both he and the other party are usually severely punished. This intensifies his curiosity regarding sex and makes it an exciting, forbidden subject. If he has been scared by the punishment and shame, he may never openly experiment in the matter again; but his curiosity is just as keen as it ever was and he daydreams on the subject. His feeling of guilt can even be strong enough to try to suppress the daydreaming and push the thoughts farther back into the subconscious. But the feeling of guilt, the latent curiosity, and the memory of the pleasure during the first experience may work together to cause a future maladjustment. The individual may have an abnormal craving for sex relationships. He may indulge in perversions, or he may recoil from all heterosexuality. When an older boy or man attacks a five-year-old girl, he may be succumbing to an impulse which has lain dormant since the time it first occurred when he was very young.

Many maladjustments, particularly in the matter of sex, have been traced back to some startling experience forced upon the individual as a child. The number of girls who have been attacked or approached by older men when very young is appalling. Young girls seldom report the incident at the time, although physically and emotionally it is usually a severe shock to their entire system. Shame and fear are always connected with it. The individual's entire attitude toward the opposite sex may be distorted. Of course she tries to forget the incident; but though she may be able to stop thinking of it afterwards, it may later on lead her to try to punish people whom she associates with the offender. Psychiatrists find that patients with certain forms of insanity have often had a disastrous experience with sex.

The problem of a sane and conservative plan of sex instruction is the most critical issue in educational theory and practice. The inertia of public opinion and the personal inhibitions of those in authority are obstacles to progress. But the tragedy of thousands of wrecked lives in our mental hospitals and in our juvenile courts and police divisions and the irony of 200,000 children born out of wedlock annually stir a storm of social protest that cannot forever be ignored.

BIBLIOGRAPHY

1. FORMAN, HENRY JAMES—*Our Movie-Made Children*. New York: The Macmillan Co., 1933. 288 pp.
2. THRASHER, FREDERIC M.—*The Gang; A Study of 1313 Gangs in Chicago*. Chicago: University of Chicago Press, 1929. 571 pp.

CHAPTER VIII

PERSONALITY AND SOCIAL FACTORS

THE group of personality and social factors includes Items 27 to 37. They are more difficult to evaluate than those of Chapters VI and VII. These factors lead the list of the five groups in distinguishing between behavior and non-behavior children. Possibly the health and physical factors of Chapter VI exercise indirect effects on these personality and social factors, so that the difference between these two groups of factors may not be as great as appears at first sight.

27. SOCIAL TYPE [1]

A child's social conduct, as we see it, is his overt reaction to his environment. His sociability depends upon interreactions with his family, school, neighborhood, and play groups, as well as upon his own life experiences and his reactions thereto. To designate his social type therefore is merely to describe his symptomatic behavior. Since this description is in terms of symptomatic behavior, it points out the direction which must be taken in readjusting him.

There are three important traits common to the socialized human being. The degree to which he possesses them determines his social adaptability. These three are:

1. The extent to which he is the "ingoing" or "outgoing" type of personality

[1] See page 70.

2. His degree of submission or aggression
3. His sensitivity to public opinion

Normal society can be divided into persons who tend toward introversion and persons who tend toward extraversion, although the degree to which each deviates from the norm may be slight. If the individual tends to be the ingoing type, he may be quiet and reserved, especially in a group. He prefers the companionship of one or two persons, rather than of several. He makes friends slowly and only after a relatively long acquaintanceship. Since he is inclined to daydream, he may have a high level of imagination and feeling which find expression through poetry, music, or art or even through scientific inventions.

The more the introvert deviates from the norm, the more he tends to withdraw from reality. He seeks fulfillment for his repressed desires and feelings by daydreaming and by night dreaming. He distorts reality in such ways as to satisfy his cravings. Because his impulses are repressed these take on strong emotional tones and his self-feelings are very much heightened. A bizarre set of values and entities may be constructed. There is also an intense "personalization" of all events that come within his notice. He takes casual remarks in a personal way and is suspicious and resentful. He may become distinctly antisocial, uncouth, and insulting. He cannot stand any teasing; he repulses the attempts of others to get his friendship. Introversion in its extreme form is typical of certain types of insanity.

The extraverted, or outgoing, type lacks the symptoms of oversensitiveness, unreality, and protracted daydreaming. He may have repressions or conflicts for which he is compensating by aggressive behavior. He needs companionship for stimulation and tends to seek crowds or gangs. He makes contacts easily because he does not set up defensory attitudes or respond with unintelligible bursts of emotion. On the whole, he is likely to be better adjusted to the actual world than the ingoing type.

The extreme outgoing type often clashes with society. He is apt to be too boisterous and to take too much initiative. In school he often gives the teacher considerable trouble because he talks too much and expresses his feelings too freely.

Unless the ingoing child withdraws into himself in an extreme degree, he is rarely considered a problem by his teachers or parents. In fact, they regard him as a model of behavior. Later, however, his recessive traits may become more marked, and it may become obvious that he is "odd," and that he is not developing along normal lines. It may then be too late to help him come out of himself and meet the world courageously.

There may be an hereditary basis for the outgoing and ingoing tendencies. It is noticeable among babies that some are always quiet while others are always making noises. Which trend the individual will follow, however, probably depends much more on the later influences of his environment. His early success or failure determines how much he expresses himself later. His early physical health gives him the amount of energy necessary to exert himself. Early encouragement or discouragement from his parents, siblings, and companions tends to set his habits of expression. If he is frequently punished for his blunders or for his protests against dissatisfactions, he may develop inhibiting fears which drive him inward. To be rejected by parents or siblings may cause him to brood over his lack of love and to seek his happiness in daydreams.

Some children are happy and voluble in the bosom of the family, but shy and shut-in at school and in groups of children. They may be overprotected by their parents and kept on a baby level from which they do not care to rise. Possibly their first contacts with people outside the home or at school were so unsuccessful and disagreeable that they lost their courage to make further trials at adjustment. The outgoing child may have had robust health and great energy when a baby. He may have received encouragement and attention for his thoughts and plans. He may have found that to express his feelings of anger or joy brought him into the limelight. At an early age he probably became accustomed to groups and enjoyed showing off before them. His protest against rejection, physical defects, or failure may have taken an overt form in unsocial acts, and undoubtedly in his drive for recognition and love he has preferred attention given him in punishments and scoldings to no attention at all.

Teachers frequently call upon mental-hygiene clinics for help in curbing the garrulousness, quarreling, and emotional expressions of their outgoing pupils. Since excessive extraversion, like excessive introversion, is likely to have an unusual cause, the sources must be sought and treated. As behavior is principally directed toward a satisfying end from the individual's point of view, another type of behavior must be substituted which will bring satisfaction, not only to himself but also to those about him. Thus to give a child attention, praise, and privileges for his quiet, self-controlled behavior may be as satisfying as giving him attention by scoldings and punishment for his loud, disturbing behavior. If his excessive enthusiasm is a compensation for failure, rejection, or deprivations, the causes underlying these factors must be removed, modified, or provided with substitutes.

Psychologists are urging teachers to make a greater effort to identify the introverted child in the primary grades so that something may be done to draw him out before his personality has become irrevocably shut in. To *force* this child to express himself or to take an active part in school is never successful. Gentle methods of praising and encouraging must be used. Any word or idea expressed by him must be recognized with extravagant interest so that he may wish to try again. Positions of honor and responsibility should be given him in order that some of his daydreams may come true. Chances for unfair competition and failure must be minimized. In the home the chief sources must be sought. The relationships and attitudes of the family must be directed toward helping this child to come out of himself.

Submission and ascendance are two opposing traits of personality, relative in value, which universally characterize the social type. If two persons of equal status come together, one is likely to stand as the master. His impulses dominate, while the other yields and adjusts his behavior accordingly. So swift is this sorting of personalities that frequently the issue is decided in the first instant by the glance and bearing of the dominant individual. It is true of course that each individual is submissive toward some people and ascendant toward others; but if an average is taken of his behavior in contact with his equals, he may be placed with some assurance at a definite point on the scale between the two extremes of complete ascendance and complete submission.

Two of the leading conditions of ascendance are physical size and energy. It is easy for a large, strong child to dominate because, without his asking it, the smaller, weaker children look up to him. The eldest child, the child thrown early upon his own resources, and the child who controls his parents bid fair to retain their ascendance in adult relations. On the other hand, some individuals feel a strong need to compensate for their lack of size, strength, and family position. Their ego drives are so strong that they try to put every person they meet into the submissive rôle. When their drive for power is too strong, they come into violent conflict with society. Other ascendant types refuse to be eclipsed, and struggle results. Children who are always fighting and who dislike taking orders are of this type. They are poor sports on the playground. They cannot accept defeat or teasing gracefully.

Leadership depends largely upon the degree to which the individual possesses the quality of ascendance. Not only must the leader have the stable character traits of reliability, of willingness to accept responsibility, and of understanding of those he is to lead, but he must also be endowed with that dynamic force which makes others wish to follow him. The origin of a submissive attitude reaches far back into childhood. Frailty, physical defect, or association with older children, if not relieved by compensation, are almost certain to lead to a nonresistive trend of behavior. Repression and cringing obedience to an austere parent, teacher, or older brother may leave the personality with a permanent mark of submission.

Not all people can be ascendant types; otherwise there could be no peace in the world. It is desirable, however, that each individual have something of both ascendant and submissive qualities—that he may yield when necessary to the dominance of the stronger and wiser and yet be able to rise to ascendance and assume leadership at times. Conditions should be arranged so that he may develop both characteristics to the best degree. Physical defects which work against a child's acquiring ascendance can be corrected. To place him among children of his size and age at school and on the playground will relieve him of his feeling of submissiveness among larger and older children. Parents should be urged to allow him to choose, plan, and express himself. The teacher can let him practice leading the group. Whatever the source may be which is causing excessive submission, it should be eliminated or modified whenever possible by the understanding teacher or case worker. When the child has developed an excessive tendency to dominate, the chief sources must be sought again. If his aggressiveness is a compensation for defects, they should be removed or treated. If he is placed in groups of children his own size, he will find it less easy to rule them. As has just been said, to rearrange the environmental conditions which cause his excessive aggression tends to moderate his behavior.

The last important quality of personality which determines the social type is the degree of sensitivity to the opinions of others which the individual possesses. There is a familiar difference between the callous person and the one who is quick to respond to social approval or disapproval. This susceptibility characterizes the person of tact, the diplomat, the "good mixer." Such a one is quick to grasp the situation in a group into which he is thrown, responding intelligently to facial expressions, postures, and tones of voice. The opposite type finds himself at an utter loss. He is always making blunders, speaking thoughtlessly, and failing to profit by his mistakes.

Lack of sensitivity to social stimuli is found among all types of personality—the ingoing and outgoing, the submissive and aggressive. The trait does not even correspond very highly with the intelligence rating. Many men of genius or high professional standing have no tact or ability to get along well with people. They may be respected but not loved. Sensitivity to social stimuli may be an original capacity. Indeed, it is difficult to learn if one has not acquired it in early childhood. There is no doubt, however, that it can be learned by long trial-and-error practice, even though at considerable pain to the individual and his associates. It can also be imitated through early contacts in social gatherings or in a pleasant home. It also seems to rise from inner peace of mind. That is, children who come from happy, congenial homes have less trouble learning it than those who live amid hatred and conflict.

28. PERSONALITY TYPE [1]

A discussion of the personality type does not mean a discussion of the whole subject of personality. Personality is the sum of the individual's physical, intellectual, emotional, and social aspects. A study of all these traits obviously covers the whole picture of the child's native and acquired character. The discussion of the social type gave the objective view of the child's emotional reactions to his environment. Personality type describes his subjective side—his temperament and his emotional depth, breadth, and change, as well as the prepotent drives or needs of his nature and its qualities.

Individuals differ in their general emotional responsiveness. At one extreme are the calm, stolid, imperturbable people; at the other stand those who are excitable, sensitive, and easily aroused. Averaging the emotional reactions to many situations, we obtain a rough central tendency, which determines the personality type of any individual. Most people have a characteristic mood. Each individual is either usually elated or depressed, optimistic or pessimistic, no matter what the fortunes of his life may be. It is noticeable that some men keep cheerful in the face of unemployment or financial loss, while others grumble and worry even in good times. The spirits of one child will remain irrepressible,

[1] See page 71.

while those of another droop at small failures or criticisms. In-consequential details will irritate one person, driving him into a fit of temper, while the same situations never touch another. Some people respond quickly with mirth or tears, while others remain lethargic.

Emotional breadth denotes the range and variety of objects which arouse one's emotions. A person may be so tied up with his family that he has no interest in anything beyond it. He con-fines his love, hate, joy, and pain to the family exclusively. His sympathy does not embrace his companions nor the rest of society. Emotional narrowness is sometimes even more marked than that. The individual may be so egocentric that he has no interest in anyone but himself, in the few persons with whom he identifies himself, or in those who continually flatter him. He may hate those who thwart or discredit him; but usually his self-love is so invulnerable that it never occurs to him that anyone dislikes him. This type of person sounds thoroughly obnoxious; but, strangely enough, such an individual often has great success in his achievements.

Many people have wide emotional interests. They are affected not only by their immediate environment but also by stories read or seen in the movies; they concern themselves with politi-cal and local events through the newspapers or by taking an active part in clubs. In an extreme degree they are the people who are always "minding someone else's business." A wide spread of emotional reaction may be only a superficial, affective re-sponse. An individual with such a spread seems capable of the most enraptured pleasure and susceptible of the deepest sorrow.

Emotional intensity which is too great may cause considerable unhappiness. When the individual hates, his hatred may be a devouring passion; his love consumes him; his rages unbalance him. When he grieves, he suffers in the very depths of his being. Thus children who feel with intensity may become temporarily unbalanced by emotions which they do not understand and can-not control without help. Probably a great number of such chil-.

dren find their way to mental clinics. Forces of their environment and conflicts of their homes which might not bother other children affect them to an extreme degree.

Emotional strength has a pragmatic value in the world's work. When a man's love for children is truly profound, he may endow an orphanage. Most of those interested in improving child-labor laws have the love of children at heart. Devotion to bettering tenements, controlling liquor traffic, eliminating vice, and furthering religious and charitable institutions usually arises from a genuine love for humanity. The love of beauty in art, music, literature, architecture, interior decoration, and scenery is evidence of strong emotional feeling for certain impersonal things.

Emotional frequency and change refer to the time factor in emotion—the rapid succession or alternations of mood or upset. Excessive frequency and change constitute instability. When an individual fluctuates often in his mood, he is said to be flighty. Reliability and responsibility are not likely to be among his better traits. He cannot be depended upon to perform his tasks with much concentration or accuracy or to co-operate along with the average group. In an extreme degree emotional instability is typical of certain forms of insanity. Many unadjusted children are classified as unstable and flighty. They may enter the classroom in a genial frame of mind but in a few minutes flare up at a slight affront. Although they may not be hard to calm, they are likely to have another upset shortly. They laugh and cry easily. Their likes and dislikes interchange quickly. They cannot concentrate or pay attention to lessons. Their minds jump from idea to idea before any one of them can be developed.

Variations in aspects of emotion relate partly to the physical constitution and its changes and partly to the nature of the life experiences.

The endocrine glands have a strong influence upon the character of emotional reactions, especially mood and change. In fact, some authors have classified personality types solely on the basis of glands. Treatment by endocrine extracts, always with a physician's advice of course, has changed or balanced many of these "glandular types."

Organic and functional conditions of the body and physical defects have already been discussed in their relation to personality manifestations. Prenatal influences, circumstances of the birth, feeding habits, and early health of the child color his later emotional reactions. The amount of solicitude and attention given a sick child is reflected in his subsequent responses, as shown under the sections on health and diseases.

Early love relations with family and nurse, especially with the mother, direct the general course of the child's emotional life. His early frustrations, failures, humiliations, losses and gains in personal property, and his position in the family all predispose his tones of feeling. Imitation of the emotional expressions of others certainly sets patterns for the child, particularly in regard to his emotional strength and breadth and perhaps even mood. Emotional breadth can even be taught the child. That is, he can be taught what objects in his environment should be loved or hated, for what causes he should grieve, and what things he should enjoy.

Then there should be considered those indefinable qualities of the personality—charm, personal magnetism, and lovableness. We may heartily disapprove of a person and find him a great trial to deal with, but we have to admit that he is charming and likable. On the other hand, many successful, upright, dependable people have no magnetism or lovable qualities. Charm and magnetism do not depend entirely on attractive face, figure, or clothes, although these contribute in many cases. Humor, wit, the quality and frequency of the smile, the softening of the face in response to people are probably intrinsic parts of charm. To a certain extent these qualities are innate traits in some people; they can, however, be partially acquired by practice in social groups. A show of interest, smiling, laughing, a good appearance, grace, ability to pay compliments, and a mildly amusing and interesting conversation all contribute to make the individual likable.

The Bureau of Children's Guidance, under Dr. Marion E. Kenworthy at the New York School of Social Work, has been using a highly successful method of diagnosing personality and behavior patterns—the "ego-libido" method. The chief essentials of this method are summarized as follows from *Mental Hygiene and Social Work,* by Porter R. Lee and Dr. Kenworthy (2): Ego and libido are the two broad trends which underlie behavior. *Ego* is defined as the instinct for self-preservation and domination. The ego needs prompt the individual to strive for prominence through self-realization. Libido refers to love values, first of all for the self, then for parents, siblings, relatives, and other individuals in the group, and finally for the mate. If an individual does not receive satisfaction or recognition for his ego needs, he may overcompensate and demand attention from school and home, often through antisocial means. If his love needs are not satisfied, he seeks a love object. He does not work for ego satisfaction, but by his work he gains loving attention from some person whose affection he seeks.

The normally adjusted person has a well-balanced proportion of both ego and libido drives. There are some people, however, who do not seem to need love. They are more interested in getting ahead and in winning power and position. Love is only incidental. On the other hand, when the love drive predominates, the individual seems to care little for his own welfare or advancement. Only a love object can spur him to achievement.

Every experience, whether physical, intellectual, or social, has its tone of feeling. In other words, there are elements of both love and ego present. Since it is not experiences in themselves which motivate conduct but rather the feeling tones which accompany them, in order to understand a child's nature it is necessary to know the feeling tones accompanying his experiences which formed his personality and behavior patterns. The fact that the same situation affects two people differently and arouses two entirely different reactions is proof of the theory that the feeling tone in experience determines behavior and personality. Two boys, very much alike, come from poverty-stricken homes where their respective fathers drink and abuse the mothers and children. One boy steals, but the other does not. If we rule out possible contributory factors and assume that poverty and the father's abuse are the instigating cause for the one boy's stealing, how shall we account for the fact that the other boy does not steal? The answer is that the chief causal factor did not hold the same meaning for the second boy—that it did not affect him with the same feeling tone.

Every experience is either satisfying or unsatisfying to the child because of the feeling tone attached to it. Every experience is either constructive or destructive from the point of view of the mature goals toward which every child must strive. Furthermore, since a child naturally wishes to repeat experiences which have brought him satisfaction, in arranging a program for developing a child, emphasis should be laid on the satisfying, constructive experiences and their substitutes. Children or adults who are described as emotionally immature are those who remain on the level at which their experiences were most satisfactory; they repeat these experiences to obtain more satisfaction, although they may have been of a destructive nature and growth-preventing.

When children do not wish to grow up but misbehave in ways much too immature for their age, they are trying to perpetuate that state in which childish actions brought attention from a beloved person—the mother or an early teacher. Society abounds in old and young who are functioning on immature levels or maintaining immature habits: children who suck their thumbs or wet the bed or who refuse to try in school, men who do not wish to work or who will not accept better jobs, many semi- or quasi-invalids, and the married person who is unwilling to accept responsibility but demands that the mate act as a parent substitute.

An understanding of the personality type, as it is manifested in the emotional reactions of the child, is necessary before a program of treatment can be formulated. It must be borne in mind, however, that no true estimate of his nature can be made from one interview. Repeated observation of his behavior and questions asked of parents, teachers, siblings, and the child himself must be directed toward obtaining information regarding the child's instinctive trends as well as his life experiences and their emotional associations.[1]

29. ANGER, JEALOUSY, REVENGE, ETC.[2]

Teachers probably refer more children to clinics because of fighting and bad temper than for any other reason. Their descriptive phrases are: lack of self-control, incorrigibility, meanness, stubbornness, poor sportsmanship.

The two general sources of anger are frustration and lowering of the self-feelings. A baby screams with rage when his hunger or love needs are not satisfied. As he grows older, he has many desires and plans which he wishes to carry to fulfillment. Many of them, not being socially acceptable or not in accordance with parental or school wishes, must be squelched. These frustrations cause feelings of resentment, anger, and hatred.

Some children learn at an early age that it is a better policy to inhibit their feelings of anger. They either become resigned to giving up their plans, or they nourish imaginary forms of revenge. The former type is the happier, more socialized being, though possibly inclined to be too unaggressive and submissive. The latter gives evidences of his secret resentments through moods of sulkiness, daydreaming, sleeplessness, loss of appetite, sudden aversions to people or things, or uncalled-for bursts of irritation at irrelevant situations.

The type that gets into most trouble is the one unable to inhibit his anger. Since the time when he was an infant, he has been accustomed to giving vent to his rage. As he was not early taught habits of self-control, he grows into adulthood a victim of his own bad temper.

Bad temper is decidedly objectionable, particularly to the

[1] For a thorough review of tests and measurements in the fields of personality and character see Watson (4).

[2] See page 72.

person against whom it is directed. It is a threat to his ego. The parent feels that his age and experience give him the privilege of dominating his offspring. Evidences of the child's anger at his domination are an affront to the parent's self-esteem. He usually punishes the child into docility, and after he has cowed him, believes with satisfaction that he has taught the child the meaning of self-control and obedience. But the child resents this unfair advantage taken over him on account of his small size and may harbor lasting feelings of hatred for the parent.

School of course is full of frustrations for the child. His wishes or impulses are seldom recognized. If he persists with them, he is forcibly frustrated. It has been the traditional duty of teachers to enforce the rules and give academic instruction according to set curricula. Not only do displays of bad temper interfere with the progress of the pupils, but they are also frequently a threat to the teacher's ego. She cannot face the opposition and disrespect of the child. Therefore she feels a strong urge to punish him by making use of her superior strength and position. The child may be cowed but resentful, or he may become offensive in his rages.

The temper tantrum may be an attention-getting mechanism. A child finds that fits of rage fill spectators with fear and force them to give in to him. The spoiled child and the rejected child both use this weapon. The former employs it through force of habit, the latter because it is a means of attracting attention. Persistent refusal on the part of adults to recognize the tantrum is the surest way to conquer it. Commending the child for self-control and other good behavior is usually an acceptable substitute.

To effect preventions and remedies, causes must be sought and treated. Poor health and poor living habits must not be overlooked as factors causing irritation and anger. Low physical resistance gives an easy access for emotional stimuli. Headache, indigestion, constipation, toxic poisoning as from bad tonsils, sinus trouble, itches, poor vision and hearing, encephalitis, and epilepsy have bad temper as one of their chief characteristics.

Lack of sleep, hunger, or poor food aggravates temper. Before expecting a child to improve his self-control, it is only reasonable to improve his physical condition.

The second principal source of anger, as we have said, is the lowering of the self-feelings. The desire to surpass and to assert the self is considered an instinctive trait in all humans. Failure in striving for recognition is decidedly vexatious. The individual seldom punishes himself for his shortcomings but has a strong impulse to punish another person or thing. When he hits his finger with a hammer, he is likely to hurl the hammer to the floor; or when he cannot make a telephone connection, he feels like tearing the instrument from the wall. In school when the child cannot get his lessons, he is inclined to blame the teacher or the children. He may punish them by activity on another level in which he excels. He may thrash his successful rival, or he may be impudent with the teacher. It takes a person of mature insight to resist the impulse to punish another and to stop to consider wherein he himself is at fault. Meanness and incorrigibility in a school child are usually caused by his feelings of inferiority. On the whole it is not the bright and successful child who has temper fits but rather the one of limited ability who cannot easily compete with his group. Some are resigned to defeat; but others, through stronger need to express themselves, are chronically resentful and wrathful.

Most cases of bad temper develop before the school age. They are bred by competition in the family life where siblings vie with one another for parental recognition. The oldest child and the one who remained the baby until supplanted by the arrival of a new one have the strongest feelings of resentment and jealousy. They may resort to violent actions in order to draw attention away from their younger brothers and sisters. Though formerly of a mild and loving disposition, they become negativistic, vindictive, and irritable. They are likely to carry over the jealousy and hatred to include all young children whom they feel like bullying and tormenting.

Parents do not intend to show partiality. Few of them ever

realize and few of them admit that they do. A mother naturally spends most time on a new baby and is able to give less attention to the older one. All the world loves a baby. Visitors and relatives cannot resist the appeal of a new child. The older one, used to receiving all their affection, feels injured and wronged by the arrival of the newcomer. He has lost his sense of security and importance in the home and inevitably develops some mechanism to compensate for it. He may try to do some actual bodily harm to his supplanter; or afraid to reveal his antipathy openly, he may hide it from his parents and lapse into dreams of revenge or delusions of grandeur which may later lead him to make active attacks against others whom he identifies with his younger brother or sister.

As the child grows older and as his personality develops, his parents and teachers naturally compare him with his siblings. Adults have apparently believed that comparisons between children would stimulate the laggards to catch up with the others. They contrast the older with the younger—usually to the former's disadvantage. There are few children who are not aroused to fury when this is done. Even though a child has never previously felt any dislike toward his younger brother or sister, he will undoubtedly begin to have feelings of antagonism. Moreover, this method of setting one against another may make the older child feel so inferior that he ceases to put forth any effort at all, or he may be so hurt that he wishes to get revenge. To have the younger brother or sister surpass him in school is a great threat to his ego. To allow two children of the same family to be in the same grade is almost sure to make trouble for one of them. The older one cannot be expected to accept this with equanimity. He is far more likely to retaliate with truancy, disobedience, temper tantrums, and malicious fighting.

It is not impossible to alleviate feelings of jealousy. Parents must never give one child more compliments, personal privileges, demonstrations of love, or even smiles than the other children. Giving the older child positions of responsibility which can bring him praise and importance or letting him take charge of the younger ones, especially in teaching them, relieves him of the necessity of competing with them on their own level. The teacher, too, must guard her actions lest she create jealousy and bitter rivalry among her students. It is difficult for her not to prefer some child above others, but to show it alienates the rest. Giving the failing child some permanent duty will make him feel that he has a place in the class.

As in disease, to find and treat the cause eliminates the symptom—and anger is a symptom. The sources to which reference has just been made—jealousy, rejection, failure, and frustration—cannot be eliminated like extracting a bad tooth. They can, however, be faced and gradually lightened. Adults must realize that a child has impulses, principles, and dreams, many of which are essential to his full development. Consequently to frustrate them is to deny him his natural personality growth. His anger and rebellion in many cases are normal and healthy reactions. Instead of being taught inhibition in every field, he should be encouraged to analyze his irritation, to exercise his judgment, and to act constructively upon his decisions. His need for love and recognition is a natural craving. His parents and teachers should understand and make an effort to satisfy it.

If fathers will trouble to find out the source of the child's anger, they will be less irritated by his wrath and better able to help him. Wives and mothers have for years borne the brunt of their husbands' and children's anger because they have sensed that it was not personal, not directed at them, but the result of other experiences in which the husbands and children have had to inhibit their rage. It is only inexperienced parents and teachers who put themselves down on the child's level and meet anger with anger. The wise adult tries to be objective and to seek out the basic irritation which has called forth the child's demonstration. Then if he is consistent, he reasons with the child and encourages him to use those same methods of objective analysis and correction.

30. FEAR, DREAD, ANXIETY, ETC.[1]

A large fraction of the insecurity of childhood is based upon fears, real and imaginary. In fact, half of the history of mankind has been built upon human fears, founded or unfounded. No child can develop positive personality traits if he lives under pressure of fear. He loses his spontaneity and his courage, or he turns Don Quixote and, assuming a false bravado, creates and fights enemies.

Early man feared the elements, wild beasts, disease, and famine, constantly warring neighbors, oppressing tyrants, vicious deities and malevolent spirits, and the unknown perils of unknown lands and seas. Many of these dreads still survive, either in fact or in folk tales and, as if they were not enough, are supplemented by fears of rapid traffic with its accidents, police, gangsters, kidnaping, murders, operating tables, fires, modern warfare, uncertain economic conditions, bank failures, and unemployment. Indeed, fear seems to be ever with us in spite of the efforts of scientists and education to dispel ignorance and make living safer. If adults succumb to these states of fear and find their motives and their efforts influenced by them, how much more, then, must a simple child, not yet arrived at the stage of reason and independence, be affected by them?

Fear is an emotion. One of the definitions of emotion is that it is a feeling which, if analyzed, disappears. Therefore if fears are analyzed to find out whence they come and on what they are built, those afflicted with them may be rid of their inhibitory bonds. They may leap ahead then with new hope and energy. It is extremely important that educators and juvenile workers help children to get a good start in life, free from the stunting effects of fear.

Fears may be divided into these four general classes:

1. Conditioned fears—those which are built upon or associated with instinctive fears
2. Fears that are acquired through unpleasant experiences

[1] See page 73.

3. Fears that are learned and imitated from others
4. Fears regarding the self, such as feelings of inferiority—physical and mental

In regard to the first class, scientists no longer believe that there are many instinctive fears but really distinguish two, upon which many of the others are built. Tests made on five hundred babies by Dr. John B. Watson revealed that the two things infants instinctively feared were sudden loss of support and sudden loud noises occurring near them. For instance, if a baby were given a bunny at the time that a loud crash happened close to him, he would be likely to be afraid of that animal thereafter. Letting him slip from the grasp when putting him into his bath might make him always afraid of water.

Concerning the second class, if the child has had an early unpleasant experience with an object or a person, he dreads a recurrence of that unpleasantness and is therefore afraid of that person or object in the future. If he is bitten or snapped at by a dog, he fears dogs. If a clap of thunder awakens him in the night or startles him when he is alone out of doors, he is afraid of storms. If a doctor is rough in his treatment or hurts him, he is always afraid of doctors. The same holds true for his attitude toward his playmates or parents or teachers. Some children hate or fear school because the kindergarten or first-grade teacher was thought to be harsh. Babies who have had many unpleasant experiences are in a susceptible state, in which they are likely to apprehend the fearful; thus, for instance, the unexpected often frightens the little child. Having had unpleasant experiences in strange places or with strange people, he dreads going to other places or meeting other strange people.

Fears that are thus conditioned into existence can be reconditioned out of existence. This is a gradual process, involving these three steps:

1. Anticipating the difficulty so that the child does not have to experience contacts with his fears often or alone without sympathy and understanding

2. Gradually accustoming him to seeing or meeting the fearsome object or situation, as giving a child who is afraid of animals trips to the zoo, animal picture books, or a small pet of his own

3. Diverting the child's attention by associating with the fear-producing situations some pleasant experience, as in the case of a child who forgets his fear of the water while he plays with a new sailboat. (This is fundamentally conditioning the situation to a new response—confidence and satisfaction—instead of fear.)

In the third class probably are found the largest number of childhood fears—those which are imitated from adults or playmates or suggested through stories. Little children are seldom afraid of snakes, mice, or worms, but they hear so much about them from adults that they soon develop a horror of them. All superstitions are imitated. It would never occur to a child to be afraid of breaking a mirror, of Friday the 13th, or of black cats if he did not hear adults talk fearfully about them. Few children are afraid of the dark until they hear stories of bogies, ghosts, and spirits which supposedly flit about in the shadows. (Fear of the dark, however, can be conditioned through a child's being frightened by some other cause while in the dark.) The fear of death and ill-health and of doctors and hospitals is often the result of the remarks of others.

Even fear of persons can be imitated. A child knows that other children are afraid of a certain teacher, and he, too, therefore fears that teacher. A bully can make a whole crowd stand in awe of him by first intimidating only one or two. School children may make little ones who have not yet entered afraid to begin school by their talk of harsh punishments, of competition, and of teachers. Fathers with their complaints about the hardships of the workaday world often make their children dread to go out and seek jobs. Thus the fathers are often responsible for what they call their sons' shiftlessness and weakness. Mothers, in their efforts to keep their daughters pure, often intimate such horrible things in regard to relationships with men that their daughters either avoid the male sex altogether or, when married, find it impossible to adjust their emotional lives.

Adults of course seldom realize that they are superimposing their own fears upon the younger generation. They think they are merely passing on the traditions of the race when they repeat old wives' tales and point out superstitious signs. It sometimes tickles their perverted sense of humor to watch a child writhe with fear in response to some hair-raising narrative. Often they are only talking among themselves about their harrowing adventures or their worries and obsessions, not realizing that children are listening and taking in all that is said. Ignorant adults and many who should know better think they are being clever disciplinarians when they scare a child into obedience. They tell him that, if he does not mind, they will have a doctor cut his ears off, a policeman will throw him into jail, or bogies will come to get him in the dark. The child who is afraid of his teacher can hardly be expected to develop many positive personality traits through school training. In spite of the emphasis which psychologists and mental specialists have for years placed upon a sympathetic rapport between pupils and teachers, it appears that there are still a few teachers who manage to create unfortunate timidities and inhibitions in their children. Sharpness and sarcasm, scolding, nagging and criticism, and threatening and warning frighten and antagonize children. Many children possess sensitivities and feelings of inferiority which are the result of the conflict in the home environment and which lead them to recoil from teachers who do not understand their sensitive natures. For such children the schoolroom may become little short of a nightmare if the teacher is the type who makes frequent use of such a negative control as fear.

A child's fears are not always apparent to the observer. The child may not be aware of them himself; he may have repressed them until they are mere vague feelings of unrest or anxiety; or he may be so ashamed of them that he refuses to discuss them. Yet adults, confessing their outgrown fears, give evidence of the acute suffering that fears can cause a little child. One woman confessed that her fear of thunderstorms was so great that the sound of a cart rumbling over a bridge made her ill. Her mother, aware of her daughter's fear, was sympathetic but, not realizing just how deep the feeling lay, did not do much to help her overcome it. Another adult told of her fear of fires. She would walk blocks out of her way to avoid certain buildings which had been charred by fire. The sight of burned wood distressed her almost to the point of nausea. Many nights she awoke with terror, imagining she smelled fire. Yet she told this fear to no one when she was young. Men have admitted that, when they were youngsters, certain adults had so frightened them in regard to masturbation that they thought they would be insane as a result of their indulgences.

Some apparent or suggestive signs of fear are sudden loss of appetite, inability to sleep, nightmare, enuresis, moodiness, taciturnity, jumpiness, and general nervousness. Lack of courage in undertaking new enterprises, timidity, stuttering, and nail biting are indicative symptoms. Forgetfulness, dislike of or hesitation in reciting, and outbursts of anger are suspicious signs in school. These manifestations may have other bases of course, but analyses often show that they are the result of various fears.

Gradually to accustom a child to seeing and meeting the things he fears can be useful in helping a child overcome those fears which are imitated from others. Reasoning with him about their origins, giving him scientific explanations, providing pleasant associations, and making jokes about fearsome situations can make him see them in a new light and thus relieve his emotional tensions.

Feelings of inferiority in children are frequently linked with fears. A child who has had many frightening experiences loses his courage. He dreads making new friends because he has been unkindly treated by former friends. He dreads passing to a higher school grade because he feared his former teacher and classmates. Not being able to win approval from them, he assumes that he cannot win approval from the new associates. Various specific fears encountered in his earlier life make him apprehensive of venturing far from the parental knee.

The child's status in the family is responsible for most of his feelings regarding himself and his abilities. The tiniest infant seems to know when he is loved or wanted by his parents. If he feels that he is rejected by one of them, he grows up from babyhood with a feeling of insecurity. His own opinion of himself is patterned after what he believes is their opinion of him; since they do not want him or do not like him, he cannot be of much importance. Furthermore, he assumes that all people hold him in the same low esteem.

The insecure child has an especially great dread of losing his parents. He therefore tries to perpetuate that state in which he is directly dependent upon them. In his fear of being pushed from the nest he devises all sorts of mechanisms for focusing their attention upon him and forcing them to keep him longer under their wing. This is the type of child who often identifies the teacher with one of his parents and refuses to assume responsibilities for his own progress at school. His actions and attitudes remain on an immature level in spite of the passing of years. This insecure, rejected child who doubts his own importance in the group frequently withdraws within himself. He is a daydreamer, who imagines himself among companions to whom he is a hero. He does not try to compete with his contemporaries. Failures and combats take on huge proportions in his mind, and he avoids further chances of failure or combat. Finally he may retire from reality altogether.

Another type of rejected, insecure child assumes the rôle of Don Quixote. He anticipates troubles. He thinks his teachers and playmates do not like him, and he imagines that they plot against him. Before they have a chance to do so, he has attacked them by some antisocial activity. He goes through the world fighting windmills. This type often becomes delinquent or criminal.

Placing the child in a group of his equals allows him to compete with a fair chance of success. A small conquest whets his appetite for further victories. He begins to have more interest in life around him when he sees that he can hold his own. Praise mingled with kind and constructive criticism spurs him to further trial.

Finally there is the opposite type of reaction, which is utterly devoid of any fear, dread, or worry and seems to be wholly indifferent to everything. A child with these characteristics may be analyzed as the person whose opinion of himself has sunk so low that he is not afraid of anything that might happen to him. There is also the cynic who has found through experience that the bark is worse than the bite. A trip to the detention home assures him that this is not to be feared. He knows that teachers and parents talk and threaten more than they act, and that policemen cannot do much more than "run you in." He seems dead emotionally. This type of child makes a dangerous delinquent. He is the despair of educators and of penologists, but psychologists usually find from exhaustive analyses that he has some vulnerable spot through which he can be reached.

Is there a remedy for the inferiority complex, this complex of feelings arising from fear? Remedies applied to adults are largely only palliative because the condition has become so deep-seated that little can be done to overcome it. There is more hope of helping a young child. Most of the work must be done by trying to change the attitude of the parent. If the child can be made to believe that he has the love and support of his parents, he is more likely to have greater confidence in affairs outside the home. When the attitude of the parents cannot be changed, teachers and social workers can act as parent substitutes. They can make the child feel that in them he has guardians who admire and trust him.

31. EXCITEMENT, SHOCK, UNEASINESS, ETC. [1]

Few people have not had at some time or another a shock or a disagreeable episode in their lives which they strive to forget. Such incidents return occasionally to unbalance their equilibrium

[1] See page 74.

for long or short periods. Though they try to push these memories farther back in their minds, there are always associations which recall them. This conflict to rid themselves of the memory and to ignore the associations may be an unconscious one, but even so it causes uneasiness, restlessness, and nervousness.

This condition may have symptoms corresponding to those which arise from other origins, such as those mentioned in the discussion of health and personal habits. But analyses of many cases in which individuals exhibited abnormal traits of excitability, uneasiness, and susceptibility to shock have revealed that their roots lay buried in the earliest period of the individual's life and were the result of some shock to the emotions. Further signs of an inner uneasiness are the individual's jumping at a car's backfire or at the slamming of a door. Perhaps he cannot fall asleep, or he wakes up at night with a start. Night sweats or distressing nightmares disturb him. He may be subject to fits of despondency, unprovoked irascibility, or floods of tears. He may talk of suicide. One or more morbid topics may be fascinating to him—such as death, murders, suicides, rape, accidents, fires, divorces, or the miseries and misfortunes of others.

In school such a child cannot concentrate. He daydreams. He forgets the question before he answers it. He takes sudden unreasoning aversions to teachers or classmates. He may cry or laugh without cause. He may even attack a playmate because the latter has made reference to some apparently inoffensive thing or act. Perhaps he gets wildly excited over an accusation or affront.

Truancy may be a manifestation of the same condition. The child is uneasy within doors. He seems to choke for fresh air. He feels unsafe inclosed in four walls (claustrophobia); therefore he wishes to seek freedom from these feelings by walking in the open air. He even feels this way at home. He goes out several times during the day or night for a walk around the block, and in summer he goes on camping trips where he can sleep out-of-doors.

Stealing is a symptom. It is seldom done just for the sake of the desired object. Probably stealing very frequently can be laid to the fact that the child, through his stealing, tries to punish some one person or society in general for a past injury. This injury or unpleasant experience is probably buried in his unconscious mind, so that when he is questioned as to the reason for his stealing, he can never give it; but thorough explorations into his past may bring the cause to light.

Sex offenses are another way in which the individual tries to avenge himself for something which still unconsciously bothers him. Boys and girls may indulge in filthy talk, write dirty notes, or scribble on fences and walls. Girls may have a precocious interest in boys, permitting great liberties and even seeking relations with men. An older boy may make attacks on little girls or little boys. The cause is in each case that the child in question is acting upon an impulse which arises from his own earlier experience with sex.[1]

What are these causes, these traumata or unpleasant experiences, which occurred in the individual's earlier life and which now lie festering their poisonous way to unsocial ends? The symptoms which we have just outlined may be the same in many cases but may have different bases. In fact, the worker who is trying to untangle this problem must not try to fit symptoms to set causes. However, a knowledge of possible causes will help him to know what to look for.

As explained in connection with Item 30 (page 233), various fears may have left an unsettling effect upon a child so that he is in a general state of uneasiness, expecting further frights. Being lost, isolated, or almost drowned or being a participant in an accident, a fire, or a collision may cause him to start or jump at loud noises or to have nightmares and disturbed sleep.

Conflict and confusion in the home leave their mark upon the child. The parents may have had a violent quarrel. Perhaps the father came home drunk and beat the wife and children. One parent may have deserted, leaving the rest of the family in want and panic. These tragic occurrences, which the child does not

[1] For a more complete discussion see Item 26, on playmates and companions.

understand at the time, leave him wondering whether they will recur. Or he may have so violently resented the situation or his emotions regarding them that he tries to forget them. He may have partially succeeded in doing so, but he may retain the general feeling of anger. The evidence of this anger shows itself when he begins to reveal certain undesirable personality traits or to commit unsocial acts.

Severe punishments and humiliations, especially in public, cause a child to harbor feelings of revenge. He wishes to get even with the person who humiliated him. Moreover, he may identify other people with that same person and wish to get even with them, too. He may partially forget the incident, but the sting rankles in his mind and sooner or later he seeks retaliation.

While the first few years in school may not seem significant to an adult, they are of tremendous importance to a young child. They provide the most exciting experiences in his life. Any school failure, punishment, or disgrace during these first few years may cause him painful suffering. He may gradually accustom himself to the routine of school and to the changeable moods of the teachers and children; he may finally learn how to meet situations and personalities; but the smart of his early failure, conflict, or disgrace may condition his whole future attitude toward school and education. Truancy or incorrigibility are sometimes a final consequence.

Practically any or all of the other sixty-five items can cause shock or excitability. The discovery of adoption, as discussed in connection with Item 54 on legal status, often causes a shock which is of deep-seated consequence to growing children.

The process of mental catharsis, clearing the mind of its unpleasant memories through talking them over with the sympathetic listener who can explain them in a new light, relieves the individual of their preying effects. Discussing harrowing experiences, emphasizing new safety devices which make recurrences unlikely, bringing up a touch of humor, and picturing the individual as an important hero relieve his dread. In going over family conflicts and disasters the worker can interpret the family's actions or reassure him of their affection for him. If there is no chance of establishing a feeling of security, the child's powers must be enlarged so that he can feel self-sufficient and able to face life alone. Traumatic sex associations or attitudes are reconditioned by giving frank sex information and scientific facts. If the child feels that other people, too, have had similar disagreeable incidents in their lives, he will have less secret fear regarding his own. Understanding their causes and effects and realizing that he has the power to live beyond them will reorient him in his outlook on life.

32. Pity, Sympathy, Enthusiasm, Etc.[1]

Pity, sympathy, and enthusiasm are not entirely dissimilar emotions. They are alike in that they are states of social consciousness in which the individual is affected by his environment. In sympathy he feels sad or glad with the joys or griefs of others. Pity has the admixture which makes him wish to alleviate sorrow. Enthusiasm has the meaning of an earnest and commendable devotion and an intense and eager interest.

These three emotional states are intrinsic parts of the personality. They add warmth, color, and depth. A person who possesses them is beloved because he understands the feelings of others. Thus his friendship is sought and his presence is desired. He has life; he vibrates; he "gives out." His enthusiasm particularly makes him alive and interesting and usually popular.

These traits are also parts of character development. The tiny baby is conscious of those about him only as the sources through which his hunger and love needs are satisfied. As he develops, he realizes that others also have selves which are similar to his own. This stage of social consciousness is of fundamental importance in human society. Its possession not only distinguishes the normal from the asocial infant but also places the social psychology of man upon a different plane from that of the lower animals. Instead of responding, like the latter, merely to the

[1] See page 76.

overt acts of his fellows, man is able to respond by sympathetic reaction to the evidences of their thoughts and feelings. In a superior stage of social consciousness the individual is not only aroused to sympathy and enthusiasm by just those persons and objects with whom he can identify himself or with whom he is thrown in contact, but he can also embrace abstract ideas and ideals. Thus he has a basis for mature intellectual pleasures and pursuits through which he can lead a full and useful life.

The two extremes of these states interest the mental hygienist because from them come various complications of personality and behavior. There is, on the one hand, the person who has emotional orgies. He becomes maudlin in his sympathy for others and lives in a chronic state of excitability wherein anyone can play upon him. "Tear-jerking" literature or sob-rousing movies stir him to the depths. Anyone's illness, misfortune, or tragedy upsets him. Either he gets an unhealthy satisfaction from such emotionalism, or he is quite volatile in his responses and changes his stand. At any rate he cannot be depended upon to relieve the conditions which he is deploring because his hyperemotionalism prevents the rest of his mental and physical system from co-ordinating toward rational ends. The extreme enthusiast may be a fanatic or an unstable dilettante. He is seldom able to carry out his schemes lucidly because of his fluctuating interests. While a fanatic's ideas may be useful to society, it is more usual that that type of person is objectionable because his ideas are too colored by his own emotional needs to be of much universal importance. The causes of his extreme radicalism merit discussion.

Personality traits are common to all human beings, but the greater or lesser degree to which they exist in some people is determined by the combined effects of heredity and environment. It is difficult to be sure just what part heredity plays, but at least it is known to provide nervous and endocrine systems which are unusually sensitive to outside stimuli. A person so endowed is likely to be easily aroused.

A child of this type ideally should live in an environment with a minimum of distracting and exciting situations. His parents should not play upon his emotions. They should take special care of his health and living habits to eliminate physical irritations. In school such a child cannot concentrate, is easily distressed by others, and jumps from one interest to another. Thus he is apt to make little progress and may be considered unstable by teachers and friends. If possible, he should be placed in a small school group where the teacher can help him reason his way through emotional crises and develop steadier habits of application.

Children of extreme emotionalism may have acquired their tendencies through having been excessively stimulated, probably at an early age. The parent with whom the child was closely tied may have made many demands on him for sympathy, or the child may have suffered at the hands of those around him in his early years and have grown up supersensitive to sorrow, so that he identifies himself with others and suffers with them. Perhaps he was allowed to read too stimulating stories or to hear and see them through radio and cinema. For lack of more normal, direct emotional experience he may have thrown himself into that of the artificial medium and indulged in the sensations to obtain release and satisfaction for his own repressed feelings. Children in large families who receive little love or attention are apt to do this, as are those in homes where considerable conflict exists between parents or other members of the group.

Children with facile imaginations that make them readily suggestible and susceptible are best helped by being provided with constructive interests and recreational facilities, especially of a physical nature. They must work out their emotions through creative efforts or tire out their sensitive nervous systems by healthy exercise. It goes without saying that they should witness or listen to few trying or overexciting situations.

While many unadjusted children suffer from an excess of emotions, a much greater number present problems for the teacher and mental hygienist because of the dearth of them. Nothing seems to arouse them from their emotional lethargy. Blasé and

world weary, they are indifferent to most of the things that
interest the average youngster at home or at school. The child of
this type is apparently devoid of sympathy and pity. He may
be so completely egocentric or infantile in his social consciousness
that he is not aware of the misfortunes of others. He is always
hurting someone else's feelings; he is inconsiderate and consequently unpopular among his contemporaries. It is difficult to
make any appeal to him when trying to help him because he is
insensitive to the opinions and moods of others.

The emotional void in the make-up of such a child may be
due to his early home training. Probably he was an only child
among adoring relatives who asked nothing of him except the
privilege of loving and serving him. The pampered, self-centered
child must be *taught* these emotions. He must acquire the habit
of considering the feelings and interests of others. His teachers
and parents must call his attention to the experiences of those
outside the home, either through literature or direct observation.
If he is unimaginative, parallels can be drawn which will suggest
to him how he would feel in the same situation. He will develop
more enthusiasm if he is left to himself and allowed to devise
his own pastimes and amusements, as well as to make his own
plans for vocations in the future.

The other type presenting a conspicuous problem is the child
who deliberately wishes to torture persons and animals, apparently taking delight in their suffering. His need to inflict punishment is often derived from the fact that he himself has received
a great deal of punishment, probably from his family. One or
both parents may have rejected him and made him feel unwanted and unliked. Perhaps they showed preference for a brother
or sister. The child in his jealousy wishes to punish that sibling
or any child whom he identifies with him. The child who enjoys
the failure or punishment of his classmates has a strong feeling
of social inferiority. He has never felt socially equal to his
neighbors. Colored children and children of foreign-born parents
feel inferior to other American children. In their efforts to equal
or surpass they are apt to become so self-centered that they are

unable to sympathize with any people whose life situations they cannot identify with their own. Moreover, since they have experienced failure and humiliation, they enjoy seeing others do so. Criminal tendencies often result.

Those children who live in homes where drunkenness, fighting, wantonness, and poverty exist òften seem wholly numb emotionally. They *must* develop this numbness, for if they continued to be affected by the tragedy in their lives, they would go to pieces completely. It is not strange that they are not aroused to react with sympathy or enthusiasm to situations outside their homes; their emotional patterns are naturally carried over elsewhere. Delinquents and criminals from this class are particularly dangerous because they have no feelings either for themselves or for society and are thus immune to appeal.

Paradoxically, the person who cannot give out sympathy has the greatest need for it. When he senses the understanding of another person, he is relieved of the necessity of feeling sorry for himself. When he ceases to look inward, he can look outward and then it is but a short step for him to notice and respond to the pain and pleasure of others.

33. INTELLIGENCE [1]

Intelligence may broadly be defined as the capacity for solving the problems of life. It depends upon observation, memory, reasoning, learning ability, constructive imagination, soundness of judgment, and general adaptability and stability. The degree of the individual's intelligence is inborn; it develops fairly steadily; like height, it reaches maturity at some time in the teens; and it sets for each individual a limit of achievement. There seems to be a general factor of intelligence on which are superimposed various special abilities, shown in artistic, musical, mechanical, mathematical, or business inclinations.

Since the last quarter of the past century there has been a strong trend toward individualization in education, psychology,

[1] See page 77.

and industry. The theory was that, if an individual's native intelligence could be determined, his value to organized society could be determined before time and money were used in training him. Experimenters therefore began devising intelligence tests. The United States Army found such tests useful in dividing the men into five general classes' of mental caliber; and intelligence tests are especially efficacious in large school systems where many types and classes of children are thrown together and must be sifted into relatively homogeneous groups, each with a curriculum suited to its mental limits.

Group tests, which are used extensively at present, provide rough measurements, giving grades of A, B, C, D, or E. They have correlated closely with scholastic achievement, and they indicate to the teacher what she can expect from each pupil. These tests investigate in a crude way different types of mental attainments; but they avoid items which have much to do with academic training, though in the advanced tests it is impossible not to depend somewhat on the child's knowledge of reading and arithmetic. The tests are timed and have directions, either printed or to be orally administered.

The individual mental tests are fairer and more reliable because the time element is less important. The Stanford Revision of the Binet Test (3) is most commonly used throughout the United States. The items cover comprehension; reasoning; judgment; rote, auditory, and visual memory; and memory for ideas. Little knowledge of reading and arithmetic is necessary. This test correlates closely with scholastic standing and with the scale of vocations. It is, however, less reliable for children of from two to five and from fourteen to eighteen, because there are too few items at the lower and upper extremes of the test. Each item on the test receives a score in terms of months, so that the total score gives the mental age of the individual. His mental age divided by his chronological age yields an intelligence quotient—popularly known as the I. Q. It is a formula of the rate of mental growth—how much of a normal mental year he accumulates each calendar year.

Performance tests do not depend upon either reading ability or the auditory knowledge of language and are therefore useful in testing children with speech or hearing defects, those of foreign parentage, or those who seem to have a general language disability. Many children who cannot understand the questions or verbalize the answers in other tests do surprisingly well on these. A good score indicates that they have a motor ability which can be trained for vocational purposes.

Further tests have been designed to discover special talents. There are tests to discover music and art talent, ability in salesmanship, and mechanical ability; and there are many tests for the particular industries and professions. These special ability or vocational tests are becoming more and more popular with mental hygienists, personnel workers, vocational counselors in the schools and juvenile courts, and charity organizations which must find work for their dependent cases.

In dividing the mental age by the chronological age, when the two are identical the result is 1.00 (or 100, as it is called). This is normality. The curve of intelligence, like the curve of chance, has the majority of cases clustering around the average, with the numbers diminishing toward both ends. Individuals with an I. Q. above 130 or 140 belong in the genius class. In the group of those with I. Q.'s of from 80 to 100 are most of the slow school children who get little farther than the eighth grade and who make average workmen. Those in the borderline group from the high 60's to 80 may or may not be able to go through the eighth grade with the average group, depending upon their stability and habits. Many of them must be placed in classes for the backward and receive a special type of training. Those with an I. Q. below 60 are properly institution cases, the lowest stratum of whom are little better than the animal in intelligence.

While intelligence correlates fairly highly with scholastic, social, and vocational achievement, still there are many instances when it does not. When a child is unable to learn or when he persistently misbehaves, the first assumption on the part of his teachers is that he is of subnormal mentality. In some cases the assumption is correct, particularly in the matter of learning. There are, however, numerous times when an intelligence test shows that the child has sufficient mentality to grasp the work at an ordinary rate if no other factors are involved. Though these factors have already been referred to in previous chapters, they may well receive further attention here.

A poor physical condition, chronic ill health, and frequent illnesses deprive a child of the necessary energy to think quickly and clearly. Poor food or lack of food or disturbed or insufficient sleep lower his resistance and render concentration difficult. Visual, hearing, and speech defects make certain kinds of work hard to grasp. Poor habits of attacking problems and lack of drive because of spoiling, neglect, or inadequate training at home are carried over into school. Feelings of inferiority brought on by too frequent rebuffs and unfair competition block a child's ability to work. Poverty and trouble in the home preoccupy his mind. Emotional conflicts divide his attention. Resentment against a parent's or a sibling's domination or rejection, jealousy, or fear of playmates keep him from applying himself to his lessons.

The purpose of the intelligence test and the intensive study into the personality and social background of a child is to determine which factors are responsible for his scholastic failures. Teachers and counselors can then work together with child and parent to help eliminate noxious elements.

Social adaptability and popularity among one's fellows do not correlate so well with intelligence as might be expected. The reason is more apparent when the two ends of the curve of intelligence are considered. At both ends the individuals are fewer in number than in the middle group or average. The average child therefore has a better chance of getting along with his equals— he has more equals in society. The subnormal child cannot keep up with the brighter. He is looked down upon for his dull wits. In his resentment he often makes himself more unpopular by trying to win recognition through some attention-getting device— usually meanness or fighting. The very bright child, on the other hand, is often out of touch with average children because he thinks more deeply and more quickly than they. Frequently he has been advanced in school too rapidly for his size and muscular strength, so that he finds himself among children as bright as he (although sometimes they are duller) but of superior stature and physical prowess. They may be jealous of the small child who rivals or surpasses them in the schoolroom and may try to get even by tormenting him. The small bright one may make matters worse by attempting to boss the older ones—a natural impulse on his part since he has more creative ideas.

A curriculum varied to fit the mental level is a better way of solving the problem of intellectual inequality among children of the same age than retarding the slow and double-promoting the bright. Many large city school systems use the former plan. Group intelligence tests divide the children into three general groups. The brightest children receive an enriched curriculum, the middle group, one of medium difficulty, and the slow group, one of minimum difficulty, while the very dull are given an individual intelligence test and are institutionalized, segregated into small classes for the backward, or given trial in the regular slow group.

Studies made of the intelligence of delinquents indicate that the majority of them fall into the dull normal or borderline group. Only 2 per cent are above average. Supernormal intelligence among children is not completely incompatible with delinquency, but delinquents of high intelligence are rare. While the proportion of feeble-mindedness in the delinquent group is not great, it is at least five times as great as the proportion of feeble-mindedness in the total population. Typically, then, the delinquent child is a dull child, but not all dull children are delinquent. Social and moral deficiency (truancy, theft, sex offenses, destroying property, assault, and stubborn disobedience) may be attributed to dullness plus several other factors. It is not strange that there are few delinquents of superior mentality. In the first place, they are too bright to be caught easily. They make use of duller children but take care to save themselves from the hands of the law. In the second place, being bright, they have less need to resort to underhanded practices because they can succeed on a normal social level. When they do commit offenses, they can be brought back to acceptable behavior more easily through appeals to their reason and ambitions, especially if they are handled by a worker who helps them see the underlying causes of their trouble.

Feeble-minded children seldom have the initiative or originality to break away from their usual ruts. They follow the lead of the majority. Although it is true that they can be made the tools of brighter children, they are quickly ruled by fear into conforming again. The problem of the child of dull average intelligence is more acute, for he tends to get into more difficulties than those of brighter or inferior intelligence. One reason is that he is not quite alert enough to succeed along normal lines easily. Any defect makes achievement more difficult and is likely to result in some compensatory activity—often of a nonsocial nature. Another reason is that he is just bright enough to be aware of his deficiencies and to resent them. His desire for attention may lead him into delinquency, since he has found he cannot win notice by any other means.

It is believed that practically all human beings are endowed with the same kinds of emotion—the same powers to feel. Unfortunately they are not all endowed with the same mental capacities. The superior or average child has the necessary intellectual equipment to keep his emotions in check. The dull child, on the contrary, when his emotional needs become too great, does not always know what to do about them. He may follow his impulses without heeding whither they are carrying him. The emotion of fear is strongest with the feeble-minded child and may inhibit his other impulses. This inhibiting emotion is not strong with the dull child because he is smart enough to realize that the law is in the hands of other human beings and that he has some chance of escaping them, but he overestimates the odds in his favor.

A suitable curriculum for somewhat dull children is extremely important if their school misdemeaners are to be ironed out.

Since their capacity to absorb purely academic work is limited, they should be given more manual arts, vocational subjects, and gymnasium work than the average or superior children. Outside of school it is the duty of social agencies interested in the prevention of crime to provide recreational centers where these children can pass their time profitably, free from the temptations which surround them on the city streets.

Great importance has long been attached to intelligence as a factor in behavior maladjustment, but it has probably been overstated. The ease of interpretation of the I. Q. and its seemingly specific nature have made intelligence a definite landmark among causes which cannot be expressed in such definite terms. This scale of behavior problems, which furnishes specific scores on additional aspects of children's qualities, should prove helpful in relieving the unjust burden which has long been thrown on intelligence and its measurement.

34. INTERESTS OR HOBBIES [1]

This is the age of the machine, when laborsaving devices have made drastic cuts in the time required for work. The father may be home long before sunset and may work only a few days a week. The mother may finish her household tasks in a comparatively short time. There is not the necessity now for sons and daughters to spend their waking hours helping the parents to keep the home going. What, then, is to be done with all this leisure?

When a person is not busy, he must indulge in time-killing devices. He may sit idly daydreaming of things he longs to possess—riches or power. He may become discontented with his lot in life and feel vindictive toward his family or society. His pent-up energy may await a match to set it afire. For this reason idlers are good material for radicals, fanatics, and the unscrupulous.

A healthy, growing child usually finds plenty of ways in which

[1] See page 78.

to spend his hours; but the majority of those who come to the attention of the mental hygienists or juvenile workers are those who, for the lack of something better to do outside of school, have got into trouble. This is especially noticeable with adolescents in high school. Although they may not have come into conflict with the law, they are often conspicuous for their lack of zest in life. They can think of no job they want to apply for after leaving school. None of their subjects ties up with anything they might do outside of school—or so they believe. Some of them spend their time at the movies or in reading stories of love and adventure, but they make no effort to emulate their heroes beyond merely resenting their own lives and hopelessly longing for better. Several have been known to spend the entire day and evening in one or two movies. In extreme cases they retire from reality altogether and are burdens upon society.

Had these adolescents acquired active interests earlier, they might have had a closer touch with their fellows. School material might have held possibilities for pleasure. Had they been accustomed to creating, they would have offered themselves for jobs where they could make good use of their habits of concentration and of their ingeniousness.

Constructive interests and hobbies play an important rôle in the building up of the personality. Resourcefulness engenders self-confidence. To know that one has something to contribute to a group gives one ease and grace and consequently brings him popularity. When the mind is occupied with concrete ideas, it has less time to dwell on little meannesses and worries. In other words, a child with good interests is more likely to develop a rich likable nature than one who has nothing to do but brood over his deprivations and difficulties. Hobbies and interests may or may not be direct preparations for future vocations, but at any rate they set good work habits. A child who can stick at a hobby until he has perfected something will persist longer at more important problems. To have no fear of attacking a job and to know how to go about it through practice on one's own projects are assets in tackling harder work.

Children do not have to be of superior intelligence to find their own interests, although the brighter ones usually do acquire very good ones. Average and dull children devise many absorbing pastimes, principally of an active and manual nature. Even feeble-minded children have a few interests which delight them. All children have a tendency to think up their own recreations. They do, however, need suggestion and guidance.

Many people who suffer from the lack of constructive avocations might have acquired them had they had them suggested at an earlier age. They may come from homes where the parents lacked education and were solely occupied in making money. A parent's interest in his child's play can stimulate in the young one a desire to impress him by more and better play projects. A teacher, too, by her sympathy, can instill in a child a taste for good hobbies. School clubs in which the children display their inventions, constructions, and collections arouse similar interests in other children.

Interests and hobbies vary in their ulterior usefulness. Movies provide relaxation and can instruct educationally by showing how the rest of the world lives, but they also often give an impressionable person false values and fill up his time so that he has no need to create anything for himself. In fact, a poor movie can have a dangerous effect. Recent studies (1) indicate that movies portraying gangsters or salacious subjects may be partly responsible for the increase in crime and moral laxity.

A poor type of literature is no better than a poor movie. Adolescent children are among the chief purchasers of cheap love-story magazines and detective and gangster publications. While reading this material may keep them off the streets and out of trouble, it is doing little to enrich their minds. Biography, travel books, and the classics are not too advanced for the average adolescent child and will broaden his understanding of the world without making him shun reality.

Music is an excellent socializing agent. The schools are doing splendid work in interesting children in singing by teaching them popular or semipopular pieces which they may enjoy also in their homes. Bands and orchestras train many children for a valuable vocation.

An interest in painting, drawing, cartooning, or sculpture may occasionally direct children into the field of commercial art, and it will always give them a source of pleasure and an appreciation of beauty. Sewing, cooking, and home decorating serve the same purpose. Writing stories, plays, or poetry requires perhaps a rarer talent, but it is always valuable. Training at school in these subjects is not only helpful but almost necessary.

Making collections is popular with all ages. Adults as well as children enjoy collecting stamps, coins, butterflies, stones, flowers, favorite poems, items of interest in newspapers, photographs, and pictures of airplanes, automobiles, architecture, and famous art objects.

Active games and athletics are favorite recreations of all children. They strengthen the physique, provide avenues for urges to act, and draw the children together in congenial groups. Gardening is an active pastime which keeps children in the sunshine and instills a practical interest in foods, flower arrangements, and possibly landscaping. Fishing, hunting, and camping have similar practical values. Dancing, too, is a beneficial activity, although unless well supervised it may lead to complications. Girls who enjoy it may desire to frequent dance halls and beer gardens where they are apt to meet undesirable companions and get into sex difficulties.

More constructive interests like woodwork and metal work, building, repairing cars and radios, inventing mechanical devices, or making improvements in the home are fully as desirable as other interests and can have direct vocational utility.

Churches and clubs are becoming more and more necessary to the development of social consciousness and adaptability. The Girl Scouts and Boy Scouts and similar organizations teach codes of social ethics as well as provide healthy and supervised activity. Many children hitherto unable to adjust themselves to a group have learned to mingle with and contribute to a gathering of their contemporaries. For those children who live in apartments or rooming houses, there should be more community and recreational centers where they can play and pursue their hobbies. Free or inexpensive camps should take more of them off the crowded city streets for at least a part of every summer.

Dramatics, too, are important as a socializing medium. Moreover, they provide a release for emotional tensions. They relieve individuals of their self-consciousness regarding their bodies. They teach ease and grace in social conduct.

To have one or more interests and hobbies similar to these mentioned is necessary to the full development of character and personality. There can be a negative aspect to this, where the child is so absorbed in his many hobbies that he has no time for school work or for a job. But it has proved easier to curtail a superfluity of interests than to instill them when they are lacking.

35. INITIATIVE AND AMBITION [1]

Initiative and ambition probably have more to do with success in the world than intelligence, social standing, or education. Two men with equal academic and mental assets can differ greatly in their achievements because one of them possesses greater drive than the other. In times of adversity or depression it is noticeable that some men still manage to have a job or at least to make money while their neighbors lack the ingenuity and foresight necessary to thinking up some scheme for securing an income. There are many men who are called armchair geniuses. They often think brilliantly, invent really clever scientific mechanisms, or plan out worth-while political and social schemes. Yet somehow they lack that initiative or ambition which makes less intelligent men bring their creations to the public eye. Extensive surveys with intelligence testing in the schools show that, while scholastic standing correlates fairly closely with intelligence rating, there are still a large number of pupils who do not care to live up to their ability. Perhaps their interest and ambitions lie in other fields. At any rate they do

[1] See page 80.

not lie in getting an education or in preparation for an occupation requiring a good education.

The lack or presence of initiative and ambition is apparent in a child as soon as he enters the kindergarten. Some children take an active part in everything. They wish to be leaders and to win praise from the teacher for their capability. They raise their hands, eager to recite. They wish to do lessons at home in order that they may learn faster. On the other hand, another child with the same mental rating and even with the same kind of home background may do only enough to get by. He is mildly interested in the extracurricular activities but makes no effort to be a leader. His school marks may be C or D, though they could be A or B. Children with lower intelligence ratings may surpass him because they have greater initiative and drive. This type of student presents quite a problem for his counselor. He may want to leave school when he reaches the age of sixteen and is often willing to accept a job unworthy of his ability. Moreover, he is not likely to put forth his best efforts even in an inferior occupation. Then again, such a child may do well through the grades but for some reason lose his drive in high school; he may lack a sense of responsibility for his own progress and fail to plan his time so that he will have hours reserved for homework. Perhaps he is too absorbed in the pastimes of the moment to bother about preparing his lessons, or he may be such an immature person that he wishes to have his parents and teachers continue to stand over him when he studies, as they did in the grammar school.

It is difficult for the average teacher or parent to instill these desirable traits in the child if they have not already appeared at an early age. To nag at him for his lack of ambition may easily antagonize him. The result is that the child hates the parent or teacher or the school or the job, becomes negativistic, and loses what little ambition or initiative he had. He may wish to show advisers that he has more spunk in him than they suspected, but he may show it by performing some unsocial or desperate act.

It is not easy to put a finger on the source of initiative and ambition. It is believed by some to be hereditary, because many children evince the traits in babyhood. They seem anxious to learn to sit up, to creep, or to walk long before their muscles will permit them. They like to try to do things with their hands and to help around the house. They make plans for the future. On the other hand, some babies are listless and lazy from the time they are born. Mothers have to make them learn to walk or to sit up, and they are unwilling to help themselves in such matters as dressing and eating. The hereditary theory is borne out by the fact that all members of certain families are commonly tireless workers, possessed with energy and drive. There may be a constitutional factor at the base of these traits, just as in general bodily conditions or in temperamental type.

The glandular system probably has something to do with a person's initiative. Various glandular secretions provide him with the necessary verve to carry out his daydreams. A child of the hypothyroid type may have ambitions, but he often seems unable to bring them to fulfillment. One of the marked hyperthyroid type may have a great deal of initiative but lack concentrated ambitions, so that he makes many movements but arrives nowhere. There are obviously many exceptions to this glandular theory; but at any rate balanced or unbalanced glandular secretions may make the individual have a tendency toward or against positive and well-proportioned traits of ambition and initiative.

Children of dynamic parents often have no initiative. They feel inadequate in the face of their parents' forceful personalities. They therefore sit back and accept dictation. This habit is carried over into school, where they do little work unless prodded by the teacher. Later they feel that they are not capable of finding or keeping a job. If possible, they remain at home, where their parents can continue to plan their lives for them. The same situation may occur when parents spoil their children. The latter find it pleasanter and easier to have things done for them instead of trying to do things for themselves. In fact, they demand that adults wait on them. When teachers or employers refuse to do this, they run home to their mothers, where they can lapse back into their infantile patterns of living.

Unsuccessful competition with a bright and successful sibling causes a child to lose his drive. The other child eclipses him and gives him feelings of inferiority which he cannot shake off. To make unfavorable comparisons between children may make one of them give up striving.

Initiative and ambition are taken out of some children in the early school grades by failure and discouragement. The little ones look forward eagerly to enrolling in school. They throw themselves with zest into activities. Because of mistakes they must be corrected or reproved. Some accept this criticism cheerfully without losing their courage. Others are soon deflated and gradually cease trying to co-operate or to succeed in the group.

The development of drive, as with other character traits, should begin in babyhood. Allowing the baby to help himself, as in dressing and eating, is the first step. Allotting him duties at home and in school gives him a chance to plan and think independently. If parents and teachers show interest in the child's games, hobbies, and dreams for the future, they are indirectly encouraging the child in his development of initiative and ambition, for their interest pleases him and he plans more of the same pastimes and makes up more of the same dreams to sustain their interests. Once his habits along this line are established, they are more than likely to follow him into adulthood.

Adults are too often callous to the emotional reactions of children. They deal out punishments and reproofs without stopping to notice how they are received. It is true that some children can be chastised and criticized indefinitely and still bob up unsquelched; but many are quickly cowed into a lethargy in which all effort and ambition have been anesthetized. Adults then reproach them for their laziness and listlessness, not realizing that it is partly their own fault. Especially with little children must they make it a point, in criticizing, to praise and encourage, emphasizing the hopeful, positive side instead of the negative.

Segregation or division of children into groups of nearly equal ability at school eliminates the heartless competition which pushes the slower child into the background. He has a chance to strive and succeed on his own level without constant fear of failure. At home, if an older or brighter child is overshadowing a brother or sister, efforts should be made to find each a companion of his own type. Vacations during which children visit in different places often send them back home entirely changed individuals. Away from the old home ruts, where they have been accustomed to reacting according to the popular opinion regarding them, they have an opportunity to shed their old habits and to blossom out into fresh personalities.

36. VOCATIONAL INTERESTS [1]

It may seem foolish to ask a school child what he wants to be when he grows up. He has of course no way of knowing what he can do and no surety of realizing his ambitions. The idea of asking him, however, is a good one because it keeps him thinking on the subject and helps him mature more rapidly. Many people arrive at working age to find themselves without plans regarding a suitable vocation or much training for one. When they thought about it at all, they vaguely intended to get some fine position with a high salary and with prestige, without stopping to consider their fitness for it or the practical steps necessary for obtaining it. Children of mediocre intelligence and only poor or fair economic status are often heard declaring that they mean to be lawyers, doctors, or teachers; yet when confronted by reality, they have to admit that they have not done well enough in the public schools to win a recommendation for college, nor can their parents send them there.

Parents are often at fault in setting vocational goals for their children which are entirely out of their reach. To compensate for their own failures, they wish their offspring to achieve where they did not. They therefore heckle them from the time when they are youngsters with visions of power and wealth. The result is

[1] See page 8).

that the children have an inflated idea of their own ability. They do not desire to accept a lesser position and, if they must do so, often perform their tasks poorly.

On the other hand, a large number of parents are so anxious for their children to get to work and bring more money into the home that they encourage them to leave school as soon as the law allows (or sooner in many cases) and to take any kind of job. Children, too, in their eagerness for monetary independence, lose sight of the fact that more education may secure them a more profitable job. They leave school to accept the first job that comes their way. The number of newsboys earning a few cents a day is an example of the number of boys who make this mistake. Girls take housework at one, two, or three dollars a week or work a few hours a day in the dime stores. Extra training in the regular school or in a trade school would have trained them better for even these jobs and so gained them higher salaries.

Another fault parents have is that of deciding on a vocation for the child when he is obviously unfitted for it or has no taste for it. For instance, they may be determined that he shall be a minister when he wishes to be a doctor, or they may want him to be a lawyer when all his talents and interests point to his being an engineer. The folly of trying to push a square peg into a round hole is apparent to everyone. The child is likely to be antagonized by parental pressure. He may give up all vocational efforts and be utterly discouraged or estranged from his parents for the rest of his life. At any rate, it is unlikely that he will succeed at the vocation of their choosing when his own definite preference is ignored.

When large-scale production was begun in this country at the end of the last century, employers had no thought but to use unskilled labor. It did not occur to them to consider the qualifications of the workman for the job. Similarly in the domestic field, housewives did not expect trained servants. The schools turned out into the work world children fourteen, sixteen, or eighteen years old, many of whom were entirely unprepared for any job. Ruthless employers hired them as apprentices or unskilled laborers at scandalously low wages and under deplorable conditions. This condition caused the thrusting out of the older family men who could not afford to accept such low pay. Later, however, when the great waste of men and materials became apparent and successful competition depended upon thrift, the employers began to realize that more efficient methods of selecting their workers must be found. The larger factories, for instance, opened schools where young men could learn the operations of their machines.

There has been an increasing demand recently that public schools should provide children with special vocational training. Almost all cities, even of moderate size, have been adding to their curricula manual training in metalwork and woodwork and sometimes courses in automobile mechanics, welding, drafting, steam fitting, tool and dye making, aëronautics, business, cooking, and dressmaking. Larger and wealthier cities have complete trade schools where the pupil can work toward a high-school degree as well as learn a definite trade and get practical experience through part-time work outside. The entrance requirements differ; the pupils usually must be fourteen years old or older, have finished the fifth grade, and possess at least borderline mentality.

The purpose of vocational training is twofold. First, it prepares the pupil for industries and professions by giving him direct instruction and practice and by familiarizing him with the demands and methods of labor, in order that he may have some idea of how to tackle a job even though he has had no actual training for it. The second purpose is to give an interesting and congenial curriculum to those children with special defects or limited intelligence who are unable to absorb much more academic work. This has been referred to in discussions of intelligence and motor co-ordination and in references to delinquent and unadjusted children. When a child finds a school subject in which he can achieve some success, he is bound to have a keener liking for school. When his mind is occupied with pleasant activity, he has less time for succumbing to undesirable influences or devising ways of punishing society for his failures and conflicts.

Vocational and intelligence tests are becoming more widely used in schools, factories, and department stores, as well as in the Army, the Navy, and other governmental services. Although they may not yet be a completely reliable description of an individual's ability, still they give a general estimate of the type of work for which he is best fitted or for which he should be trained. Most organizations have their own examinations. The state civil-service departments have tests for almost every type of work. Psychological and mental hygiene clinics can furnish information on the subject to anyone interested.

37. GENERAL BEHAVIOR [1]

It may seem to be somewhat of a paradox to insert an item on general behavior in a scale for the analysis of behavior. Naturally the problem cases selected for analysis and study offer difficulties in behavior or they would not be referred. In Table XII of Chapter XII this item leads the list of the sixty-six factors in differentiating between behavior and non-behavior groups. An inspection of the behavior data from all the cases shows that some cases are much worse than others in their behavior; there is not a perfect correlation between the severity of malbehavior and the total score on the behavior scale. Within the behavior group itself the Pearson correlation between this item and the total score is only .369, which ranks it forty-first of the sixty-six items.

There is one justification for inserting general behavior among the factors of motivation. Malbehavior becomes established from certain causes; but in turn, after the habits of malbehavior have become chronic, general behavior becomes a cause as well as an effect. Usually by the time an advanced and aggravated case comes to the attention of the guidance clinic, bad behavior has become so firmly entrenched that it is difficult to know what were the original inciting causes and how much was naturally bad behavior if we can characterize it as such. On pages 15-17

[1] See page 82.

of Chapter II there is a discussion of behavior mechanisms to which the reader is referred for a much more complete discussion than will be repeated here. In the earlier chapter we have pointed out hidden and unseen causes of malbehavior which the parent and teacher do not usually understand. The boy in question steals; the parent wants his stealing cured at once. But experience shows that the stealing is an indirect result of some troublesome factor such as fear, parental rejection, or poor ideals in the home. The treatment does not consist in punishing for the stealing, possibly not even in admonishing him not to do it any more, but in the removal of the basic causes of worry. Stealing will tend to disappear if the case is taken in its early stages; but if stealing has become a habit, it may not tend to disappear when the original causes are removed. Such a process tends to take some time; it cannot be hurried. Yet the parent or teacher demands immediate relief, as though it were no more difficult than waving a magic wand or leaving it all to the finding of the I. Q.

Another reason for including general behavior as a factor among the motivating causes is the desirability of analyzing the character of some children whose general behavior is not very bad but who show some possibilities of later maladjustment. In the non-behavior group to which we have referred there were certain cases in which the general behavior was almost ideal, but analysis of the possible factors of maladjustment showed a dangerously low score. It would be enlightening if such cases could be analyzed and studied to learn whether general behavior maladjustment or some special phases of behavior difficulty tend to drift out of adjustment. If they happily do not become unadjusted, there is need of discovering what factors in the social constitution act as a preventive for the many predispositions to malbehavior. These causes could then be contrasted with the overt malbehavior cases that yielded to the temptations of the environment.

Finally the inclusion of general behavior as a motivation for maladjustment gives some recognition to the lay persons who still insist that the external or overt behavior is an important part of the diagnosis. No doubt there is some value in facing these direct products of behavior and in trying to cure them by direct methods; but the subtle causations underlying them in obscure and hidden factors of the environment must eventually be studied.

This item closes the series of the past three chapters which have dealt primarily with the child, in his health and physical factors, in his personal habits and play factors, and in his personality and social factors. There remain two further groups of factors which are important in his adjustments, the parental and physical factors of the home and the home atmosphere and also the school adjustment. These factors will be presented in the next two chapters.

BIBLIOGRAPHY

1. FORMAN, HENRY JAMES—*Our Movie-Made Children*. New York: The Macmillan Co., 1933. 288 pp.
2. LEE, PORTER R., and KENWORTHY, MARION E.—*Mental Hygiene and Social Work*. New York: Commonwealth Fund, 1929. 309 pp.
3. TERMAN, LEWIS M.—*The Measurement of Intelligence*. Boston: Houghton Mifflin Co., 1916. 362 pp.
4. WATSON, GOODWIN B.—"Tests of Personality and Character," *Review of Educational Research*, 2:185-270; June, 1932. Washington, D. C.: American Educational Research Association, a department of the National Education Association.

CHAPTER IX

PARENTAL AND PHYSICAL FACTORS OF THE HOME

THE present chapter covers parental and physical factors of the home, Items 38 through 55, inclusive. They are all items which are quite independent of the child as to their origin, but nevertheless they all have their effects upon him. They are the best illustration possible of the facts that a child can neither make all of his own environment nor control its effects upon him.

38. AND 39.   INTELLIGENCE OF FATHER AND MOTHER [1]

The intelligence of parents plays an important rôle in the behavior fortunes and misfortunes of children. It is a factor which probably cannot be measured by the direct method of intelligence tests unless there is unusual co-operation and the parents volunteer. As a substitute the worker must usually make an estimate after one or more interviews. Breadth and quality of vocabulary, quickness of reaction, use of abstract or concrete thinking, and insight into the social problems of children are all clews to the mental alertness of parents.

After making liberal allowance for the influence of many other factors, one may conclude that the mental acumen of parents affects the attitudes and behavior of children. The more intelligent parents gain insight into children's problems through study and explanation. They are able to take an impersonal and detached attitude and sublimate themselves and their feelings for the greater good and welfare of the children. They can adjust

[1] See page 83.

themselves to long-time goals rather than look for the satisfaction of immediate desires. There are a few parents with high intelligence who are unfortunate in their personality and emotional developments. They capitalize their mental insight in undesirable ways to further their own selfish desires and accordingly are hard to impress or change about their children's problems.

Parents with inferior intelligence gain little insight into their children's lives. They do not comprehend the changing social conditions in which children are growing up; they refer all matters back to their own childhood, with which they believe they are still familiar. In some cases the children are actually brighter and more mature mentally than such parents, and yet they find that they must yield to parental authority when wisdom cannot prevail. Mentally inferior parents tend to live narrow, self-centered lives and to interpret all life's incidents in a personal and individual manner. Anything which does not conform to their meager standard is considered disrespectful and rebellious. In such instances the discipline and atmosphere of the home are destructive and negative factors in the child's training.

Differences in intelligence between parents are apt to cause family discord, which in turn contributes to juvenile delinquency. If the mother is much superior to the father, she is able to reverse the traditional leadership of the home with disastrous consequences. If the mother is markedly inferior, the father may feel that a double burden of duties falls on him. In the event of a backward child, direct blame by the brighter parent will often fall upon the duller. Adult intellects of wide mental difference do not and probably cannot think together harmoniously about common marital problems. If the one with more intelligence and wisdom can assume the leadership by common consent, a great step has been made toward domestic tranquillity.

One of the chief obstacles to harmony in matters of intelligence lies in the little understanding which either party may have of the fundamentally inherent nature of mental brightness or dullness. Frequently matings are made with a vague recognition of differences or inferiorities; but the brighter one is certain that he can improve the other by his (or her) own mental brilliancy. While psychologists admit that anyone of average intelligence can probably make better use of such intelligence with added experience and with maturity, they doubt the ability of anyone to change inherent mental acumen to any very appreciable extent. However, the problem is seldom faced with such insight. In time the slower one in intelligence is sometimes called "dumb-bell," "idiot," "moron," and similar uncomplimentary terms. These appellations do no good but afford an unholy and cruel outlet for the feelings of the brighter one. For the slower one, the problem becomes more acute.

Students of heredity and psychology are aware of the fact that there is a wide range of mental differences among the children of a family whose parents are both of average intelligence. This phenomenon is analogous to the differences in mature height shown by a large family of children with parents of average height, a condition which goes unquestioned as being natural. Two parents of average ability sometimes have one very superior child who eventually excels in a university education and another child who barely completes the elementary grades.

There has been much agitation among social workers and reformers in the past few years to solve society's problems by the sterilization or sex restriction of the mentally subnormal, and some states have statutory provision for such practices. While certain cases of marked feeble-mindedness are probably thus eliminated, it would soon become a question as to how far up the mental scale such a policy should be extended. There is marked religious opposition as well as individual resentment on this question. A long-time study of effects in certain states which now permit these practices will eventually point to a solution.

In solving the problems of the individual behavior case when the parental intelligence appears to be below par, the course of treatment must lie in appealing to the judgment and ability of the child himself and in the exercise of a reasonable degree of supervision and probation by agencies outside the home.

In making social diagnosis according to levels of intelligence, the social worker and the psychologist must make suitable modifications in their procedure for this variable factor. In the case of the more intelligent parents if there is a desire to co-operate, there is a grasp of the unfolding of events in the behavior sequence with little or no direct instruction. It is analogous to the ease with which a very bright pupil learns to read with a minimum of teacher direction. Conditions are quite the opposite with the mentally slow parent; he has to be shown the problems in very concrete and specific terms. The worker may virtually have to take on a supervisory and dominating rôle to establish the desirable point of view. The parent usually accepts this condition gladly and profits from the direct advice. This condition is parallel to the important rôle of the teacher in instructing dull children, when every step must be explained, emphasized, and reiterated. However, there are social agencies and mental-hygiene clinics which implicitly believe that there is *one* method, usually the one for the superior, which is the only acceptable technique for all cases. Such practice is no more feasible than trying to find one universal method by which all children should be taught. Flexibility of approach and method with respect to mental differences is a most important requisite for successful programs of mental hygiene.

40 AND 41.   EDUCATION OF FATHER AND MOTHER [1]

Within certain broad limits education is circumscribed by intelligence, but these limits are very broad. Education and training in adulthood may capitalize intelligence for much greater fields of endeavor than has been commonly assumed. Experiences may be broadened for a person of average intelligence by the exercise of a multitude of functions on an average level in the same manner that a first grader can gain a wide experience by reading many primers and first readers. Unless materials are entirely beyond his comprehension, he can gain much enrichment with profit

[1] See page 84.

at his own level. The bright parent can expand his knowledge by the wealth of scientific and literary material at his disposal; the mentally slow can with help find plenty of reading matter suited to his grasp.

Any child profits greatly if there is a spirit of education and mental inquiry in the home. He gets direct benefit and he establishes a good attitude of his own from the subtle example set for him. He finds the home a pleasant place to live in and does not seek undesirable things outside. An intelligent parent who understands the child's abilities and caters to them through suitable material finds this informal and supplementary education a source of profound happiness and parental satisfaction. A home that is barren of culture for children of superior mentality loses its hold on them; they seek satisfaction elsewhere.

Both parents find it difficult to share alike in keeping up a standard of education and experience. Fathers usually have the advantage since they form many contacts in business and professional pursuits. But these contacts also divide their interests so that they may put forth less effort in setting a suitable standard for the home. Mothers tend to profit less in the way of continued experience and training if they limit themselves closely to the affairs of the household. They see fewer people and often become limited and provincial in their outlook. A story is recalled of a farmer who testified at the insanity hearing for his wife: He did not know why she should go crazy; she had been right there working in the kitchen for thirty-five years.

In homes where the daily routine of ordinary things has gradually taken the lead, children get no stimulation for their school work. They feel that school is something entirely apart from home, something apart from life. The home cannot share any common program with the school, and the entire field of normal relationships becomes disrupted. While this procedure may pass as the normal and average practice, its effects upon the life of the child are vicious and devastating.

The adjustment worker can perform wonders for such homes if she becomes aware of this problem. Modern circulating libraries can reach any rural community. Magazines are available on any topic, including child study; there are books to be read for pleasure and for information; and articles on science, invention, and travel are always at hand. The radio, which is found now in nearly every home, affords a rich variety of entertainment and education which was unknown a decade ago. Adult education is taking on a new meaning; it is no longer limited to a few foreigners seeking aid for their naturalization papers or for a speaking knowledge in English. Parents and other adults are now seeking new attitudes, new information, and additional training in their chosen professions. They find pleasure in pursuing their avocations, in riding their pet hobbies, and in keeping abreast of the times. Other agencies of adult education are the various child-study clubs sponsored by schools and churches. The parent-teacher movement is having a steady, significant growth and promises to stimulate and continue parental interest in education. Education of the future will receive greater influence from adult endeavor; when this influence is better developed, parents, children, and the schools will have many more common grounds of interest than exist today.

42 AND 43. AGE OF FATHER AND MOTHER AT BIRTH OF CHILD [1]

The age of parents at the birth of the child is an important factor in the parental attitude toward children. Parents who are in the early twenties at the birth of their first child probably have more physical strength and endurance than parents who are in the late thirties or forties when their children are born. Younger parents are less disturbed than older ones in their routine of living by loss of sleep and worries of infant illnesses, and they are usually more tolerant. The older parents possibly find that disturbances tend to create feelings of rejection and rebellion against children for disrupting their long-established routines of living. This subtle animosity toward children may be enhanced if the child born late happens to be an unwanted child.

[1] See page 86.

In making these general statements the individual exception must be kept in mind. Often parents who are older have wished for children and in having their wishes fulfilled suffer none of the feelings that have been suggested. But in maladjusted children the factors first mentioned frequently have operated. At times the younger parents are not well adjusted to the period of child rearing; they may not have wanted children until a later time, and they feel a distinct interference with the freedom which they had contemplated. From a certain traditional point of view it seems to be the predominant practice to have children in the twenties rather than in the thirties and forties, and any departure in the direction of the later ages is potentially a cause of maladjustment.

The younger child of a large family may suffer from some of the unfavorable reactions referred to, since his parents are in the older age group at the time of his birth. The older children exercise certain tendencies toward the younger child, as will be discussed in Items 52 and 53. Children born later in large families may fall heir to physical weaknesses or lowered vitality on the part of the mother. Many of the cases of Mongolism, in which the child is mentally subnormal and possesses features of the Mongoloid type unnatural to his race, arise from such enfeebled maternity.

Aside from the physical disabilities which may overtake the children born in the later life of their parents and aside from the mental attitudes of intolerance, the older parent is less able to enter into the spirit of play and understanding of children. It should not be claimed that all parents fall into such a classification, but there is in some a trend in that direction. Some persons seventy years of age make suitable adjustments to small children; but they are the exception rather than the rule. The person of forty-one is just twice as far in age from the one-year-old as the person of twenty-one; such a span of years cannot help but make a difference in understanding children. Although parents do become adjusted to children, it is more difficult for children to become adjusted to parents or to grandparents whenever they must live with them. A small girl recently gazed in awe at a wizened eighty-year-old great-grandfather and asked if he had really ever been a baby at some time. Children do not find it so easy to enter into the spirit of play and competition with older parents as with younger ones. Such parents cannot so easily run races with them, swim so far, or laugh with the spirit of youth. If these factors are present, subtle barriers develop and the children seek other outlets. Parents also instinctively look for recreation and avocation within their own age group rather than in the wild and strenuous pastimes of early childhood. Differences in age between children and parents have the potentialities of maladjustment, although many such relationships are successful in spite of these differences. A careful observation of the actual parental and child attitudes will determine the effect in any individual case.

In making a readjustment of behavior cases which present these difficulties, the burden of change falls heavily on the parents. Since the physical fact of age difference cannot be changed, the only avenue of reform is in the parental attitude. It takes much will power and determination to establish or to re-establish psychologically sound contacts between parents and children. The approach can be made by taking on some activity in which the child is known to be interested, so that his enthusiasm may carry him over the obstacles of indifference or previous failure to cooperate. The age factor may not be a problem; it is only one of many problems which may exert some influence, and its dangers and possibilities for maladjustment should be recognized. In Chapter XIII the age of the father at the birth of the child stands ninth from the top of the list as a cause of maladjustment; the mother's age is twenty-ninth in the list of sixty-six causes. In differentiating between behavior and non-behavior cases in Table XII of Chapter XII, these age factors fall into the least important third of the range, indicating that non-behavior cases also have many discrepancies between the ages of parents and children.

44 AND 45. HEALTH OF FATHER AND MOTHER [1]

Good health of parents is an asset in the behavior adjustment of children. The atmosphere of the home is more wholesome if strength and virility prevail. Parents who are healthy and well are able to carry on their work; they proceed in their duties with a feeling of confidence and security which reassures the children. It may not occur to parents that their health makes any difference to children, but it certainly affects their mental attitudes in many instances.

In case the father is ill, he loses his place as breadwinner for the family. His worry spreads a dark blanket of gloom over the entire household. If he is confined to bed or to his chair and is in a helpless condition, it is easy for the family to lose all hope. Debts for groceries and doctors' bills pile up, and payments on the home become overdue. There is a spirit of repression, laughter does not ring through the house, and the children find it more agreeable playing at the homes of their playmates. The home or family as a unit in social life begins to disintegrate. In time the mother goes out to seek work; the home then becomes even more neglected and less time is given to the children.

If the mother is ill, the problem is equally bad. Unless there are older children to carry on with the housework or unless help is secured, the household soon gets into a state of chaos. Children imitate the example of their home and become careless of their clothing and habits of personal cleanliness and orderliness. If clean and mended clothing is not available, the temptation to slump is easy to follow. In many instances the appeal of the mother to maintain the former normal standard is effective, but sometimes it is not.

From a fine sense of duty children, when there is continued illness in the house, frequently abandon all play and participate in the household duties. They often present sad and pathetic pictures of little old men and women, adults before their day. The spirit of youth and play is gone. On the other hand it may per-

[1] See page 87.

sist, and the children may play in the schoolroom, much to the distraction of pupils and teachers who do not understand their motives. Any disciplining or restriction from the school tends to arouse a vague feeling of injustice, and the last avenues for childish expression fade away.

Not only are homes with much illness disturbed in their mental attitudes; but wherever a continual stream of minor illnesses, aches, and pains is prevalent, the attitudes are also far from ideal. Children gain the impression that their parents are seeking alibis for avoiding their duties. They practice the same techniques successfully but disastrously in terms of the patterns of honesty and fair play. Some children are so adept in these matters that they carry them over into all play activities and particularly into school. If the teacher happens to surmise what the problem really is and sets about to cure it, additional complications arise. The child feels that his bluff is called. Yet his parents practice the same techniques and no one is able to stop them; further feelings of injustice rise in his childish mind. No worker can deal very long with problem cases without unearthing many vicious circles based upon these conditions.

Parents may expect children to understand why they are ill or the victims of accidents, but such comprehension is the exception rather than the rule. If the disability causes too much inconvenience to children, they openly blame parents for being careless. Parents are chided for exposure to colds, and at times they are reminded that illness is their reward for continually urging the children to be overcareful of their own health and safety. Not long ago the unemployed father of a nine-year-old girl insisted on seeing that she got safely to and from school, much to the disgust of the girl herself, who wished to go with her playmates. On his return home alone from one morning trip to school he was killed by an automobile. In his case he may have felt a vague insecurity about traffic which he expressed toward his daughter, but she did not share with him this feeling or its fatal results.

Whenever illness, either severe or light, affects either or both parents, the consequences in the children's behavior are difficult to foretell. The best safeguard is to avoid illness and maintain a vigorous and aggressive state of good health. Naturally some illnesses and accidents are unavoidable, but the mental outcomes should be recognized and dispersed wherever possible.

46 AND 47.   PERSONALITY OF FATHER AND MOTHER [1]

When the parents' health is poor the children may make some allowance, but there is among children less understanding of poor personality traits of their parents. The parent who is nervous or irritable or loses his temper quickly sees his or her behavior reflected by the children. The personality adjustments of parents are very important in determining the attitudes of children; within the behavior group the factors of both father's and mother's personality fall in the first third of the sixty-six items.

A study of the non-behavior group with respect to the personality of parents reveals little difference between them and the behavior group of parents. The probable difference in children's behavior may hinge on the poor personality of behavior children acting and reacting on parents' personality, plus other undesirable factors. In other words, the parents of behavior children are not seriously worse than others in personality, but these traits occur in unfortunate combinations with other traits. In Table XII of Chapter XII the personality of mothers has a difference of 1.18 points on the scale between behavior and non-behavior groups, while the father's difference is only .93 of one step. From this standpoint the personality of the mother in behavior cases is more inadequate relatively than that of the father. The personality differences between fathers and mothers are not very marked.

The parent who has a noble personality accomplishes marvels for his children without conscious effort but through the silent examples of control and social restraint. He is able to talk without embarrassment to his children about undesirable traits, stressing traits that are worth while. He is not a hypocrite or an

[1] See page 88.

impostor in doing it. Nothing is quite so futile as to harangue children about controlling their temper when the lecturer is never able to practice control himself. Under these conditions the child loses respect for the parent on account of the latter's weaknesses and the irony of the situation. In such cases it would probably be more effective to remain silent and allow the child to learn the desirable virtues wherever he may find them. However, the parent with personality weaknesses may try to make amends for his own shortcomings by resorting to an artificial moralizing with his children.

Children tend to copy their parents whether the model be good or bad. It sometimes seems easier to copy the bad than the good, but no one knows just why this is true. The undesirable traits may be similar to the instincts and hence have a broader foundation in their appeal. If a parent becomes hysterical, the child can scarcely control or be expected to control his own hysteria. One of the best illustrations is the fear of thunderstorms instilled into children by the fear of the parent, usually their mother. In turn, she may have been reared under similar circumstances and be able to do little to control herself.

The parent who is stern and cold causes much unhappiness and uneasiness in children. He is considered old and unreasonable; the children make loud complaints about him to youthful playmates. But instead of copying these traits they follow the trend of some other father who is known to be less severe. It is little wonder that young children from severe homes are easily led away by the enticing kindness of some cunning stranger who would eventually seduce them. Either extreme of sternness or overemotionalism is bad for children; possibly the former can be remedied somewhat by the child's admiration of other adults who have more desirable traits.

In a program of re-education there should be much more hope of change in parents' personality than in such traits as intelligence. The parent who has a bad temper may be conscious of it and may seek for means of diagnosis and cure. The person who is indifferent to the appeal of children may be reached through some channel by the resourceful worker. In many instances the inadequate traits of personality have been a gradual evolution which has proceeded so slowly that it is not realized. Parents may be encouraged to see themselves through the eyes of others and to get a new perspective. Whatever can be done will be of immense service to children unless the difficulty is not detected or remedied until after long years of harm have already passed and child attitudes have been firmly established. One of the best virtues upon which to build is the almost universal desire upon the part of every parent to hope for better things for his children than he himself enjoyed. The criminal seldom wishes his son to be a criminal, too. He often sets a high standard to offset his own weaknesses. The work of restoring and improving obvious faults of personality is fraught with difficulties for the worker, but it is usually worth the risks that are involved.

48. OCCUPATION [1]

The problem of the father's occupation may offer some complications which enter into the behavior pattern of the children. It is a broad general question the answer to which is affected by the philosophy of classes or privileged groups in a modern social order. In other words, is it actually "better" or should it be considered "better" to be a professional person, such as a physician or attorney, than to be a laborer? Should it be "better" or merely a different choice, with one as good as the other? There are several aspects of the problem worth consideration.

The authors feel that equality of all occupations is more nearly an actuality than is commonly believed. Although certain professions appear to receive a larger economic return within a period of time than certain other occupations, they necessarily must do so or the profession cannot be practiced. The case of the physician illustrates the point. He must complete a high-school course, next an undergraduate course of three or four years, four or five years' additional work in a medical college, and one

[1] See page 89.

or more years of interneship in a hospital and then wait for two or three very lean years to pass while he is building up a successful practice. He is nearly thirty years of age by the time all this training has been completed. Probably he has had to borrow heavily or has assumed an obligation to his parents which he feels morally responsible to repay in part. All these debts must be settled with interest out of the first years of earning. If he can become a leader in medicine, he has a fair chance to break even and justify his investment of years and money; but the path has not been easy nor illuminated with the bright lights of a "privileged" class. Eventually he may find his satisfaction in his service to humanity.

In contrast to the physician's case is that of the boy who starts out in some "lowly" type of unskilled or semiskilled labor. He can begin as early as sixteen or eighteen years of age; during his twenties if labor is scarce, he commands a good wage and easily gets a fifteen- or twenty-year start on the physician. Moreover, he has no investment-for-training debts to repay. His is a small investment with immediate return; the physician has a large investment and a long-deferred return, with no absolute assurance of a large return. When this kind of analysis of occupations is made to young people or to their parents, the so-called advantages of the "higher" or "white-collar" occupations over the others tend to fade out and the entire range of occupations is much more nearly on a common level than is ordinarily supposed.

The selection of occupation should not be in terms of supposed economic advantage but in the light of mental and temperamental qualities. The individual endowed with a large amount of abstract mental ability will eventually find an occupation to his liking which requires his talents. The individual with a different type of endowment will find greater interest and satisfaction in an occupation suited to his own ability. These mental and educational differences should not be thought of as better or superior, but as individual variations. Methods of reporting school marks, measures of vocational aptitudes, and measures of intelligence, all tend to set up assumptions of superiority or inferiority; but while all these devices are necessary and essential in a plan of education, there is an urgent need for a more fortunate terminology.

Parents are also at fault in being apologetic for their lowly occupations, which they declare their own children shall never follow. Eventually the children may follow them, but with the shadow of the condemnation which has been pronounced upon them from childhood. It is probably too much to expect of human nature that eventually every type of occupation will be considered as good as any other, or that virtue really lies in accepting an occupation suited to one's tastes and abilities and doing it well. A great many of the social stigmas, feelings of inferiority, and futile comparisons which lead to behavior maladjustments could be alleviated if such ideal philosophy could even be approached. Parents who are ashamed of their occupations and never mention them to their children set up a feeling of restraint between themselves and the children. If parents are apologetic, children become even more so and regard the occupations or the parents with a feeling of scorn. These attitudes may affect undesirably the initiative, ambition, and vocational interest of their children, which were discussed in Items 35 and 36.

The parent with no occupation, the loafer, or the ne'er-do-well who occasionally accepts a few days' work when it is forced upon him is not much of an example or inspiration to his children. If they succeed, it is not on account of him but rather through their determination to make good by way of self-justification. This type of father is not to be confused with the unfortunates who are unemployed on account of hard times. In many instances these latter are able to keep up a high morale under almost impossible conditions. The more recent policies of requiring a work assignment to earn maintenance has introduced a much better psychology and an attitude which is reflected in the home.

Occupation may be no cause for difficulty with parents if it is handled wisely in all of its aspects. If subjected to the malpractices which have just been discussed, it can become a virulent cause of juvenile delinquency.

49. Economic Status [1]

To a certain extent economic status is often parallel to occupational choice and the conditions mentioned in the preceding item. However, there is not a perfect positive correlation between them. If there were, all the unskilled laborers would be poverty stricken, and professional people would be rolling in easy wealth. But such is not the case.

The discrepancies between type of occupation and acquisition of worldly goods are dependent upon several factors which reveal home attitudes, habits of parents, and other factors that may affect the child's behavior adjustment. Parents with a modest income frequently save enough to buy a comfortable home because the family is small; their health is good because it is wisely safeguarded; and a sane budget plan is adopted and practiced. Very little is bought on the installment plan, or at least such buying is kept within reasonable limits. In contrast to this type of modest but effective thrift are the experiences of the wealthy business men, speculators, and movie actors who rise to the heights of multimillionaires and then crash to reputed pauperism. The cause of their downfall is often overinflation of credit which must be retired; in other instances it comes from a steady orgy of extravagances after earnings have been curtailed.

If parents are extravagant and spendthrift, the children easily follow their example. Such children have no idea of money values. They have never learned how big a dollar is when it has to be earned; all they know is how small it is when it is to be needlessly squandered. Many live in the belief that later they will begin to save money, that their wages will become magically greater, or that some prudent investment will prove to be a lodestone. Such miracles do happen, but they are distributed in such scant ratios

[1] See page 91.

that relying on them alone is a poor gamble. From such conditions and the home conversations that go with them, children gradually believe that money is always easy, that there is nothing to worry over, and that the family will always get along some way or other. It is little wonder that teachers find that these same children do not put much effort or purpose into their school work.

It is of course ironical that during periods of economic depression, business crashes, and bank failures, those who have been prudent and frugal sometimes see the earnings of years swept away. They naturally become discouraged and have no heart for further effort. Various attempts at insurance of bank deposits, the regulation of speculative investments, and federal pay-off for closed banks are a recognition of the serious injurious effects of outright losses of life savings, particularly when a large proportion of the population is affected.

Whenever a family goes to the extreme of continually complaining about great poverty, with or without cause, children get a depressed attitude. They feel guilty in asking for small amounts of spending money, and parents are reputed to be stern and deaf to childish wants. The children may develop feelings of insecurity and inferiority which are not warranted by the actual condition of the family budget. Such a case is known of a girl who spent her early adult earnings on expensive shoes and a constant round of the best seats to shows and concerts while her parents were in actual need. She really wanted to help them, yet felt a compulsion to spend money extravagantly as an antidote for her long period of childhood poverty. She might as logically have thrown ten-dollar bills in the fire as far as results to her parents were concerned. Parents frequently err in thinking that discussion of money is unnoticed by small children; but it seldom passes without their comment or without childish exaggeration and misinterpretation.

Children should be wisely introduced to the value of money. They may pay for their clothes or assist in shopping for groceries. A budget allowance for them should be set aside even from a modest family income. Part of this allowance should be budgeted for savings and part for spending as they themselves may choose. As they reach adolescence, it is usually beneficial for them to find some way of earning small sums for themselves. Above all they should make some plan of saving from their first adult earnings and continue to observe a budget through their twenties and thirties. The wise use of money can be practiced to advantage by the poorest and by the wealthiest. Values will be realized in terms of children's attitudes and behavior adjustment.

50. HOME LANGUAGE [1]

In studying all sixty-six factors for their possible effects in behavior maladjustment, it should not be assumed that every factor which has undesirable elements in a physical sense necessarily carries with it actual emotional or social maladjustment. The presence and use of a foreign language in a home may have no effect whatsoever in terms of behavior adjustment, but the authors believe that such a situation is the exception rather than the rule. In any case it is desirable to discuss the possible effect of all factors and leave the interpretation of the individual case to the judgment and insight of the worker.

Language difficulty in itself is often a potent cause of social trouble between the family and the current neighborhood practice. If all the members of a large community—neighbors, the storekeeper, the postman, the salesman—speak some foreign language, and if the newspaper read by the family is printed in that language, the difficulties due to the foreign language are naturally at a minimum. But all these agencies seldom uniformly use the foreign tongue; certain neighbors speak only English, and the public school uses English alone. Barriers arise between the foreign-language family and the others; embarrassments, suspicions, awkwardness, and restraint tend to become the rule. The parents often develop social aloofness as a means

[1] See page 92.

of escape, or feelings of inferiority prevail. When such social phenomena operate in the home, the adjustment to the normal social processes for parents and children is thrown out of balance.

A second factor of maladjustment is the advantage which the children soon gain over the parents in the mastery of the current language, which is with few exceptions English in this country. The children learn more rapidly because they are young and adaptable, they do not feel inhibitions about expressing themselves, and they get more practice in speech at play and at school than the parents do. Mothers particularly, with limited experiences outside of the home, suffer most from language isolation. In any event children make more rapid progress with English.

After the children have become more proficient, they begin to correct mistakes of their parents; they even ridicule them, so that the parent eventually decides to escape by abandoning all attempts at English using only the foreign tongue, with which he is more familiar. The parent falls in the esteem of the child in this respect, and naturally all of the other parent-child relationships become colored and affected to some degree. The child gains an additional advantage in becoming the interpreter between parents and the various agents of business which come to their door and must be met in some way. Sometimes this interpretation works to the disadvantage of the children if it has to do with a complaint which concerns them. A case is recalled in which the child acted as an interpreter to his father with the message that he had been truant from school. The reward for his honesty in translation was a sound flogging by his father. There are many complications in the home resulting from a division of the home language.

The most serious problem with respect to foreign families is the rift between the social customs of the ancestral country and those of the new environment. The language difficulty itself is a factor causing divergence between parents and children, but it is aggravated by the differences over standards of living, practices of discipline, and similiar matters, which the children more quickly assimilate and interpret in their own ways. In brief, there is a clash between the conservatism and the autocratic powers of the father in discipline and the liberalism and freedom for children in modern American civilization. The children play with others who sympathize with them in their common experiences. They form gangs to play on the streets and in vacant lots or roam the river fronts, railroad tracks, and dump heaps. Item 26, on playmates and companions, deals with certain related phases of this problem. Shaw (1) in his studies shows convincingly the psychology of these social phenomena, and Thrasher in *The Gang: a Study of 1313 Gangs in Chicago* (2) emphasizes the effect of gang life on these children.

Such problems arise among the laboring classes who live in the poor tenement-house districts near the business and industrial areas of large cities. Shaw shows that the kind of nationality living in these areas makes no difference in the number and character of the juvenile delinquents. In the Chicago areas there has been a long procession of different nationalities in these districts, first north Europeans, then Polish, Italians, Greeks, and more recently Mexicans, but with the same results. Juvenile delinquency and adult crime, which cost millions of dollars annually, foment in these areas. Therefore the problem involves much more than merely the discrepancies of language understanding and practice. It should be remembered that there are distinct trends toward delinquency in these neighborhoods, though not all children become delinquent who live there. There are other factors of personality and individual differences in intelligence and interests which must operate in addition to language and to ideals of discipline.

It is becoming evident gradually that unreserved welcoming of immigrants of certain classes into certain areas of large American cities does not result in an unmixed blessing. The melting pot does not completely melt; at least some of the elements and factors do not mix or fuse, and there follow disastrous consequences to individuals and high cost to society and government. The remedies and preventions exceed the recommendations that can be made in discussing one factor of a behavior scale. The larger social issues must be solved and individual adjustments planned. Classes in English for adults, social and recreational centers, and an improved standard of living are necessary for the cure of these evils if immigration continues to be accepted. At present language difficulty offers many possibilities for maladjustment. It will be noted in Table XII that it comes last in the list in distinguishing between behavior and non-behavior groups; yet many serious cases of maladjustment do arise within the behavior group from language handicap.

51. OTHER ADULTS IN HOME [1]

Homes vary in number of adults from no one besides the child's own parents to a house full of aunts, uncles, grandparents, roomers, or boarders. Children are influenced by the presence and attitudes of these individuals, who play an important rôle in the training of children. One domineering male roomer set himself the task of disciplining a ten-year-old boy, whose parents were pleased to be relieved of the job. The child did not relish this plan and ended it by taking a gun belonging to his self-appointed master and dangerously shooting at random in a playfield near home. No damages were inflicted; but in the investigation the parents were reminded of their duty, and the roomer was sent on his way, sadder and wiser.

At this point it is well to make some estimate of the amount of experience which may arise from mere presence of a number of people in any household, including the brothers and sisters. The number sets up a series of contacts between pairs of individuals, and the ratio of contacts to numbers increases rapidly with the addition of members in the family. The following illustrations will help to make the point clear. Where there are only husband and wife, there are the attitudes of husband to wife and of wife to husband. These attitudes may not be identical and probably should be considered as two distinct relationships.

[1] See page 93.

There are two of these relationships in a family of two persons. But when the baby enters, there are not only the two relationships between husband and wife, but also two more between mother and baby and two more between father and baby, a total of six relationships or attitudes between individuals. These all tend to interplay upon one another. For example, if the father is antagonistic toward the mother, there is some effect upon the baby; so all six relationships are important in the child's family adjustment. It is to be noted, then, that increasing the number in the family from two to three raises the number of relationships between them from two to six, a threefold increase in the actual number in the family. If a fourth member comes into the family, the number of relationships is increased by six, or by the two sets between the new member and each of the former members. The number has increased from six to twelve with a number increase from three to four. For a $33\frac{1}{3}$ per cent increase in the number there is an increase of 100 per cent in the relationships. Five in the family, or a 20 per cent increase from four, raises the number from twelve to twenty, or $66\frac{2}{3}$ per cent. The number of relationships in any family is the number in the family times one less than that number. In a family of ten members there are ninety possible relationships between individuals.

There are certain advantages and disadvantages in large numbers in a family in terms of the general social atmosphere which exists. If all of the relationships between all members of the family are cordial, if they all do kindly acts, and if they all speak well of one another, the growing child gets a wealth of good social experience from living among a large number of such relationships. But if there is a poor attitude, with jealousies, accusations, and special privileges, the experience is a distressing one for a child of tender years. One maladjusted boy lived in a home with his mother, two of her sisters, her husband's father, and two male roomers, a total of seven members. All of the forty-two relationships were bad. Certain people could not sit on certain chairs or use this or that, and the boy reveled in the discord and delighted in helping to stir it up. He had acquired a wealth of experience in antisocial practices which would last him to the end of his days. In the matter of relationships between members of a household the mere number is not alone significant; the attitudes and maladjustment growing out of them are the important factors in children's fortunes.

Grandparents are naturally apt to indulge grandchildren, often to the dismay of the parents, although sometimes they may be unduly harsh, requiring quiet and many unreasonable restrictions. Adult roomers are often unscrupulous with children of the opposite sex in actual malpractices or in interfering with their play and projects. The economic gain from their maintenance scarcely balances the harm which they often do. There are cases in which the relationships and attitudes between adults and children are happy and wholesome, but parents should carefully check up from time to time to ascertain the true status. The behavior and non-behavior groups which were studied showed little difference in the effects from adult contacts, but a larger sampling might easily have shown a greater trend toward difficulties in the behavior cases.

52. Number of and Position in Siblings [1]

The number of brothers and sisters may have a profound effect upon any child. It was shown in the preceding section that, if the numbers are large and the attitudes undesirable, the effects are harmful. The only child in the family is also to be considered in this discussion and, since there are many popular conceptions and misconceptions about him, he will be studied first.

It cannot be denied that certain elements in the environment of the only child tend to make a spoiled and overindulged individual. He is the only one, the center of attraction, and the sole receiver of affection and attention. If this situation is not controlled by the parents, the only child can easily become the victim of spoiling and all the concomitants that go with it. Since the stage is set in the only-child pattern, the chief cure is either

[1] See page 94.

to inform the parents of the danger or to let their own good reasoning and intuition guide their course of child training.

During the period of babyhood the problem is not very different for the only child from that of siblings; a certain amount of personal care and attention are commonly required for all infants. The chief difficulties for the only child arise when he is old enough to be among and play with other children. At this point the attitude and practice of the parents are crucial. If they realize the importance of social contacts with other children, opportunities are either afforded or at least not opposed when the child finds them for himself. He learns how to share his things with others and practices give and take in play, and his training becomes practically identical with that of the child who has small brothers and sisters of his own. The opposite extreme is the child who is not allowed to play with other children. The parents do not wish to contaminate their child with the children of the neighborhood, who run the streets, shout, and sometimes get their clothes dirty. They solve the problem in the simplest way for themselves and avoid trouble by keeping their child away from it. But he, sadly watching the others from the window, is piling up a mountain of feelings and emotions which will have their reactions later. Many times these shut-in children are not sent to kindergarten but wait until they are of the first-grade age or possibly until they are seven years of age, since the parents are trying to prolong isolation as far as possible. This type of child is the one most in need of the kindergarten experience, which is designed to enrich and develop the social intelligence. When he is at last permitted to join a group, he finds it extremely difficult to meet large numbers of children; he finds himself in a new world, a complicated and heartless world. It is easy for the other children to make him the victim of all kinds of social embarrassments. In the midst of all these worries he cannot concentrate upon his school work, he makes a poor record, and he now has two major worries instead of one. If he is fortunate in having an agreeable personality and has not become disturbed by the other children in his period of probation, he makes the adjustments with some success and comparatively few scars on his emotional life.

Naturally we have described an extreme case by way of illustration. Not all cases of only children conform to this pattern. They probably range from this extreme to the opposite, where there is free play, with a variety of contacts with other children, accompanied by the inhibition of the parents' own predispositions to spoil them. Most only children fall between these two extremes; probably the majority of them are near the average, which is not very different from the average of siblings. For these reasons we cannot expect to find that all only children are problems from the standpoint of behavior; in fact, the average of their social contacts is probably not greatly different from that of other children, if at all. Whatever difference there is lies in the treatment and training of the individual case rather than in the fact of being an only child.

If there are several children in the family, there may be serious effects and consequences for any child. Children in the same family differ from one another in many respects—in looks, personality, intelligence, size, habits of work, and all the other traits that human nature ever shows. All these differences make the children react in different ways to one another and to their parents, and their parents to them, as will be discussed in the next section. In this section only the general trends of behavior are considered.

The older child in a family of two has problems of adjustment which arise from being the older child. Until a second child is born he enjoys all the privileges and woes of an only child. But when a second one is born, particularly when the older is about two or three years old, he suddenly finds that he has not only lost his favorite position but is eclipsed by a new individual. He sees the baby being held, dressed, and fed at the expense of attentions which he formerly received from his mother. He does not know that he had such experiences himself, or that as an only child may have received even better care. The time and maturity factors are not intelligible to him; even his parents may be unaware of them. He feels a sense of insecurity and jealousy and becomes unhappy and rebellious. When wise parents detect such trends, they try to neutralize them by giving the older child time and attention, dressing him, and helping him occasionally a little more than is necessary so as to keep him encouraged. These patterns of behavior are common in the older child, but they are less apt to occur if he is five years of age or older. Then the competitions are not keen, and he accepts the baby as someone for him to love and attend. However, if the older child has taken on the worst characteristics of an only child, the longer the time between him and the second child, the more violent his reactions may become.

The second or younger child has his characteristic problems inherent in being the younger or smaller. As he gets old enough to walk and play actively, he soon finds that he cannot do what his older brother does. He tries but falls and gets hurt. His older brother may add a note of scorn and sarcasm to his failure, which intensifies the smart. He toddles up the street as fast as he can go, sobbing because he is left behind. He runs a race with hopeless and continuous handicaps; possibly he catches up in adulthood, but the victory is hollow for by that time at any rate he understands its nature. In the meantime during the early years of childhood he has had many embarrassing and worried moments from these apparent inferiorities.

His troubles multiply from another source when the third child is born. He was previously at least secure with his parents as the baby in the family, but now he goes through all the agonies and troubles which were experienced by his older brother at the time of his own coming. In some cases these conflicting drives tend to neutralize one another, but often they tend to be supplemented and amplified. In clinical practice with behavior problems often the middle of three children is the problem child, disclosing this cycle of characteristics.

If there are more than three children in the family, there is a continual procession of problems of these three types passing in review. The family life for the children is not necessarily a uniform and happy composite of common elements but a diverse array of mixed, tangled, and confused patterns which neither the parents nor the children understand or know how to solve without instruction and interpretation. It is something of a miracle that problem children are not more numerous.

Parents go through the greatest possible sacrifices to provide for their children food, shelter, protection, and all the physical necessities of life, yet expose the children and themselves to the subtle and hidden dangers in their very midst of misunderstood social attitudes and relationships within the home. Often these perils are much more dangerous and devastating than those which parents really anticipate and try to avoid.

53. ADJUSTMENTS TO SIBLINGS [1]

In the preceding section maladjustments were discussed which arise from number and position among siblings. The discussion is here continued in terms of the differences between the qualities and characteristics of children and their effects upon behavior patterns.

Children differ within the same family in their many traits. Members of some families are more alike than in other families, but in all families differences exist to some degree. It is an unsolved problem for social research to evaluate the amount of emotional adjustment in terms of the uniformity or disparity of traits of family members. The importance of these differences has been discussed in earlier sections. In Item 15 the privileges and favors granted to the good-looking were considered. In the immediate family such a member feels consequences due to the jealousy of the less favored members and to favoritism shown by the parents at the expense of the other siblings. Many other factors, particularly those covered in Items 27-37, inclusive, are a psychological parallel to looks or appearance.

Consciously or unconsciously parents become aware of differences and mold their treatments accordingly. Psychologists fre-

[1] See page 95.

quently try to keep secret from parents knowledge of the actual mental status of their children in terms of the intelligence quotient; but no confidences are actually betrayed in telling, since the parents really know the facts anyway. The chief danger from parents occurs when comparison is made between a brilliant child and a merely average child who is thought to be very backward if not virtually feeble-minded. The slower of the two children may be continually stimulated and nagged to do better and to emulate the achievements of his brother or sister. The intention of this practice is to produce better effort, but it may result in an intense hatred or in a complete slump in all effort.

In many of the social qualities likenesses or differences between parents and children tend to create problems of adjustment. The quiet, retiring girl may find an unusual bond of affection with her quiet and retiring mother. The noisy, boisterous brother does not understand this sister, and far less does she understand him. Sometimes radically different and opposite traits attract people to each other, sometimes they repel. Little reliable information is available about these phenomena and their effects upon different types of individuals.

Among the children themselves all these differences afford an interplay of character and personality clashes or accords. The combined or cumulative effects over a period of years gradually play a derived rôle of their own, supplementary to the original causes. Screaming and rage from a twenty-year-old girl rang out in a certain home one night from causes of a perfectly logical nature. She was an ambitious girl, steadily employed, and self-supporting, with a sister two years older who apparently had none of these traits. The older one presumed upon the younger by wearing her clothes, and in this particular instance she had left a fine evening gown soiled and untidy. There was no time to have it ready to be worn by its owner and no sense of responsibility on the part of the borrower. Many similar incidents occur between children in some families with varying degrees of emotional feeling and response.

In suggesting remedies for these divergent trends with their attendant antipathies there is no one approved method of procedure to be offered. If parent and child or child and child can recognize that there is an element of danger in blaming and fault-finding, with clashes likely over problems that are inherent in individual differences, a more reasonable practice of self-restraint will be observed. Yet too much self-restraint has its dangers and eventually may burst the bonds and create a tremendous break between the persons in question. A knowledge and understanding of fundamental differences in temperament usually prove to be valuable. The ways of ignorance and misunderstanding have made for much unhappiness and maladjustment; an experiment on a large scale with analysis and understanding could scarcely do worse and bids fair to be an improvement. A study of certain families who are known to be well adjusted among all their members would afford concrete and positive suggestions for the improvement of other less fortunate families.

In the relationships between siblings there is an unusual social situation between twins. Are they often behavior problems? What characteristics are unique in them on account of being twins? Frequent complaints are heard of minor infractions of school discipline, mostly from taking advantage of the confusion as to their individual identity. Twins tend to merge their personalities into identical patterns, which probably results in lessening the radical and extreme practices of both. The merging may even go as far as to remove all feeling of individuality. For example, if one twin falls and soils his clothing, his brother must stop his play and change his clothes, too, for no reason at all so far as his own actions are concerned. Cases of triplets, quadruplets, or more recently of quintuplets must tend to even greater uniformity and merging of personality and character patterns, which are probably initially similar by condition of birth. Any combination from twins to quintuplets is recommended for those families who sigh for uniformity among their children. Extreme habits of dependence on each other may occasionally inject severe problems into the lives of twins.

54. Legal Status [1]

The state recognizes that it has certain rights over parents in the protection of their children. Parents are usually unaware of or at least unconscious of any authority superior to their own since such power is not frequently invoked. But whenever a child is physically abused, abandoned by his parents, or exposed to moral and social hazards, the state removes him to safer and better quarters. Considerable attention was focused upon this problem not long ago by the state enforcement of an operation on a child whose parents refused to permit it.

In this matter, as well as in many others, the physical aspects of abuse, neglect, and cruelty receive much more consideration than mental and emotional maltreatment. The latter is much more difficult to prove since it does not produce visible and tangible evidence. Social agencies are reluctant to take these cases into court, no matter how obvious the damage or how sure they are of the effects, because of the strong probability of losing the decision.

In society, children are found from one extreme of a happy home with their own parents to the other extreme of having no regular home and being boarded about temporarily with or without the jurisdiction and supervision of some state-authorized agency. There are various intermediate steps between these extremes, all of them with certain characteristic emotional results. The feeling of insecurity, a factor which is seldom actually recognized, may cause much unhappiness and concern to children. They find it difficult to make adjustments to new homes, particularly among strangers, or they become adept in setting a standard of their own if they are frequently moved to new homes. That the number of cases of unadjustment based on this cause is so small is a tribute to the fundamentally good intentions of those who accept children for boarding care or for adoption.

The demands of adults to adopt children greatly exceed the supply. If some disaster caused one third of all the children to

[1] See page 97.

become homeless, they would all probably be readily absorbed into private homes without recourse to state homes or colonies. Parents with large families sometimes adopt one or more additional children from their relatives or sometimes from strangers.

The entire matter of child adoption is so closely attended by emotional factors that the state agencies are forced to use a great amount of restraint and common sense in guiding decisions and placements. They advocate delay in placement until the child is old enough for reliable measurements of intelligence and estimates of personality traits. A most unfortunate example of haste recently came to our attention. A family adopted a six-weeks-old baby boy from a maternity hospital to compensate for the disappointment over the stillbirth of their own child. Within the year they had another child of their own and later three more children. Their ardor for the adopted boy became less, in part on account of their own children and in part because of the gradual but sure evidence that he was of mixed blood. During his early teens he was for several years on a farm with the adopted mother's mother, who refused to believe the fact about his paternity. She attempted to make full amends for the abuse and rejections of the foster mother and her children by indulging him with everything at her command. Later on account of the grandmother's age and economic condition she had to return him to her daughter, who with the rest of her family was in need of public charity. The supervisor of the welfare agency discovered the social implications of this situation. A thorough mental examination disclosed defective intelligence on the boy's part which qualified him for immediate and permanent placement in the state home for the feeble-minded. He will probably find this solution a happy escape after the sixteen years of wretchedness for which he was in no way responsible.

There are many other cases in which adoptions are unfortunate for all concerned. A large number of adopted children are reported to mental and child-guidance clinics as unstable and maladjusted. The foster parents are often vague about the natural parents, exhibiting real or professed ignorance. But sometimes they admit that the child was born illegitimately of an unfortunate girl by an alcoholic father who was a ne'er-do-well and who was always on the road. Just how much part heredity has played in these cases it is hard to determine, but the rejection by the foster parents after a long period of antisocial trends transfers to the advising agency a serious problem. It is of course poor psychology to raise too many questions and doubts about the heredity if the foster parents wish to make a new trial, but it is well for them to realize the gravity of the earlier influences.

The factor of emotional adjustment in the home, whether it be a foster home or not, is a matter of vital importance. The home is incidental to adjustment factors, and there are many foster homes in which the adjustments are many times more satisfactory than in natural homes. The phrase "a left-handed welcome," once coined by a fourteen-year-old girl in the foster home of an aunt and uncle, expresses a multitude of things having the form and substance but not the strength and reality of naturalness. It is something of a reflection upon parental treatment of children that many children from natural homes at some time or other express doubts as to their real legal status. They must feel that their parents display little consideration for them.

The question of telling children about their adoption offers many difficulties. Some foster parents have a firm resolve never to divulge the fact; they want to eliminate any doubt as to the adopted child's real ancestry. With babies and very young children who would not understand the matter is delayed, and then excuses for continued delay are found regardless of the desirability or undesirability of the course. Another practice is to tell the child in as matter-of-fact a manner as possible if he happens to ask the question. The desire to know one's parentage is an impelling one, and the search for clews furnishes one of the most thrilling themes for movie or drama. There is danger, in not telling or in denying the fact, that the child will some day know, remember, or find it out. In such a case the child receives a cruel and sometimes mortal shock, while his confidence in his foster parents is entirely destroyed.

In the question of legal status the physical and legal factors are much less important than the spirit and attitudes which accompany them. These latter elements determine adjustment or maladjustment.

55. BROKEN HOME [1]

Some of the discussion of legal status applies equally well to this topic. Broken homes have always been reputed to be a major cause of juvenile delinquency, but in the analysis of specific cases there is less evidence to support this fact than had been supposed. In differentiating between the behavior and non-behavior groups in Table XII of Chapter XII, broken homes stand fifty-fourth in the sixty-six items. This rank indicates that broken homes are not among the more frequent or serious causes of behavior difficulty in children. The crucial element, as in many other factors, lies in the handling of the problem. Unbroken homes are often much worse in their applications of mental hygiene than broken ones. Although there may be only one parent in the home, if that one has a sympathetic understanding of children the problem is solved to a great degree. This is true whether the other parent is dead or separated from the family.

There are at least three phases or variations of broken homes worthy of mention. The first situation exists when both parents remain in the home but with continual conflict over all of its issues. If this condition is evident to the children, the psychological effects are among the worst that can be imagined. They sense controversy, they may even take part in it, and in some cases they learn how to play one parent off against the other and thus add to the confusion of issues. All respect for the authority of either parent or even for adults as a class is destroyed. Children usually have respect and veneration for the opinions and ideals of adults, particularly of their parents; and when these are swept away for any reason, much of the stability of childhood is undermined.

[1] See page 98.

The second situation occurs when the child lives with the parent who is the less desirable either in the eyes of the child or in actual emotional adjustment. If the child is better adjusted to the other parent but denied the right to live with that one, the door of opportunity for good mental health is closed. The child does not understand why this limitation is placed upon him, and he looks upon life as a great injustice. He avoids the home as much as possible, seeks comfort in the gang on the street, airs his troubles to sympathetic ears wherever he can find them, and by these processes finds his unhappiness increased rather than lessened or softened.

A third type of social situation which gives rise to injurious results is living alternately with one parent and the other when each one tries to undermine allegiance to the other during the sojourn. A twelve-year-old boy who had had such an experience was finally brought into a child-guidance clinic at the desire of both parents. He had played the game better than they had anticipated and was insolent to both and quite beyond their control. He had completely disrupted his school program, and part of his downfall was due to change between two schools several times. Neither parent would accept him in the end. A new environment in a foster home was arranged, but it would require long residence in a desirable foster home to counterbalance the damage which had been inflicted on him.

For those workers who are especially anxious to solve difficult problems of behavior maladjustment, attention is invited to obvious cases of problem children from broken homes with their attendant attitudes and derived outcomes. The next few items in the following chapter deal with certain phases of this general situation.

BIBLIOGRAPHY

1. SHAW, CLIFFORD R.—*Delinquency Areas*. Chicago: University of Chicago Press, 1929. 214 pp.
2. THRASHER, FREDERIC M.—*The Gang: A Study of 1313 Gangs in Chicago*. Chicago: University of Chicago Press, 1929. 571 pp.

CHAPTER X

HOME ATMOSPHERE AND SCHOOL FACTORS

THE factors which are presented in this chapter grow out of the home atmosphere and the school environment. They include such items as recreation for the family, ideals of the home, and attitudes toward the child. Many of these items show greater differences between behavior and non-behavior children than do items from the other classes of factors.

56. GENERAL HOME ATMOSPHERE [1]

General home atmosphere is a difficult and subtle factor to evaluate. It should not be confused with general furnishings, with neatness or orderliness, or with kind of furniture. Whether the home be elegant or humble matters little if there is a wholesome atmosphere. There is little need to elaborate upon the importance of home atmosphere. Those who have been fortunate enough to live in a favorable one understand its blessings; those who have been unfortunate in this respect realize the limitations which it imposes upon them.

Home atmosphere can be evaluated in terms of its holding power on all the members of the family. If the family is a happy, sympathetic, and understanding unit, the home can make an effective appeal. If it is distinctly otherwise, the home is a place to leave promptly with or without pretext. Society seldom has at hand plenty of suitable substitutes for the home; the child who must seek his contacts outside his home runs a grave risk of

[1] See page 99.

social and moral degeneration. Recreational facilities beyond the home are the most meager and of most doubtful value in those urban areas in which the homes are poorest in home atmosphere; and they are best in the best neighborhoods. It is extremely important to have and to preserve a desirable home atmosphere.

In the home in which conditions are practically ideal with respect to home atmosphere, the children feel a sense of security, confidence, and happiness which carries over into their attitudes toward school work, into their play relations with other children, and into their vocational outlook. Children become involved in emotional tangles in their play activities and in their dealings with teachers and many others in their daily life. They often wish for and need some line of activity to clear away these difficulties; in a congenial and understanding home opportunities for doing so are always at hand. In the home in which satisfying attachments are lacking, the germs of childish anguish often grow and foment into mental illnesses at adolescence or in adulthood.

In a poor home atmosphere the child also loses the supreme desire to worship and emulate his parents. That trait seems to be universal in the human race. If the conditions are so bad that the children feel and express contempt toward their parents, one of the greatest social and moral values of the home is absent. In like manner the desire of parents to live up to the best which children expect of them suffers badly in the home of poor atmosphere; such a home easily leads to the children's seeking contacts and pleasures elsewhere. Children from such homes are apt to form strong attachments to social workers, Scout leaders, or any adults who seem truly interested in them and in their problems. In the homes of the best atmosphere such tendencies are seldom in evidence in the children.

Home atmosphere is something which cannot be made or unmade in a moment. Heredity and the training which the parents have brought from their own early experiences play upon it as important conditions. It is difficult for any individual to set standards for his adult living very different from those of his childhood home unless he has the fortunate guidance of someone who has been more favored in his early training. Home atmosphere is affected by many factors which are listed in this inventory of behavior causes, such as limitations of parents or differences between parents in intelligence or in education. The comparative ages of the parents and their offspring affect their feelings of tolerance or sympathy for them. In fact, there is probably no item in the entire list which does not play its part in affecting home atmosphere.

Among the significant causes are those in which the parents believe their duty toward childhood lies entirely in attending to physical cares. Good food, clean clothing, and personal cleanliness completely engross the mother, and the drive for economic security engages the father. They feel that thus they are most dutiful and ideal parents, but the children may sense no sympathetic understanding. It is one of the first steps in the cultivation of proper home attitudes in parents to disabuse their minds of the expectation that their children are going to be grateful now or later on for physical comforts if the mental ones are always allowed to languish. One may sometimes sense in homes of good economic security that such lacks are very marked; while in the homes of the poor there is often partial compensation for physical discomfort in a better mental understanding. In any particular home the cross current of causes is so baffling that it almost defies diagnosis, yet the effects upon children and parents are usually obvious.

The factor of general home atmosphere offers one of the greatest challenges to constructive social work. If improvements can be made, the entire mental and emotional life of the child may be transformed; if no change can be made, the hands of society are practically tied with respect to that particular child and his problems. Removal to a foster home or to an institution is not entirely a substitute for a desirable home.

Education during either the high-school or college period or immediately preceding marriage in duties and in how to avoid dangerous pitfalls would be one of the most effective means of building and preserving home atmosphere. When marriage is not undertaken with too blind a belief that anyone can be changed or reformed to fit the ideal, one important step will have been taken. The process of trying to reform one's mate in the first few years commonly ends disastrously, and a desirable home atmosphere is much more difficult to recover than to maintain before its dissolution. Constructive home atmosphere and healthful parental attitudes may be likened to two people holding a heavy pole upright between them. There is little strain or trouble as long as each is mindful of the other's rights and feelings; the pole stands balanced with little assistance. But when either begins to shove or pull this weight off its balance, it is too much for the other to offset and a crash occurs. Prevention is many times more effective than remedy; it is much easier to keep the pole erect than to try to lift it back into place.

It is possibly too much to hope that merely diagnosing and explaining the sources of difficulty in home atmosphere will bring about a change for the better. Events keep recurring which recall the old issues, and the factors which mar the home atmosphere persist. However, enough experience has been had with discouraging cases of poor home atmosphere to furnish hope that much may be accomplished even in very bad conditions. As the children grow toward adolescence and adulthood, they are often able to do what their parents were unable to do. The improvement of home atmosphere continues to be one of the important factors in the reduction of behavior problems. Its possibilities are unlimited.

57. IDEALS OF HOME [1]

The general home atmosphere includes phases known as ideals. These ideals are all-important in the development of children. If there is laxness in ideals on the part of the parents, it is hard for the children to be superior. When home ideals are the very highest, however, children may develop lower standards on account of outside influences or from predisposing trends in their

[1] See page 101.

own personality. Both of these causes are matters partly outside of the control of the home; but when the home itself is the main cause of the downfall, a pathetic picture of childhood experience is presented.

Among the worst possible causes of poor ideals is laxity in matters of social contact. Some homes even go to the extreme of promiscuous sexual relationships. The children become aware of what is happening; there may even be commercialized vice which is witnessed by the children. Children may either take the line of least resistance, or their better natures may prevail. They may revolt and determine to live their lives above such degradation. It is this latter drive for the better which helps to raise standards or ideals above the slough into which they might otherwise sink.

Other low ideals may arise in connection with honesty. If children know that their parents continually lie as a matter of habit, they may quickly acquire the same habit. In the early years of their lives children may be merely confused and mystified, but eventually they learn what is really taking place. One wonders if such parents ever feel qualms of conscience when they see their children taking up the same practices of which the parents themselves are sometimes the victims. There are all degrees of dishonesty, from deceit about money in large amounts to lies about being ill and unable to meet undesirable appointments. Some of the practices are merely witnessed by children; others are performed with their help and connivance. The child who is told to answer the door and say that mother is not at home becomes a party to the deception, either willingly or unwillingly.

Among the more common examples of deceit are the reports of the birth dates of children for school records. The child of four becomes quite a problem at home; he is taken to school and entered in the kindergarten as a five-year-old. If he is large and mentally superior, he may make the adjustment; often he does not. He is warned to say that he is five instead of four. It just happens that one of the most frequent incidental questions asked of young children by adults is their age, so that he has to face this question constantly. If he happens to dislike school or finds it difficult, the deceit which he must practice to remain in school becomes an additional strain.

In cases where five-year-olds are started in the first grade as six-year-olds, they are not mature enough mentally for the school work if they are of average intelligence or less. Since they cannot master the reading and other formal subjects, they sit in a semi-indifferent mental condition and allow their minds to wander. After they have repeated the grade two or three times, they become so dissatisfied with school and so averse to reading that they no longer try. Finally the teacher decides they must be mentally subnormal. Mental examinations and investigations are made which bring out the facts of average ability and the true birth date. But the damage has been done, the child is not a candidate for any type of special class, the regular teacher does not have much opportunity to help him, and he is the victim of well-meaning but destructive parental deceit. It would not be surprising to find him eventually joining the army of maladjusted children. Schools have seen so many children suffer from these practices that many of them are now requiring a birth certificate for admission.

There is another type of home ideals at the opposite extreme from the types already considered. It includes false standards of extreme honesty, piety, and sanctity. Parents and children try to live on an artificial plane of goodness which is beyond the wildest hopes of a saint. If the children take this idea too seriously, they are always worried that they have done something wrong or committed some unpardonable sin. A case is recalled of a quiet girl of ten years who rated herself very low on a self-rating scale of usual habits of living, play, and school known as (1) *Telling What I Do*. Her teacher could not understand the low rating, for she was a model student both in studies and in conduct. A home investigation disclosed a very strict and puritanical standard, about which the child had been reproached so much that she had a marked inferiority complex. After discussion of some of these attitudes by the entire class her ideas changed, she became much happier, and she later rated herself much higher in her own estimation. If her tendency had not been discovered quite accidentally by the self-rating test, she might have become an inhibited and maladjusted individual at adolescence or later.

In programs for the re-education of maladjusted children there is always a great urge and drive to correct those children who have shown aggressive traits of nonconformity. It is necessary also to discover those of a quiet and retiring nature who may have outbursts at a later time. People are always surprised to learn that such children have become problems because they were "absolutely model" in early childhood. Extreme quietness, shyness, or timidity should be recognized as conditions calling for case studies of children; there will be many such cases.

The home with high ideals, practiced in a wholesome way and without artificial strain, is not likely to have behavior-problem children. It is the highest duty of society to provide such homes for all children.

58. RELIGION [1]

The authors approach the problem of religion as a factor in behavior motivation with much caution, with a feeling of reverence, and with a desire to encourage religious observances as a means of curing the ills of maladjustment. There are a few negative factors in this process which merit discussion. It is rather the absence of religious influences or the presence of badly perverted religious forms which seem to contribute to the woes of behavior children.

In many of the maladjusted children there is a complete lack of religious influence and training. They have never attended church or Sunday school or at least have not been in attendance for many years. They hear no beliefs discussed and they are ignorant of the splendid moral lessons which are to be gleaned from the Bible stories. Under such circumstances it is little wonder that they live a limited and antisocial life with its unfortunate consequences. Practically all of the churches, creeds,

[1] See page 102.

and religions are advocating and preaching a code of moral living in terms of modern social conditions. Those persons who entirely ignore some form of religious belief miss one of the greatest opportunities of adjustment to the complications of present-day life.

Religious worship may act as a wonderful healing power for those who are in deep trouble of any kind. Those bereaved by the loss of a close relative find comfort and solace. The poor, the homeless, and victims suffering from war or invasion seek it as their last and only haven of refuge and comfort. It would be presumptuous to imply that the values of religion needed any defense or justification in our brief discussion. At best, all that is intended is a brief but sincere tribute to religion's deep and underlying values. All kinds and types of religions have their values, and the adjustment worker of one religious faith should be able to endorse heartily the practice of another belief as a means for the positive rehabilitation of the moral and religious aspects of life.

In the matter of different church denominations and affiliations troubles sometimes arise over children. One parent is of one denomination, and the other of a different one. Each is trying to claim the children for his own beliefs. The children become conscious of conflict and eventually solve their own problem by accepting a third denomination or by staying away from church altogether. The conflict may continue between the parents, and each may well blame the other in such a fundamental matter.

Another source of conflict arises when one parent is very religious and the other never makes any profession of faith whatever. Sometimes it is the father, sometimes the mother, who does not go to church. This rift in the family accord may take some violent turns if the nonattending parent interferes with the church attendance or practices of the other or of the children. Tolerance and respect for the views of the husband or wife might prevent some of these difficulties.

There are instances in which overindulgence in religious practices causes an emotional and nervous upset. A fourteen-year-old girl was hysterical and almost completely unbalanced on this account. Her parents were ardent followers of a certain creed which practiced excess in sensational conversions and drew dire pictures of punishment for those who were in sin. They had sold their home and moved to temporary quarters next door to their place of worship so as to be conveniently near. They attended services every night of the week until late hours, when the pitch of emotional excitement became very high. Their daughter was required to go. She absorbed the most undesirable elements of the experience and became completely fatigued from loss of sleep. It did not seem to be showing a lack of respect for religion, then, when less excessive practices of worship were urged. Any agency or clinic for adjustment of problems runs afoul of such situations frequently. It should be noted that it is the malpractice of religion rather than religion itself which is at fault.

Another type of maladjustment over religion arises when a child is forced to attend some church against his will. For various reasons the child may be conditioned against it; what seems the easiest solution to the parents is to order, rather than to study the causes and modify the attendant motivations. Children may become so conditioned against any form of church worship that they rebel and never join a church even in adulthood. One young man accounted for such an attitude by an experience which occurred when he was forced to lead a young people's meeting at the age of fourteen and suffered the agonies of the bashful adolescent. The use of force on children as a substitute for other avenues of appeal is as futile in religion as in any other situation; even the backing and authority of religious practice cannot overcome the destructive effects of the method.

There are some cases in which religious practice causes maladjustment by its spasmodic and variable application. The forms of religious worship are followed on Sundays with liberal support to the cause in service and money, but the parents treat their own children throughout the week with abuse and cruelty. Subconsciously there is often more ardent devotion on the part of the parents the following Sunday to absolve them from any sin or ill intent. The children who are victims vaguely feel some discrepancy. Whenever the gap between religious theory and practice becomes too great, there is another case of maladjustment.

It is hoped that all these incidents are exceptions rather than common practices. In the main, religious practice and belief do untold good. Analysis of unadjusted cases tends to raise one's appreciation of the importance of proper religious observances.

59. Family Recreation [1]

The recreation of the family is a crucial item in the adjustment of children. In Table XII it stands among the first third of the sixty-six factors in differentiating between behavior and non-behavior groups. Within the behavior group it has the highest correlation with the total score, which is interpreted to mean that the worst behavior cases had the poorest family recreation and that the less severe cases of malbehavior had considerably better recreation.

The recreation for the family has many implications for social adjustment among its members—between father and son, mother and daughter, brother and sister, and younger son and older son. In recreation there is relief from the tensions of work and daily living. There is encouragement of informality and an opening for confidences that otherwise remain unspoken. In the spirit of play children at unexpected times suddenly release their inhibitions and disclose their most secret confidences. If these are received in the same earnest and sincere manner in which they are given, bonds of confidence and understanding are greatly strengthened. Any parent or anyone else who works with children knows how futile it is to beg a child to tell something at some required time; but plenty of important facts pour out spontaneously under the liberating powers of co-operative recreation.

Recreation for the family also releases inhibitions for the parents, who profit greatly if they can really relax from their usual routine. Probably the greatest curse of modern life is the

[1] See page 103.

continual drive to be working. Even with a shortened working day and with periods of enforced idleness there is still an excuse to be busy at something rather than to be enjoying some kind of recreation. The spirit of rush and get there cannot be shaken off even in recreation if it fastens its tentacles too strongly upon the worker at his job. It is unsafe to make general characterizations of national trends, but in Europe the rank and file of the populations seem really to enjoy the freedom and leisure of their spare time. They stroll about, lie on the grass, or saunter off on short hikes. In their midst the American tourists rush about madly, jostling one another and being in a great haste to get nowhere at all. The American who perhaps wonders whether his different style of clothes marks him off from the natives, seldom understands that it is his hurried actions that are different. In like manner the hurried adult tends to strain and scurry about even on his vacation by mapping out a tour which is two or three times too long for the time available. He eventually completes his tour within the allotted time by long hours of speeding past fleeting landscapes, which are scarcely glimpsed from the corner of his eye as he fixes his gaze on the narrow ribbon of concrete ahead of him. He probably ought to have a month for rest after the vacation is over before resuming work. Children do not get the maximum vacation benefits out of such harrowing experiences.

In a sane and calm program, recreation is not crowded into a concentrated period of two or three weeks but is scattered throughout the year with a little every day. At these times the adults should lay aside their cares and really enter into the spirit of play with their children. If the children even direct or supervise the play, it is a splendid thing for them and adds to the relaxation of parents. For the moment children dictate policies, which is good training and experience. They can also participate equally on the adult level by sharing in games with enough handicap in their favor so that the chances of winning equal those of losing. There are thousands of ways in which this handicap may be accomplished. In checkers the father takes fewer men, and this reduction can be rescaled whenever it gets too strenuous for him. In games of strength and skill, such as quoits, the boy can have a shorter distance for throwing. Whatever the type of game, some handicap can usually be arranged for equalized playing. It is real competition which brings out the best effort in adult and child.

There is a natural tendency for children to prefer playing with others of their own age. It is somewhat of a problem for parents to get inside this magic circle a part of the time; but if they have been faithful and resourceful in the early days, they will probably be rewarded in the later. In many homes the recreational program is a co-operative activity even into the adult years of the children. There is little emotional or behavior maladjustment.

In some of the worst types of homes the parents have but limited insight or no insight at all into the social possibilities of recreation. It is easier to remain at work or at least to be aloof. They toil and toil, believing that they will be rewarded by the thanks of their children at some later time. But sad to relate, these thanks are seldom forthcoming. All the physical comforts afforded to children are merely taken for granted by them, but there is apt to be appreciation for the interest and co-operation which come from a program of recreation.

If a supervised program of recreation could be introduced into all the homes where there is behavior maladjustment, the problems of delinquency would tend to disappear. Such home programs always require outside aid for promotion and supervision, but the expense is worth the effort in terms of lesser ultimate expense for juvenile courts and houses of detention. The question of family recreation is one of the greatest challenges to modern society. It has many implications for behavior.

60. PARENTS' SOCIAL ADJUSTMENT [1]

The adjustments of the parents to society in general, to each other, and to children have a profound influence upon the atti-

[1] See page 105.

tudes of their children toward them. Parents vary over a wide range of differences from those who are versatile in social intercourse to those who have little or no knack for it. Those of wide experience can bring a wealth of opportunity to their children through the examples set within their home. Most homes fortunately have at least some degree of adjustment which benefits the children, but some do not. The effects and results of social adjustment will be considered more specifically.

In the families where there is a minimum of social life the attitudes of parents toward affairs are apt to be colored or biased by unusual points of view. They are less tolerant of children, of their play, of their behavior, and of their seeming immaturity. The adults live a self-centered and selfish life with a limited perspective. Their own aches and pains become unduly magnified; they feel persecuted, and even the minor activities of the children rise to occupy an all too important place in their thinking. Children naturally retaliate when they feel too much intrusion on their liberties, and an armed neutrality is set up between them and the adults. Not only are the parents unhappy but they also make their children miserable.

When there is no social adjustment or recreation, there is no holding power over the children aside from physical force, which is always ineffective. They seek social contacts of their own and readily find them among others who are suffering from similar injustices. They may fall in with unscrupulous adults who try to exploit them and who may teach them sex perversions or the practices of stealing, swindling, and vandalism. Children eventually develop a certain amount of social intercourse; whenever it is lacking in home life, it is found elsewhere.

Boys are often picked up by the police for stealing the property of railroads. Frequently when they are brought into court, the parents do not know where they have been and take no interest in how they happened to get there. In such cases the court frequently solves the problem by removing the children from their homes into its own custody and by finding foster homes of much better standing. In cases where the malpractices are not so flagrant, the adjustments may be made within the home by an improvement in its attitudes. An appeal for the welfare and bene- fit of the children usually offers an avenue of approach, although it sometimes fails of full capitalization. The greatest difficulty in such problems often lies in the inability of the parents to see any connection between the immediate factor of poor social adjustment and the larger effects on the attitudes and ideals of the child. Since they do not understand any of the mechanisms of mental activity, only the simplest rudiments of comprehension can be expected. In fact, an emotional appeal on behalf of the children is one of the most effective of controls if anything at all can operate.

The results of poor social adjustments have usually accumu- lated for a long time before the case comes to the attention of anyone. Habits of poor social contacts have been established almost beyond hope of change. The children have become set in their resistance to parental indifference. If no progress can be made within the home on account of the ironclad habits, the worker must expect to build by using the general social and rec- reational facilities of the community, such as community houses, play fields, Boy or Girl Scout troops, or whatever else may be available. It is to the discredit of the larger social units that in those areas where these facilities are most needed, they actually do not exist or are found only on a limited scale. Few homes are owned; no one is able to pay taxes nor clamor for such outlets for their children. Unless the entire community realizes the gen- eral nature of the problem, invests money, and has a genuine interest, the people in these unfortunate areas can do little by themselves. If it could be realized by the adjacent groups that the problems growing out of poor social adjustments eventually come to visit them in personal attacks on their own girls in their own neighborhoods, in robberies, and in the appalling expenses of court and police costs, some progress might be made with the problem. These serious effects cannot be kept away from the more favored neighborhoods by merely ignoring them. The total expense of providing recreation centers, workers trained in recreation, visiting teachers, or social workers for the homes to remove trouble before it is deep-seated would be much less than is now actually paid to arrest and punish those who are the worst products of our neglect. Dividends would also be paid many fold in happier children and parents.

Parents' social adjustment is among the first third of the sixty-six items in distinguishing between behavior and non-behavior groups; it is also in the first third in the correlations of this item with total behavior score. There are social maladjustments among families located in the more fortunate districts of a city, and the problems of behavior maladjustment may sometimes be as bad here as in the poorer areas. The maladjustment factors of children are no respecters of homes, classes, or neighborhoods; they are common factors which affect any kind of area. Their importance should never be underestimated.

61. DISCIPLINE [1]

The methods of discipline used with the child eventually become an important issue in maladjustment. The child responds naturally although negatively to injustices which he has received. He makes certain answers through behavior or through verbal reply in self-defense. These manifestations are interpreted as deliberate breaches of discipline and hence subject to punishment. The entire enterprise of discipline has many ramifications, some of which merit discussion.

Corporal punishment is always a topic that confronts the psychologist or the social worker. Should it be used or not? When? What methods should be used? The answers must necessarily be a question: What effects does it have on the behavior of the child? If it merely makes him more stubborn and resistive, it seems futile. It is usually an admission that the parent does not know what to do and finds a release for his own feelings through its use; but the cause has not been touched.

[1] See page 106.

The use of reason and persuasion, with assistance to insight on the part of the child himself, is much more effective. There are undoubtedly instances in early childhood in which the child cannot understand danger and when physical punishment is the only effective means of securing compliance. But such punishment should be of a limited sort if it is used at all. Many times children balk at doing what is not necessary or essential, and they justly feel a grievance. The use of corporal punishment much after the age of school entrance is a lame substitute for rational persuasion; yet there are many cases in which it is continued through adolescence.

Much corporal punishment that is used is ineffective; but there are instances in which it is effective, as in the case of the maladjusted boy who was sent to a certain private school on account of his behavior. He was very haughty and boasted that nothing could affect him because the school did not use corporal punishment. The constitution and by-laws of the institution were suspended for a brief period to correct this impression, and no further difficulty resulted.

Our concepts of punishment have greatly changed, for it has not been many decades since corporal punishment for adult offenders was widely practiced by the courts of law. It was even recommended and used on dumb animals, as when cows were given court sentences for kicking individuals or trespassing on property. These crude measures are being or have been replaced for both adults and animals in a way which forshadows that children may some day also be left out of the picture of physical punishment. If they do not really comprehend their acts or if they are acting on impulses that are stronger than parental fear or inhibitions, punishment is not effective. It is effective, however, in another sense in the devastating attitudes which attend it. This is true both of physical and of mental punishment. The child becomes sullen, resistive, secretive; he feels that he is treated unjustly. These effects tend to offset, usually much more than offset, the gains from having one's way about an issue by the might of adulthood.

There are two extremes in the matter of childish responsibility for actions. The one attributes adult perspective and comprehension to all acts of children; under this theory children are punished often and severely. The other extreme attributes no responsibility or insight to the children; they are given full reign and unbridled license. In the latter case the children may openly brag that they are not responsible. Both extremes produce children with characteristic attitudes. Responsibility for property and concepts of right and wrong develop slowly and with periods of doubtful mastery. If the parent assumes greater mastery than is present in the child and punishes accordingly, there is a further stunting of growth, just as a pasture is ruined if the feeding is permitted too soon or if too much is taken before the growth is complete.

There are parents who have absolutely no control of children, even of very young children. They seem to have no force of character themselves, and they even proclaim in the presence of their children that they have no control. They marvel when a stranger is able to get their child to sit still or to co-operate in anything. After a few years of such lack of authority the child becomes wild and unruly, possibly much worse than he would be if he had been definitely placed upon his own responsibility for all of his acts. He can act with unbridled license, for he does it under the tacit sanction of the parent.

A well-meaning but ineffective mother once brought two boys, aged eight and ten years, to the clinic for examination and disposal. She had never gained control of them, the culmination occurring the evening before in the complete wrecking of their apartment. They locked her out when she went for groceries; when she returned they made faces at her through the window, broke all the light bulbs, smashed the dishes and furniture, and ran the water over the floor and down to lower floors. The orgy was finally stopped by the police. There followed a long period of re-education and attempt to gain adult control; the outburst was the culmination of years of ineffectiveness in discipline.

Much of the trouble in discipline is the establishment of a long and unreasonable list of restrictions and "dont's." The child actually becomes confused and could not honestly pass a memory test on the complicated code of behavior laid down for him. His simplest solution is to ignore all of it, which is what he often does. The development of responsibility in the child first for simple and later for more important issues is the best assurance of a sane level of discipline. The consequences of prohibited acts should teach their own lesson. The child is warned that the stove will burn; he finds out by trying, and the lesson is effective. Naturally the child must be guarded and warned of more fatal errors, but the self-taught lessons are the most effective. The development of responsibility carries over into other fields, and a habit of responsibility is invaluable, particularly at the time of adolescence.

Children of the same family do not respond to the same methods of training and discipline. It is amusing to note the amazement of parents who have successfully reared two or three children when a younger member of the family does not fit into their plans and they are at a loss as to what to do. There is often much damage to morale and to understanding between parent and child before the adults acknowledge defeat and appeal for outside aid.

In the case of behavior children the adjustment agency, which usually begins to work when conditions are at their worst, is expected to make a sudden and complete transformation. The really constructive work on discipline must be done through parental and adult education; problems must be prevented rather than remedied. Serious cases of bad discipline are the effects of treatment, but later the effects become causes of further misunderstandings and maladjustments. Discipline should be an attitude and a state of mind rather than the enforcement by physical or mental suasion of a code which is beyond the comprehension and ability of the child to follow or of the parents to administer.

62. Attitude Toward Child [1]

The parents' attitude (2) toward the child is a legitimate factor to incorporate in a series of motivations for behavior adjustment or maladjustment. It is fifteenth among the sixty-six items in distinguishing between behavior and non-behavior groups and is third in importance of correlation with seriousness of maladjustments among behavior children. The more difficult the problem, the more undesirable is the attitude. This may be the case as a logical outcome; the child is rejected on account of his behavior record. It is difficult to know whether behavior record or parent attitude came first, but their interplay upon each other finally brings about a sad state of affairs.

Some children are unwanted by their parents. The parents may try to forget these deeper feelings after the child is born, but they are not always so successful as they believe. Little ways of neglecting the child are practiced, or the parents are impatient where tolerance and patience are demanded. Sooner or later the child takes on a vague feeling of coldness or unresponsiveness; he becomes rebellious, and in turn he is treated with further indifference or with unreasonable punishment and restriction. There is the same vicious circle here as in other factors of maladjustment, with interlocking of cause and effect.

There are countless ways in which the attitude toward the child becomes distorted. If there is a dislike or antipathy between parents, his very physical resemblance to one or the other parent is a cause of trouble. Or he may resemble some renegade member of one family who is distasteful to everyone. He may have objectionable habits or mannerisms which he has either inherited or acquired by example. Such ways, which the parents hated and despised in their own childish experiences, unwittingly exercise their subtle effects on the child. The effects may even subconsciously be felt by the parents themselves, or they may exist as conscious though vague impressions.

Throughout all of the periods of childhood there are incidents

1 See page 107.

which may lead to rejection or partial rejection of children. In babyhood there are many cares, sacrifices, and trials which demand personal sacrifice. At the time of early schooling if the child does not succeed or lead the class, his mental ability may be doubted. Later at adolescence he is seen to undergo periods of doubt and indecision which do not harmonize with the more settled habits and attitudes of his parents. Finally he should be independent and able to support himself although there may be no work to be found. All these factors may have a cumulative dubious effect on his parents' attitudes toward him from year to year.

Whenever these phenomena operate to a greater or less extent, the child not only feels resistant to his parents, but he also worries and is submerged in feelings of insecurity. He goes about in a mentally confused state and shows pathological symptoms, such as lying, stealing, truancy, and cruelty to animals or children. He really does not always know that he does these things; in fact, he may often be honestly surprised if he is discovered going through the teacher's desk for money. His professed innocence is seldom believed by anyone. After such behavior he is further rejected and more downcast in his outlook.

In bringing about more desirable attitudes, it is necessary to analyze and understand the fundamental causes of poor attitudes. These attitudes can sometimes be changed for the better when their true nature is really understood. Another constructive measure is to look for the more pleasing and desirable traits in children instead of magnifying their undesirable ones. The psychologist may discover favorable qualities in his examination and personal interview. Many times parents are seen to shrink mentally and almost physically with self-reproach when some worker praises their children beyond what they would ever dream of doing or ever actually do.

In no other situation is it so important to see the constructive and better side of children as in the development of desirable attitudes toward them. In satisfactory parental adjustment there is a happy reflection of one's own efforts; in unsatisfactory, there is but wretched mockery of oneself and one's efforts at child care and training. If there is any place in which the psychology of childhood needs to be understood it is in building wholesome attitudes toward children. Yet parents are left after their own education, even after university training, with no knowledge of these matters. They are guided by their own "intuitions"; they learn by bitter experience and by the sad fate of their children. The investments which education ought to make in training for parenthood, as a required course or as an elective, would be many times repaid by the gratitude which parents would feel in being successful with their children.

63. Child's Attitude Toward Home [1]

In the last twenty-five items, 38 through 62 inclusive, many factors have been presented which affect the child. They are factors and situations which arise out of the home and over which he has little control. Yet he is affected by all of them, by some items more than by others. Through all of them he develops certain attitudes, antipathies, likes, pleasures, and displeasures. In this section his attitudes toward home through all these influences is considered.

In his early years the child does not feel or comprehend many subtle acts against him, but he is conscious of the more obvious slights or deprivations. He senses such situations as a home characterized by flurry and confusion and responds in like manner, but he may not detect downright dishonesty, lying, or a poor moral code. He lives in terms of specific pleasures and displeasures, mostly concerned with his own personal comfort or discomfort. However, his subconscious mind may be stored with certain impressions, or even the conscious mind itself may retain memories which are recalled later with new meanings and interpretations.

His attitudes toward the home are noticeable whenever he is classified as a behavior problem. They rank ninth among the

[1] See page 109.

sixty-six items differentiating between the behavior and non-behavior groups, whereas the parents' attitude toward him ranks fifteenth. Within the behavior group Table XIII (page 355) shows that this item ranks tenth in the positive correlation with the total score, whereas the parents' attitude ranks higher, at third place. These facts may be interpreted to mean that the children who are the worst by the entire scale are judged to be slightly worse by their parents than the children judge their homes, as indicated by their attitudes toward them.

Children do not always disclose their real feelings or attitudes toward their homes. They are young and small, and the home and adults awe them so that they dare not voice their real feelings. But if there are unreasonable restraint and a score of mal-practices, they store up their feelings as effectively as parents; they remain quiet, play away from home, become secretive, or do anything which is a relief from the home and its tensions. Such children badly need a friend at court, someone to make tangible their confused and buried desires.

Parents are often unconscious of these hidden attitudes and without knowing it blunder along through many situations which hurt the feelings of their children. In diagnosing a case the question of how the children really regard their parents or feel toward them brings merely a puzzled and worried parental response. It is a very delicate assignment for the parent to try to find out how his children feel about him; often he cannot find out, except that he discovers hidden barriers which he did not know existed. A vivid experience is recalled in which a foster boy was taken tentatively for adoption. At one time he, became unmanageable, and his foster parents removed him for safety to the detention home. He would never return to them and proclaimed his hatred loudly for having clothes given him with the proviso that he must be good and want to stay if he was to keep them. It finally took a personal interview to convince his well-meaning foster parents that he was in earnest. Later they found it desirable to move on account of the gossip which he had spread about them in the neighborhood. If one is really to know children and their attitudes, he may find them out in the confidences which come to light regarding the recreation for the family (Item 59).

When their attitudes become undesirable on account of mal-treatment at home, children frequently rebel at a later time, that is, when they are mature enough to realize that advantage was taken of them on account of their youth and inexperience. This condition suggests the importance of always treating children on a fair and square basis for long-time results. Whenever they are betrayed, their confidence in human nature is destroyed; then the effects are particularly bad because the betrayal comes from within their own home. Eventually children may discover that being resistive and developing poor social and personal attributes agitates their parents. These attitudes then become a source of revengeful satisfaction to the children. After affairs reach such a stage, the attitude of the child toward his home becomes a real factor in the motivation for malbehavior. As is often the case with other causes, if this condition is discovered late in childhood or in adolescence, it is difficult to do anything about it. A change of home status or a new home environment may be the only solution.

Some children are endowed with a vivid imagination and be-lieve they are maltreated when there is really no justification for their belief. Such feelings cannot be dismissed as groundless; parents frequently underestimate their significance. It would be well for adults to realize that, for practical purposes, within the child these unjustifiable charges of maltreatment may pass for true. It is advisable to avoid any grounds for suspicion of poor treatment as well as the actual practice of maltreatment.

Parents commonly make the error of believing that children are eventually going to be grateful to them for all the physical comforts and provisions of a home, such as good food, a warm shelter, and protection. But children almost universally take these items for granted. They really judge their home by the attitudes which have been shown to them in word and deed. If a parent has liberally provided all the physical comforts but has been harsh and unsympathetic, he is considered a failure by his children. If the child feels that he has been treated with kindness, sympathy, and understanding, he happily forgives poverty and physical misfortunes. These attitudes cannot be bought for money, nor are they respecters of money, classes, or persons. It is more of an accomplishment to rear children happily in a hovel than to ignore them in a palace; the pathos of the situation lies in the fact that ignoring, maltreating, and poverty too frequently go together.

Children's attitudes toward home can sometimes be improved by pointing out the good qualities of their parents. Explaining some of the simpler problems of adult life and reiterating certain ideas which the parents are trying to inculcate, when undertaken by the worker, often do much more good than the parents' own efforts. There is no one royal road to the diagnosis of attitudes. Even the adjustment worker may not know how to find the way; at least attitudes do often become evident after a short period of acquaintance and confidence. While they are difficult to detect, the effort to understand them is well worth while on behalf of both child and parents.

64. School Attendance [1]

Poor attendance at school is frequently symptomatic of maladjustment in school. It also leads to disrespect for any kind of law or authority, since school attendance is required by statute. Moreover, it leads to bad associations and to companions who take the truant down the road to delinquency. Poor attendance is a result and finally a cause of maladjustment. There are several of its phases which merit consideration.

When poor school attendance is mentioned, children twelve years of age or older usually come to mind. Adolescents are more apt to be truants than are young children, but there are some children not more than six or seven years old who begin the practice at this early age. They play away from home and appear to be attending until the other children return from school; or

[1] See page 110.

they claim illness and stay out on the slightest provocation. They persuade their parents to keep them out for various reasons, such as helping take care of the baby or going shopping with them. An examination of the attendance records of some adolescent truants showed that many of them had records for irregular attendance from early childhood. Even a slight amount of absence in the early years is probably symptomatic of the initial stages of truancy. When these young cases are studied intensively by means of this behavior scale, many factors of maladjustment are often discovered.

The various reasons why parents keep children out of school are of interest in behavior diagnosis. With young children they feel that absence can easily be made up and hence is of little consequence; although this is really contrary to fact in a modern, busy school program. They may be expressing hidden resentment over their own failure to complete certain grades in school themselves, and they may feel a need and desire to punish someone. There are cases in which the parents have no such feelings but must have the children help in the home on account of illness or assist with the earning of money wherever they can. The attitudes and feelings of parents should be thoroughly understood in a study of the school attendance of their children.

Poor attendance may be a direct result of the experiences of the child in school or of its imagined effects, which are often equally bad. Schools are becoming aware of the effects of school work that is too hard or too easy for the mental status of children. Bright pupils have sometimes been considered truant when they have stayed out to read in libraries books which were more interesting than their required assignments. A recent case of this kind in the juvenile court had some awkward yet comical aspects.

The children who are slightly below average in intelligence are more apt to be truant. The school program is a little too difficult for them; they do it poorly, repeat many grades, receive poor marks, and under such circumstances can hardly be expected to be happy and enthusiastic about school. Many of the modern school systems of large cities are attempting to adjust courses of study and methods of instruction to meet the various mental levels so as to secure greater interest and better attendance by mentally slow children. There remains much to be done to make this type of adjustment better understood and really effective. It is true that, unless these adjustments are made, schools are directly or indirectly responsible for loss of interest and for truancy. Schools generally offer aid and inspiration for the great majority of pupils, but they should not hesitate to go to any limit to meet the needs of the duller children. One of the reasons for the undesirable attitude of many slow children is that each teacher sees these children as members of her particular class for one or two semesters and does what she can for them while they are with her, but no one else knows these children very well and often no one becomes aware of their problems with respect to the whole school program from beginning to end.

Whenever truancy begins, children find companions who sympathize with them. They get much comfort and understanding from one another and perhaps form a gang against their homes and school. If their record at school has been poor and they have no particular goal in school, it is easy to lose interest and stay away. Often a change to a school where their records are unknown or where trade, technical, or vocational education is offered may arouse interest again. An adjustment clinic should provide for examinations in vocational aptitude, should know the facilities which various schools offer, and should have some authority to recommend and effect transfers.

Good habits of school attendance should carry over into habits in industry; poor habits probably carry over also. If the latter are not immediately effective, they are apt to become so after the novelty of a job begins to wear off. The idle boasts of the school truant that school habits are of no value and that he can make good in industry in spite of them present a futile and pathetic picture. Industry and business automatically set a high standard at the level of the best of their workers; those with less ability or those who are not in regular attendance soon fall by the wayside.

Workers should always discount the tales of woe which truants relate about school. Many of them are not true; but school people for their part must face these alleged situations as well as maintain their own beliefs and well-intended practices.

65. SCHOLARSHIP [1]

There is an old adage that "nothing succeeds like success," which may have its converse, also true, that "nothing fails like failure." Regardless of the merits of school work for any pupil, the one with good marks feels that he is a success while the one with poor marks considers himself a failure. Since schools give a great range of marks from excellent to failure, there are some results of scholarship which should be considered.

The child who receives splendid marks throughout his school experience feels that he receives a just reward for his efforts. He faces the future with confidence. If he actually earns all these marks, he has had constructive training; but if he has been able to get them with a minimum of effort on account of his superior mental ability, he may have acquired a false sense of superiority. Later, when he meets real competition in some profession where there are minds equally brilliant and equally endowed with energy and ambition, the competition takes on a more serious and possibly tragic nature. He encounters mental strife and confusion—the result of a long-time belief that little effort and energy are required to succeed in school or in business. The often-expressed belief that college students are poor workers and unfitted for constant application to stern duty may have many elements of truth in it. In order to be effective, standards of scholarship should be gauged according to the individual mental powers of the pupils, and those standards should be reasonably well attained. The abuses in the present handling of superior and mentally gifted children need correction.

The mentally slow become the victims of poor marks because they are often judged by the standard set for the average or the

[1] See page 111.

mentally superior. They at least have the advantage of having to put forth real effort to meet these standards; but they cannot do the impossible, they cannot perform beyond their mental maturity, and the strain of trying to keep up the pace is too much for them. They feel the injustice of being required to work at a maximum and then receiving only mediocre marks as their reward. The schools by tradition have set a uniform standard; those pupils who rank below and above that standard suffer in actual achievement as well as in habits of work, in general attitudes, and in belief in themselves. But again it must be said to the credit of the most modern school systems that they are making adjustments to this problem as the importance of the range of differences is being realized.

There is a fundamental question as to whether or not a mentally slow child should be rewarded with excellent marks, representing his satisfactory mastery of a minimum standard, or should be made aware of his limitations with respect to the entire range of mental differences. By giving a bright pupil good marks, it may be that we give him a false impression of his ability; by giving him a mark for achievement which is low for him though above the general standard, we may establish in him at the same time a feeling of inferiority. The answer hinges on whether or not all adults compete on a general standard or whether they compete within classes. While there are general competitions common to all classes, the real competition seems to be within groups. For example, an attorney is successful or not with respect to all other attorneys and not with respect to laborers, carpenters, or motormen. The issue is so general and far-reaching that it cannot be conclusively proved or disproved at this point.

Children are always receiving marks, some poor and some good, which leave their impressions on the recipients. The child who always gets poor marks typically grows indifferent, discouraged, and disgusted with school. If he is to be trained in habits of success on even a limited scale, there must be used for him some system of marks which gives recognition to his efforts and achievement. In order to safeguard the high standards needed for graduation from high school with college entrance requirements, a standard examination should be offered in which the limited student may find where he stands with respect to the better group.

From 5 to 10 per cent of all children fail or repeat grades each year, with heavy failures in the first grade and in the fourth and fifth grades. In some systems the failures reach a greater number. These failing pupils frequently recognize the justice of their records, but some do not. These become a minority who are rebellious toward education. Their parents and others of their family share their feelings. The good will for education suffers some setbacks. It is not suggested that school standards be lowered so that every pupil shall pass with good marks, but rather that the marks shall be explained so that children and parents may be satisfied.

The child who is a failure in school finds it easy to become a failure at home, in play, or in any other life activity. Poor scholarship may become a major cause of general maladjustment, along with other causes. Behavior children are poorer in scholarship than non-behavior children, and scholarship ranks tenth among the sixty-six items in differences between the two groups. While to a certain extent poor scholarship is merely the result of many factors, it soon becomes a cause and hence is listed among the incentives to behavior maladjustment.

66. Child's Attitude toward School [1]

In many of the behavior problems studied it was found that the children's attitudes toward school were bad. This statement does not really explain anything new, for the experimental children were selected chiefly on account of their poor school behavior. The members of the control group were chosen because they were model in their school behavior. As a result, this item stood second among the sixty-six factors in distinguishing between behavior and non-behavior groups. There is a tendency to put a certain

[1] See page 113.

general charge of "badness" against the behavior group, since the poorest and the best in the total score of the behavior group make nearly the same scores on this item. The resulting correlation is .193 with a total score, ranking it fifty-ninth among the sixty-six items.

There are behavior problems arising out of the home situation, out of play, and out of neighborhood contacts; but few of these cases were reported for special study, since teachers originated most of the nominations. Many of the nonschool cases would undoubtedly be school problems, but some might not be; in fact, the school sometimes acts as a safe haven from troubles elsewhere.

The causes of poor attitudes toward school are many. If a pupil has failed for several semesters or if there has been a long series of school marks below average, little real enthusiasm for school may be expected. If he has sought ways of entertaining himself in school instead of doing tasks which were beyond him, the ill will of the teacher is gained. The evils of this practice were suggested in the preceding section on scholarship. Pupils of slow mental ability, as a group, tend to suffer from a poor standard of scholarship, with its resulting low marks. Maintenance of a good morale toward school by a better motivated system of marking is one of the most urgent problems of school philosophy and administration.

The modern city school offers an enriched program of studies which widens the appeal of education beyond what was offered a few years ago. In the traditional curriculum the three R's were stressed, mostly by textbook problem and oral recitation methods The teacher dominated the situation, and there was little opportunity for the pupil's self-expression. The revised methods for the traditional as well as the later subjects require much more responsibility and self-reliance from the pupils. A pupil with no interest in school or one with no sense of responsibility in a general way finds it difficult to adjust himself to these conditions. He must study and plan of his own accord, or his failures quickly become apparent. Since life requires ability to make adjustments the modern philosophy of education places this responsibility upon the child at an earlier age than formerly.

The newer subjects of the curriculum have introduced a much greater variety of social situations for children to meet. The program of the school auditorium is designed for this very purpose. Unstable and behavior children cannot readily make these vital adjustments. They do not get along with others; they do not know how to co-operate; and in these situations, which are similar to adult problems, they fail to become adjusted. The programs of the gymnasium and the playground furnish further examples of the modern school's approach to education. From the standpoint of the school it might be much more simple to return to the former procedures and avoid some of its present troubles about maladjusted children, but it is a more constructive step to face the problems of social adjustment and find ways of solving them.

The maladjusted child in school often feels that the school is discriminating against him. He tells a plausible story to anyone who will listen; often his parents fully agree with him. As a result the family physician, the juvenile judge, the probation officer, the social worker, and the psychiatrist tend to have a badly distorted picture of all school procedure from the biased reports of a small minority of the maladjusted. There is probably some discrimination against these children in school; no one can deny it. It is too much to expect from human nature that there will be no personal feelings about behavior children. But the authors have seen many instances in which the problem case has been given a new start in a strange school, only to become entangled with the same kind of trouble in a short time. There is a constant interchange of such cases among public schools or among public, private, and parochial schools, with substantially the same results in most instances. The schools generally make an honest attempt to adjust all children, since failure to adjust them is somewhat of a reflection on the school itself. Beyond certain reasonable limits, however, it is desirable to effect a transfer when whole classes become disrupted by one offender.

But whatever the cause, it is lamentable when children become maladjusted in school. It means something akin to failure in other situations outside of school itself. The school is the place where children are to be studied and understood. If that function cannot be performed satisfactorily, the avenues of child growth are closed with impassable detours. Education should be the source of inspiration, growth, and splendid accomplishment; but if children cannot meet their tasks at this level, as measured by their poor attitudes, it is a sad commentary on some forces in human nature as seen in maladjusted children. In facing this problem the schools cannot give all the privileges to the maladjusted children, nor can they sacrifice their scholarship standards merely to make children feel happy and successful. At best the schools go more than halfway in solving the problems of malbehavior, but the special adjustment worker and individual diagnostic and remedial programs are needed. The present manual offers this type of service to education and to social work.

BIBLIOGRAPHY

1. BAKER, HARRY J.—*Telling What I Do*. Bloomington, Ill.: Public School Publishing Co., 1930. 4 pp.
2. Fitz-Simons, Marian J.—*Some Parent-Child Relationships*. New York: Bureau of Publications, Columbia University, 1935. 162 pp.

PART IV

CASE STUDIES, STATISTICAL EVALUATIONS, AND CONCLUSIONS

CHAPTER XI

ILLUSTRATIVE CASE STUDIES

Throughout the previous chapters, as well as in Chapters XII and XIII, attempts have been made to show that the Detroit Scale of Behavior Factors differentiates or distinguishes between children who are behavior problems and those who are not. The various steps or gradations between behavior and non-behavior cases can be distinguished in terms of the total score on the scale.

Seven case studies are presented in this chapter to verify the conclusions that have been presented in the earlier chapters. One case from each of the seven letter ratings is presented. These cases have either been developed and studied by regular members of the Detroit clinic staff or by those who have had experience and training equivalent to the standard of the Detroit clinic.

Case 1—Behavior Rating A

S. A., a boy twelve years of age, was studied as a model case of good behavior to discover what factors were favorable or unfavorable. He earned a score of 314 out of 330 points, with a rating of A. The summary of his 66 behavior factors is as follows:

Summary of Factors

CATEGORY	NUMBER	WEIGHTED SCORE
Very poor	0	0
Poor	0	0
Fair	3	9
Good	10	40
Very good	53	265
	66	314

It will be noted that there are no factors rated very poor or poor and only three that are fair. These three are children's diseases, Item 3; home duties, Item 18; and vocational interests, Item 36. S. A. comes from an excellent family, in which his training has been of the highest character. His score of 314 points verifies the behavior scale since he presents almost ideal factors of behavior.

CASE 2—BEHAVIOR RATING B

G. M. made a score of 294 points, with a rating of B. She was a fourteen-year-old girl and was selected as a model child in terms of behavior. The summary of her behavior factors is as follows:

SUMMARY OF FACTORS

CATEGORY	NUMBER	WEIGHTED SCORE
Very poor	0	0
Poor	2	4
Fair	7	21
Good	16	64
Very good	41	205
	66	294

Her poor items were No. 32, pity, sympathy, enthusiasm, etc., in which she is known to be rather extreme, for example, becoming nearly hysterical at some pitiful sight or experience; and Item 52, on the number of children in the family, in which she is next to the youngest of eight children and somewhat inclined to be spoiled and petted by the older members of the family. The entire range of items and general impression coincide closely in showing that she is quite a model child from the standpoint of behavior.

CASE 3—BEHAVIOR RATING C+

M. I. had a behavior score of 275 points, with a rating of C+. She was a thirteen-year-old girl and was selected as a nonbehavior case. The summary of her behavior factors is as follows:

SUMMARY OF FACTORS

CATEGORY	NUMBER	WEIGHTED SCORE
Very poor	2	2
Poor	3	6
Fair	9	27
Good	20	80
Very good	32	160
	66	275

She was an extremely large girl for her age, with an adult height of 5 feet 4 inches and a weight of 101 pounds. To the best of our knowledge there was no evidence that this extreme size was a serious factor in any kind of maladjustment. Her other very poor item was No. 52; she is an only child. However, Item 26 showed that she had many friends and was well adjusted among them.

Of the items that were rated poor, Item 1, on early health, showed that she had been ill a great deal when very young. Item 11, on motor control and co-ordination, showed that she was very much advanced, which corresponded closely to her size as described in Item 10. As a small child she had had several convulsions and seizures, but there were no serious lasting effects.

She was selected as a non-behavior case, for it is evident that there are but few factors not distinctly favorable.

CASE 4—BEHAVIOR RATING C

M. S., a boy fourteen years of age, who was selected as a behavior problem, was in a high type of school and in an excellent neighborhood. He had a behavior score of 246, with a rating of C. The summary of his items is as follows:

SUMMARY OF FACTORS

CATEGORY	NUMBER	WEIGHTED SCORE
Very poor	4	4
Poor	9	18
Fair	10	30
Good	21	84
Very good	22	110
	66	246

One very poor item was nervousness, Item 13; he was continually shifting and moving about at his school desk with some jerking of his head. Neurological and physical examinations were recommended to the parents. Home duties, Item 18, showed that he had no regular assignments and comparatively little sense of responsibility in these matters; Item 27 disclosed an introvert type of child, with very few friends; Item 52 showed an only child, with the mother taking too much interest in his petty ailments and his social adjustments. It was recommended that he be allowed more leeway in making social contacts.

The items which were rated 2, or poor, are as follows: speech defect, pity and sympathy, initiative and ambition, general behavior, mother's intelligence, home attitude toward child, scholarship, and child's attitude toward school.

The case of M. S. illustrates very well the problems of children who are considered as seriously maladjusted cases in good localities. In terms of the total behavior situation throughout a metropolitan area, these problems seem to be no more than those of the average child. At least some of the cases which follow are by comparison much poorer in behavior.

Case 5—Behavior Rating C—

D. M., considered as a behavior case, was a fifteen-year-old boy, with a score of 218. The distribution of his items is as follows:

SUMMARY OF FACTORS

CATEGORY	NUMBER	WEIGHTED SCORE
Very poor	5	5
Poor	13	26
Fair	22	66
Good	9	36
Very good	17	85
	66	218

He was considered as an extreme behavior case in his locality, which was somewhat above the average. The five very poor items were as follows: Early health, Item 1, seems to have had a considerable influence on his problem, as his father particularly was very indulgent to him on account of his health. Item 29, on anger and rage, shows that he was inclined to yield to fits of anger easily and was frequently picked on by other children. Item 36, vocational interests, seems to be very negative on account of his health, poor scholastic record, and too much parental indulgence. Item 48 shows that the father is an unskilled laborer, doing truck driving and janitorial jobs, with some possible feelings of inferiority about it. As to Item 65, D. M.'s record was consistently poor, with D's and E's, which reflect in part his poor vocational interests.

The items rated poor are as follows: Degree of vision defect, Item 7—he always had very poor vision in one eye, but the other eye was approximately normal. His father was rather opposed to making any adjustments to improve his vision. Item 5, accidents—he was hit by an automobile, with minor injuries, and two years before he had broken his nose in a bicycle accident. Item 15—he was very unattractive in appearance because of his crossed eyes. Items 16 and 17—his early care and present care were poor. Items 19 and 20—he ate meals at irregular times, hurried his eating, and was rather fussy and disagreeable about what he ate. Item 33 showed an I. Q. of 76 on the Stanford-Binet Test, which explains some of his difficulty in making adjustments to regular grade standards. Item 35, initiative and ambition, showed him not very ambitious. Items 40 and 41, education of both parents, showed that they had completed only two or three grades and in European countries. Item 61—his discipline was inconsistent and modified by pity on account of his physical health. Item 66, his attitude toward the school—in this respect he was poor because the regular school work was too difficult for him. The parents refused to place him in any type of special class.

It seems that in D. M.'s case, in the next two or three years of school, vocational and social adjustments would be critical factors in determining whether he would make a successful final adjustment or whether this combination of factors would tend to carry him downhill.

Case 6—Behavior Rating D

A. P., fifteen years of age, rated D. He had a score of 201 points and was enrolled in a school for behavior problems. He was transferred to this school on account of the complete failure in his scholastic duties, truancy, and tardiness. The summary of his sixty-six factors is as follows:

Summary of Factors

CATEGORY	NUMBER	WEIGHTED SCORE
Very poor	9	9
Poor	11	22
Fair	23	69
Good	14	56
Very good	9	45
	66	201

The very poor items are as follows: Item 21, time of sleeping—he stayed out until 12 o'clock or later. Item 25, later recreational facilities—he sometimes played on a recreation field, but more often was observing adult sporting events or loafing around beer gardens. Item 26—his playmates and companions were mostly older boys, some of whom had been in detention homes. Item 27—he stole coats and other articles of clothing. Item 28, personality type—he wished he were three or four years older to do just as he pleased, and he desired much attention. Item 29—he had no control over his feelings of anger or revenge and resented any correction which the teachers or parents tried to give. Item 36, vocational interests—he wished to be a big business man or physician, objectives obviously quite beyond his capacities. Item 37, general behavior—he seemed to enjoy stealing and being a leader of other boys. Item 61—he was brought up under very strict supervision until a short time previously, when his father had died. His mother was able to do nothing with him afterward.

The eleven poor items were as follows: No. 18, home duties; No. 19, conditions of eating; No. 22, sleeping conditions; No. 30, fear, dread, anxiety, etc.; No. 33, intelligence; No. 34, interests or hobbies; No. 39, mother's intelligence; No. 40, father's education; No. 41, mother's education; No. 49, economic status; and No. 51, other adults in home.

It is evident that the behavior scale has discovered a large number of factors which are very unfavorable to his best social and personality development. Upon the basis of these various items and the record of delinquency which he had already established, it seems evident that further trouble must follow unless conditions can be radically changed for the better.

Case 7—Behavior Rating E

I. J. was a boy fifteen years of age, with a score of 190 points on the behavior scale. He was enrolled in a school for behavior-problem children after having been transferred from a junior high school on account of truancy and disobedience. He was repeating his grade for the third term. The summary of his results is as follows:

Summary of Factors

CATEGORY	NUMBER	WEIGHTED SCORE
Very poor	11	11
Poor	13	26
Fair	25	75
Good	7	28
Very good	10	50
	66	190

He has eleven items which are rated very poor as follows: No. 18, home duties—he had no home duties. No. 27, social type—he was inclined to be antisocial and worldly wise. No. 28, personality type—he had a low emotional tone. No. 29—he was inclined to give way to fits of anger. No. 35—he had no initiative and ambition, he did not want to work, and he claimed he could feed himself by stealing food. No. 36—he had no vocational interests except that he wished to loaf around a brewery. No. 37, general behavior—he was defiant and cowardly and inclined to fight, steal, and lie. No. 40—his father was illiterate in both Polish and English. No. 52—he is the youngest of a family of six children. No. 64—his attendance at school was very poor; he went to shows or loafed around the railroad tracks when he was not in school. No. 66—his attitude toward school had always been resistant; he believed that he was being discriminated against on account of his continued truancy.

His thirteen items which are marked poor are as follows: No. 6, slight speech defect; No. 15, unfavorable appearance; No. 23, too much emphasis on dreams; No. 25, merely played in the streets; No. 32, pitied animals but not people; No. 34, very poor interests or hobbies; No. 41, mother partly literate in Polish; No. 45, mother's health poor; No. 48, occupation that of mill-wright, but unemployed; No. 56, general home atmosphere; No. 61, discipline divided, father too strict, mother too easy; No. 62, parents believed he was going to be bad; No. 63, inclined to be indulged by his mother and attached very closely to her.

His case is one of the worst which have been studied at the school for behavior problems. Many of his factors have become firmly established as to their undesirable effects. It would take a great amount of time and effort to bring about desirable changes in him.

Conclusion

These seven cases illustrate differences in children's behavior and in the factors which motivate them. The latter cases obviously have many more undesirable factors than do the ideal behavior cases which were presented first.

For those cases that were enrolled in behavior schools social workers attempted to remedy and improve these conditions according to the methods and suggestions offered in Part III, "Interpretation of the Sixty-six Factors."

Although these latter cases seem to be about as bad as can be imagined, it is noted that their score is slightly better than a rating of 3 for all items. Although they are extreme cases, theoretically one could find children with ratings as poor as 66 points, that is, with a rating of 1 for each factor. In other words, the extremely bad cases that are actually known are still about three times as good as the theoretically worst child that could be imagined. In general, the rank and file of average and model children closely approximate the maximum or optimum conditions of society.

In the next two chapters the statistical evaluation of the Detroit Scale for the diagnosis of behavior problems will be presented.

CHAPTER XII

THE VALIDATION OF THE BEHAVIOR SCALE

THE Detroit Scale of Behavior may possibly find its greatest usefulness in the informal and subjective evaluations of behavior which the various items afford. Its uses in this field are analogous to the opinions and impressions of the trained psychologist in observing the general reactions of a subject to a mental examination. Such impressions may be quite aside from the actual mental age or intelligence quotient. However in the fields of both psychology and behavior interpretation the objective score affords values which should not be discounted or overlooked. Considerable information has been gathered as to the statistical objectivity of the Detroit Scale, which will be presented in this chapter.

DISTRIBUTION OF SCORES ON NON-BEHAVIOR AND BEHAVIOR GROUPS

In Table VIII (p. 345) are the distributions of total scores for three groups of children. The non-behavior group and behavior group I were interviewed and studied by social workers and teachers who were enrolled in a course on the psychology of behavior offered in a Detroit university by one of the authors in four consecutive school years. The general psychology of behavior was discussed and the detailed psychological possibilities of the sixty-six items were considered. Each member selected at least one non-behavior case and one behavior problem for intensive study. The second behavior group, which was studied by a trained psychologist, consists of pupils enrolled in the ungraded school for behavior-problem cases. The selection of cases in the training courses was required at a comparatively early date, before much specific information as to the nature of the Behavior Scale was divulged. Thus the selections could be made chiefly on the basis of the usual external behavior symptoms that are ordinarily observed by teachers and parents.

An inspection of the distribution of scores and the medians of the three groups discloses some striking differences. The statistical significance of the differences between the medians will be presented in the next section. The median for the non-behavior group is 285 points, for the behavior group I, 220 points, and for the behavior group II, 205 points. In the non-behavior group there are two cases below the medians of the behavior groups and several others just above those medians. All of these cases were supposed to be rather normal children but were found to exhibit a surprisingly large number of factors which might eventually predispose them toward maladjustment. There are three cases in the behavior group I above the median for the non-behavior group and several near that median. These cases were known to be the "worst" which could be found in certain of the better neighborhoods, and by comparison with a high local standard they seemed relatively bad. Others of these high-score cases probably represented a strong personal bias of a teacher or worker to a few specific symptoms which were supposed to be sure indications of impending "confirmed criminal tendencies." Actual analysis failed to disclose many serious causes in these cases. The behavior group II, which had been segregated, is undoubtedly of a more serious type than the behavior group I, which represented individual cases of maladjustment enrolled in the regular grades, although these two groups seem to have much in common in behavior characteristics.

SIGNIFICANCES OF THE DIFFERENCES BETWEEN GROUPS

An inspection of Table VIII shows that the non-behavior group, as a group, was much different from the behavior group I, which was matched with it, and that the second behavior group scored lower than the larger behavior group I from the regular grades. The question of immediate interest is whether these differences between groups are *real* differences or differences arising merely from chance. This question may be answered by the application of the appropriate formula for the standard error, from Garrett (1), page 129, for calculating the reliability of an obtained difference between two averages, as follows:

$$\sigma \text{ (difference)} = \sqrt{\frac{\sigma^2 \text{ (av. 1)}}{N_1} + \frac{\sigma^2 \text{ (av. 2)}}{N_2}}^{1}$$

If the obtained difference is equal only to the standard error of the difference, there would be eighty-four chances in one hundred that the difference would occur again in two entirely new groups of cases. If the difference is twice as great as the obtained difference, the chances rise to ninety-eight in one hundred; and when it is three times as great it rises to practically one hundred per cent. For the distributions of cases of Table VIII these differences are as follows:

For the non-behavior group versus the behavior group I, the difference is 23.3 times the standard error.
For the non-behavior group versus the behavior group II, the difference is 29.0 times the standard error.
For the behavior group I versus the behavior group II, the difference is 4.9 times the standard error.

It is of interest to report that, when only sixty-seven pairs of cases were at one time available in the non-behavior group and behavior group I, the difference was 18 times the standard error; the median for the non-behavior group remains unchanged and the median for the behavior group has risen only three points in score after tripling the number of cases. There is a real difference between the two behavior groups in Table VIII although the two distributions tend to overlap to a certain extent. It is evident therefore from these measures of probability that the Detroit

---

[1] σ, or standard deviation, is the square root of the average of the squares of the deviations of the scores from the averages of the scores.

TABLE VIII. DISTRIBUTION OF SCORES FOR BEHAVIOR AND
NON-BEHAVIOR GROUPS

SCORE	NON-BEHAVIOR PROBLEM GROUPS	BEHAVIOR-PROBLEM GROUPS	
		GROUP I	GROUP II
321–325	8		
316–320	7		
311–315	8		
306–310	9		
301–305	12	1	
296–300	12	2	
291–295	18		
286–290	15		
281–285	27	3	
276–280	16	2	
271–275	14		
266–270	13	5	
261–265	2	1	
256–260	4	4	
251–255	4	5	
246–250	1	9	
241–245	1	11	
236–240	2	8	1
231–235	2	13	1
226–230	2	13	1
221–225	2	16	4
216–220		15	3
211–215		11	8
206–210		13	7
201–205		11	3
196–200		11	4
191–195		5	9
186–190	1	11	3
181–185	1	6	4
176–180		2	
171–175		1	1
166–170		1	1
161–165		3	
156–160		3	
151–155			
146–150			
141–145		1	
136–140			
131–135		1	
126–130			
121–125		1	
Totals	181	189	50
Medians	285	220	205

Scale of Behavior makes decisive distinctions between groups of behavior and non-behavior cases.

MEASURES OF RELIABILITY

There is only one form available for the Detroit Scale of Behavior factors, so that the customary correlation between alternate forms cannot be computed. However, the reliability coefficient has been found for the split halves of the odd-numbered versus the even-numbered items. The Spearman-Brown correction formula has been applied to determine the reliability for the entire scale. The results appear in Table IX.

TABLE IX. CORRELATIONS OF SPLIT HALVES OF BEHAVIOR SCALE

GROUP	NUMBER OF CASES	PEARSON	SPEARMAN-BROWN CORRECTION
Behavior group I.............	189	.792	.884
Non-behavior group...........	181	.821	.902
Both groups combined.........	370	.930	.964

These correlations disclose a very satisfactory reliability of the scale, with the combined groups producing the best correlation on account of the great range of dispersion of scores. It is of interest to note that the control group (non-behavior) produces a slightly better reliability than the behavior group, which would verify the hypothesis that their elements of adjustment might be expected to be more uniform and consistent than the elements of the maladjusted ones.

Fifty cases were selected as a random sampling and rescored by one person. Three of the cases had variations of less than five points from the previous scoring, and the remainder were identical. It would be desirable to gather the data on the same cases independently by two different workers. Two cases have been reported twice by different workers in different years. One case fell from 215 to 208 points, the other increased from 195 to 199 in score. Both had continued to be behavior cases, which caused the second report to be prepared. These samples of reliability indicate that the scale tends to be consistent in its measurement of the same individual.

At the present time many adult cases of delinquency are known which were problems in childhood. The records of all social agencies and clinics are mute evidence. The Detroit Scale of Behavior can help in locating them in childhood. A member of the Detroit clinic staff, through a special adjustment class to which she was formerly attached, recently made an informal review and follow-up of several cases known to her. She was able to scale her information and found that the cases which were at or near 240 points have been generally well adjusted since that time but that those scoring about 200 points or less have continued to be maladjusted. Much more information of this type is needed for the final solution of the problems of maladjusted children.

The question of reliability raises a serious and fundamental issue as to the desirability or undesirability of high reliability in second or later examinations. If social work in adjusting behavior cases is to be effective, there should be a change not only in the overt behavior of the case but also in the causes which evidently have led to maladjustment. It would be interesting to speculate upon how much change could be effected and by what methods, so that the scoring categories of the sixty-six items could be raised to more desirable and more nearly ideal conditions. Doubtless some items are more susceptible to improvement than others. For example, a child with defective vision (Item 7) may have his vision corrected and thereby raise his score for that item. Most of the physical and health items could probably yield certain improvements. Such items as eating habits or conditions of sleeping might easily be susceptible to change. The items of education of child and of parents may undergo changes. This scale is not designed to find certain factors which are predestined to remain at the same level of ineffectiveness, but rather it is devised to find what factors in the present status of a given case are operating and what can be done to improve upon them. In any event it should not become too prognostic of unfavorable conditions which may confidently be expected to remain unimproved. Through its application and reapplication to the same cases of maladjustment the effectiveness of social work may be measured and the factors may be discovered which are little susceptible to change. The prognosis of the residue of extremely difficult cases should finally become more evident.

DISTRIBUTION OF ITEMS BY SCALE VALUES

A tabulation was made of the scale values of the items for the behavior and the non-behavior groups to determine the average number of items in each scoring category. The results are shown in Table X.

TABLE X. DISTRIBUTION OF ITEMS BY SCALE VALUES

CATEGORY	SCORE VALUE	NON-BEHAVIOR	BEHAVIOR
Excellent................	5	37.6	16.9
Good....................	4	16.3	13.9
Fair....................	3	9.0	17.5
Poor....................	2	2.2	11.3
Very poor...............	1	0.9	6.4
Totals................		66.0	66.0

Table X shows that the average behavior-problem case has 17.7 of his sixty-six items marked "poor" or "very poor"; whereas the average non-behavior case has only 3.1 such items. This difference seems to be significant, so that the behavior problem may be said to be about six times as serious as the non-behavior problem. On the other hand, in the "good" and "excellent" items the average non-behavior case scores almost twice as much as the average behavior case. These numbers represent the average distribution of items and individual cases. Individuals in either group may vary widely from it. If causes tend to work together in subtle but vicious combinations, the number of items in the "poor" and "very poor" categories may show how serious are the problems confronting behavior-problem children.

SIGNIFICANCE OF THE INDIVIDUAL ITEMS

By means of a detailed tabulation of scores on all sixty-six items for the non-behavior group and the behavior group I, it was possible to compile the distribution of scores of every item for the two groups according to the five scoring categories. Comparisons were then possible as to the average score earned by the two groups on each of the sixty-six items. The distributions for two items, in Table XI, will illustrate the procedure.

TABLE XI. DISTRIBUTION OF SCORES FOR TWO ITEMS BY CATEGORIES

CATEGORY	SCORE VALUE	ITEM No. 34 (INTERESTS OR HOBBIES)				ITEM No. 15 (LOOKS OR APPEARANCE)			
		NON-BEHAVIOR		BEHAVIOR		NON-BEHAVIOR		BEHAVIOR	
		Frequency	Weighted Score	Frequency	Weighted Score	Frequency	Weighted Score	Frequency	Weighted Score
Excellent..	5	114	570	27	135	100	500	23	115
Good......	4	42	168	42	168	70	280	98	392
Fair.......	3	16	48	49	147	7	21	21	63
Poor......	2	1	2	18	36	4	8	43	86
Very poor..	1	8	8	53	53	0	0	4	4
Totals.........		181	796	189	539	181	809	189	660
Average or mean		4.40		2.85		4.47		3.49	
Difference in averages		1.55				0.98			

It will be noted in Table XI that for Item 34 (interests or hobbies) the non-behavior group made an average score of 4.40 points and the behavior group a score of 2.85—a difference of 1.55 points. This is a greater difference than between the two groups for Item 15 (looks or appearance), which is only 0.98 points. It is apparent, therefore, that interests or hobbies are more significantly related to differences between behavior and non-behavior than looks or appearance.

The differences between averages of score distributions for all sixty-six items for the non-behavior and the main behavior groups have been computed and the items arranged in the order of these differences, with the largest difference indicating the most significant item and the smallest difference indicating the least significant item. This arrangement of items is shown in Table XII, pages 350 and 351.

TABLE XII. RANK ORDER OF APPARENT IMPORTANCE OF SIXTY-SIX ITEMS

RANK ORDER	ITEM NUMBER	ITEM	NON-BEHAVIOR AVERAGE	BEHAVIOR AVERAGE	DIFFERENCE
1	37	General behavior....................	4.72	2.26	2.46
2	66	Child's attitude toward school..........	4.87	2.70	2.17
3	61	Discipline...........................	4.67	2.57	2.10
4	28	Personality type....................	4.62	2.60	2.02
5	32	Pity, sympathy, enthusiasm, etc........	4.68	2.82	1.86
6	35	Initiative and ambition..............	4.44	2.60	1.84
7	29	Anger, rage, revenge, etc.............	4.51	2.73	1.78
8	27	Social type........................	4.54	2.77	1.77
9	63	Child's attitude toward home..........	4.62	2.89	1.73
10	65	Scholarship........................	4.36	2.66	1.70
11	34	Interests or hobbies...............	4.40	2.85	1.55
12	56	General home atmosphere..............	4.66	3.11	1.55
13	25	Later recreational facilities............	4.25	2.74	1.51
14	26	Playmates or companions..............	4.43	2.96	1.47
15	62	Attitude toward child...............	4.61	3.18	1.43
16	60	Parents' social adjustment............	4.40	3.02	1.38
17	13	Nervousness........................	4.52	3.15	1.37
18	57	Ideals of home.....................	4.58	3.26	1.32
19	31	Excitement, shock, uneasiness, etc......	4.56	3.28	1.28
20	59	Family recreation...................	4.20	2.93	1.27
21	33	Intelligence........................	4.62	3.36	1.26
22	36	Vocational interests.................	4.09	2.83	1.26
23	17	Present self-care....................	4.62	3.39	1.23
24	18	Home duties.......................	4.37	3.15	1.22
25	20	Eating habits......................	4.30	3.12	1.18
26	47	Mother's personality.................	4.40	3.22	1.18
27	19	Conditions of eating.................	4.28	3.13	1.15
28	24	Early recreational facilities............	4.30	3.16	1.14
29	64	School attendance...................	4.73	3.62	1.11
30	14	Personal hygiene and clothing.........	4.63	3.53	1.10
31	21	Time of sleeping....................	4.43	3.33	1.10
32	16	Early self-care.....................	4.49	3.47	1.02
33	15	Looks or appearance.................	4.47	3.49	.98
34	58	Religion...........................	4.37	3.39	.98
35	41	Mother's education..................	3.76	2.80	.96
36	11	Motor control and muscular co-ordination	4.67	3.73	.94
37	46	Father's personality.................	4.31	3.38	.93
38	30	Fear, dread, anxiety, etc.............	4.67	3.82	.85
39	39	Mother's intelligence................	3.79	2.94	.85
40	49	Economic status....................	3.63	2.86	.77
41	38	Father's intelligence.................	3.69	3.06	.63
42	23	Dreams............................	4.48	3.86	.62
43	48	Occupation........................	3.12	2.52	.60
44	40	Father's education..................	3.46	2.89	.57
45	2	Child's present health...............	3.92	3.36	.56
46	45	Mother's health....................	4.20	3.65	.55
47	22	Sleeping conditions..................	3.89	3.35	.54
48	1	Child's early health.................	4.48	4.00	.48
49	6	Degree of speech defect..............	4.25	3.79	.46
50	8	Degree of hearing defect.............	4.85	4.41	.44
51	10	Size for age.......................	4.61	4.17	.44
52	44	Father's health....................	4.42	3.98	.44
53	43	Mother's age at birth of child..........	4.27	3.87	.40
54	55	Broken home.......................	4.89	4.50	.39
55	54	Legal status.......................	4.83	4.50	.33

TABLE XII. RANK ORDER OF APPARENT IMPORTANCE OF SIXTY-SIX ITEMS
—*Continued*

RANK ORDER	ITEM NUMBER	ITEM	NON-BEHAVIOR AVERAGE	BEHAVIOR AVERAGE	DIFFERENCE
56	7	Degree of vision defect..............	4.63	4.33	.30
57	51	Other adults in home................	4.54	4.25	.29
58	5	Accidents..........................	4.67	4.40	.27
59	42	Father's age at birth of child..........	4.11	3.91	.20
60	53	Adjustments to siblings..............	3.70	3.51	.19
61	12	Convulsions, seizures................	4.94	4.76	.18
62	3	Children's diseases..................	3.41	3.24	.17
63	4	Serious infectious diseases...........	4.57	4.46	.11
64	9	Degree of orthopedic defect...........	4.89	4.83	.06
65	52	Number of and position in siblings......	3.73	3.65	.08
66	50	Home language	4.17	4.25	−.08

The rank order of the items in Table XII merits some discussion. The social and personality items tend to be found among those which make the greatest distinction between behavior and non-behavior children. Items on the home habits and the characteristics of parents occur chiefly in the middle third of the group, while the health and physical defects seem of least importance, falling in the lower third. It should be noted, however, that the health items do differentiate, and that the only item which showed a negative trend was home language. The reason for this result with regard to home language is that few children in these studies chanced to come from homes where a foreign language was spoken. If the number of cases were extended to a wider sampling, this item would certainly make a better showing, since children with foreign parentage, as a group, tend to become delinquent oftener than the native stock. It should be added that this phenomenon is not limited to any particular nationality and is complicated by other factors besides language, such as poor economic and social status, as well as by the clash between parental authority and a new set of customs and ideals.

It is of interest to note that the intelligence of the child ranks twenty-first in order of difference between the two groups, barely qualifying to enter the first third of the items. Many of the personality and social factors show a greater difference. This fact is tangible proof of what competent psychologists have always tried to emphasize, that there are other factors operating in behavior patterns; except with psychological workers there has always been too much faith that intelligence was the chief and only component of behavior maladjustment. The authors share a belief that intelligence is an important factor but that other factors are also significant, as shown in Table XII.

In the section of this chapter dealing with the significance of the differences between groups the technique for determining the statistical significance of differences was discussed.[1] Applying the same formula to the items of Table XII, we find that all but the last three items show reliable differences between the behavior group and the non-behavior group. The fourth item (serious infectious diseases—sixty-third in rank order) has an actual difference of .11 in averages, which is 1.2 times the standard error of the differences. According to Garrett (1), eighty-eight times in one hundred the same difference would occur. All the other items become much more significant in their differences. Item 55, in the fifty-fourth rank order, has a difference which is 4.7 times its standard error, and Item 28 (personality type of child—fourth in rank order) has a difference which is 22 times its standard error.

All the evidence which has been presented in the various sections of this chapter shows that from a statistical point of view the Detroit Scale of Behavior meets the requirements for reliability and validity, both as a total scale and in its individual items. Its usefulness in diagnosing and prognosticating has already proved of value, but it has a further practical value in supporting the subjective opinion of the teacher, the social worker, the psychologist, and the psychiatrist as to the nature of the individual problem.

BIBLIOGRAPHY

1. GARRETT, HENRY E.—*Statistics in Psychology and Education.* New York: Longmans, Green & Co., 1926. 317 pp.

[1] See page 344.

CHAPTER XIII

INTERCORRELATIONSHIPS BETWEEN BEHAVIOR CAUSES

WITHIN certain limits the diagnosis and interpretation of behavior problems have necessarily been matters of subjective opinion upon the part of experienced workers. The Detroit Scale attempts to supplement subjective opinions by objective scores; but the measurement and evaluation of the sixty-six items themselves still continue to be somewhat subjective, as is the interpretation in terms of the specific factors in Chapter V. When subjective opinion is made as objective as possible in terms of the scale, however, certain definite relationships between factors come to light which would otherwise remain obscure and undetected. A vast amount of detailed work has been done to bring these relationships to light, and further work will be pursued on them after this first report has been presented. Eventually some of the more subtle and hidden relationships between behavior factors will be brought to light, though only a few of the more obvious ones are presented here.

CORRELATION PROCEDURES

The Pearson product-moment method of correlations has been used throughout, but with certain limitations in mind. There are five steps in the scoring of each item. The step intervals should be of equal value to employ this correlation technique. On

353

account of the very subjective nature of the content it is difficult to determine whether these steps are equal or not, but in the absence of such information it seemed fair to proceed on the assumption that in most instances the steps are approximately equal.

Correlations have been computed between total scores and scores for specific items or factors mostly within the behavior group of 189 cases, where the average was between the second and third steps. These correlations tend to run higher than the same items in the non-behavior group of 180 cases, in which the average score was usually between the fourth and fifth steps. In other words, the dispersion or range of scores tends to be smaller for the non-behavior than for the behavior group. When both groups are combined, the resulting correlations tend to be even higher than for either group alone, except where the narrow range of non-behavior scores tends to affect the linearity of the lines of regression.

Correlations of factors with total score.   In Table XIII are shown three sets of correlations of the sixty-six items with the total score. The first columns show the correlations between total score and all factors for the 189 behavior cases, the second set of columns shows them for the 180 non-behavior cases, and the third set shows correlations for both groups combined. The sixty-six items are arranged in the order of correlations within each group, ranging from highest positive to lowest positive correlation, since no negative correlations appeared in these particular relationships. Each correlation actually contains the score for the specific factor included in the total score, but some experimental elimination of these factors from the total score resulted in a reduction of the correlation by approximately .04 for the larger correlations and of .01 for the lower ones. In other words, a correlation of .660 was reduced to .620 and a correlation of .120 to .110, none of which made any material difference with final results.

TABLE XIII. CORRELATIONS OF FACTORS WITH TOTAL SCORE

RANK ORDER	189 BEHAVIOR CASES			180 NON-BEHAVIOR CASES			BOTH GROUPS COMBINED		
	COR-RELATION	ITEM NO.	ITEM	COR-RELATION	ITEM NO.	ITEM	COR-RELATION	ITEM NO.	ITEM
1	.699	59	Family recreation	.663	65	Scholarship	.800	61	Discipline
2	.637	57	Ideals of home	.616	25	Later recreational facilities	.791	63	Child's attitude toward home
3	.600	62	Attitude toward child	.583	14	Personal hygiene and clothing	.751	62	Attitude toward child
4	.598	56	General home atmosphere	.569	35	Initiative and ambition	.747	25	Later recreational facilities
5	.575	25	Later recreational facilities	.558	61	Discipline	.739	26	Playmates or companions
6	.562	19	Conditions of eating	.542	39	Mother's intelligence	.733	37	General behavior
7	.560	20	Eating habits	.539	63	Child's attitude toward home	.728	35	Initiative and ambition
8	.555	21	Time of sleeping	.536	19	Conditions of eating	.728	65	Scholarship
9	.551	42	Father's age at birth of child	.524	40	Father's education	.728	28	Personality type
10	.547	63	Child's attitude toward home	.513	27	Social type	.712	57	Ideals of home
11	.526	49	Economic status	.512	38	Father's intelligence	.703	27	Social type
12	.525	33	Intelligence	.507	16	Early self-care	.696	56	General home atmosphere
13	.514	61	Discipline	.506	17	Present self-care	.690	29	Anger, rage, revenge, etc.
14	.514	26	Playmates or companions	.500	47	Mother's personality	.685	66	Child's attitude toward school
15	.503	40	Father's education	.497	62	Attitude toward child	.684	59	Family recreation

TABLE XIII. CORRELATIONS OF FACTORS WITH TOTAL SCORE—*Continued*

RANK ORDER	189 BEHAVIOR CASES			180 NON-BEHAVIOR CASES			BOTH GROUPS COMBINED		
	COR-RELATION	ITEM	ITEM NO.	COR-RELATION	ITEM	ITEM NO.	COR-RELATION	ITEM	ITEM NO.
16	.498	Father's health	44	.496	Early recreational facilities	24	.682	Parents' social adjustment	60
17	.495	Mother's personality	47	.495	Mother's education	41	.676	Conditions of eating	19
18	.491	Fear, dread, anxiety, etc.	30	.490	Parents' social adjustment	60	.662	Time of sleeping	21
19	.477	Parents' social adjustment	60	.475	Father's personality	46	.651	Eating habits	20
20	.475	Father's personality	46	.472	Time of sleeping	21	.650	Intelligence	33
21	.472	Early recreational facilities	24	.458	Child's attitude toward school	66	.649	Mother's personality	47
22	.468	Personal hygiene and clothing	14	.457	Eating habits	20	.644	Mother's intelligence	39
23	.450	Mother's education	41	.454	Religion	58	.635	Excitement, shock, uneasiness, etc.	31
24	.438	Mother's intelligence	39	.438	Personality type	28	.633	Father's personality	46
25	.408	Home duties	18	.428	Mother's health	45	.620	Personal hygiene and clothing	14
26	.405	Child's present health	2	.394	Home duties	18	.612	Pity, sympathy, enthusiasm, etc.	32
27	.405	Vocational interests	36	.393	Pity, sympathy, enthusiasm, etc.	32	.609	Home duties	18
28	.405	Religion	58	.377	Excitement, shock, uneasiness, etc.	31	.594	Religion	58
29	.394	Mother's age at birth of child	43	.375	School attendance	64	.592	Nervousness	13
30	.382	Occupation	48	.368	Sleeping conditions	22	.588	Present self-care	17

TABLE XIII. Correlations of Factors with Total Score—*Continued*

RANK ORDER	189 Behavior Cases			180 Non-behavior Cases			Both Groups Combined		
	CORRELATION	ITEM NO.	ITEM	ITEM	ITEM NO.	CORRELATION	CORRELATION	ITEM NO.	ITEM
31	.380	50	Home language	Anger, rage, revenge, etc.	29	.365	.585	34	Interests or hobbies
32	.379	34	Interests or hobbies	General behavior	37	.365	.570	36	Vocational interests
33	.369	38	Father's intelligence	Fear, dread, anxiety, etc.	30	.364	.566	38	Father's intelligence
34	.365	31	Excitement, shock, uneasiness, etc.	Dreams	23	.354	.558	44	Father's health
35	.360	22	Sleeping conditions	Father's age at birth of child	42	.354	.557	64	School attendance
36	.356	28	Personality type	Looks or appearance	15	.343	.543	15	Looks or appearance
37	.354	54	Legal status	Motor control and muscular co-ordination	11	.314	.541	11	Motor control and muscular co-ordination
38	.351	29	Anger, rage, revenge, etc.	Degree of orthopedic defect	9	.307	.534	40	Father's education
39	.351	51	Other adults in home	Ideals of home	57	.306	.530	41	Mother's education
40	.345	35	Initiative and ambition	Family recreation	59	.306	.494	48	Occupation
41	.340	37	General behavior	Father's health	44	.304	.491	16	Early self-care
42	.339	65	Scholarship	Child's present health	2	.279	.489	42	Father's age at birth of child
43	.326	12	Convulsions, seizures	Vocational interests	36	.278	.488	49	Economic status
44	.318	64	School attendance	Intelligence	33	.275	.441	24	Early recreational facilities
45	.304	32	Pity, sympathy, enthusiasm, etc.	Broken home	55	.270	.438	2	Child's present health

TABLE XII. CORRELATIONS OF FACTORS WITH TOTAL SCORE—*Continued*

RANK ORDER	189 BEHAVIOR CASES			180 NON-BEHAVIOR CASES			BOTH GROUPS COMBINED		
	CORRELATION	ITEM NO.	ITEM	CORRELATION	ITEM NO.	ITEM	CORRELATION	ITEM NO.	ITEM
46	.295	5	Accidents	.269	13	Nervousness	.416	43	Mother's age at birth of child
47	.292	15	Looks or appearance	.260	43	Mother's age at birth of child	.415	23	Dreams
48	.278	23	Dreams	.253	52	Number of and position in siblings	.413	22	Sleeping conditions
49	.272	11	Motor control and muscular co-ordination	.246	50	Home language	.406	30	Fear, dread, anxiety, etc.
50	.264	27	Social type	.241	8	Degree of hearing defect	.404	45	Mother's health
51	.257	17	Present self-care	.234	48	Occupation	.361	50	Home language
52	.254	55	Broken home	.230	10	Size for age	.353	55	Broken home
53	.236	53	Adjustment to siblings	.230	51	Other adults in home	.348	51	Other adults in home
54	.224	8	Degree of hearing defect	.227	1	Child's early health	.347	54	Legal status
55	.218	52	Number of and position in siblings	.222	53	Adjustments to siblings	.335	7	Degree of vision defect
56	.212	13	Nervousness	.220	49	Economic status	.334	5	Accidents
57	.209	1	Child's early health	.193	5	Accidents	.319	4	Serious infectious diseases
58	.200	45	Mother's health	.187	6	Degree of speech defect	.317	8	Degree of hearing defect
59	.193	66	Child's attitude toward school	.168	34	Interests or hobbies	.291	1	Child's early health
60	.189	9	Degree of ortho-pedic defect	.154	4	Serious infectious diseases	.273	12	Convulsions, seizures

TABLE XIII. CORRELATIONS OF FACTORS WITH TOTAL SCORE—*Continued*

RANK ORDER	189 BEHAVIOR CASES			180 NON-BEHAVIOR CASES			BOTH GROUPS COMBINED		
	COR-RELA-TION	ITEM	ITEM NO.	COR-RELA-TION	ITEM	ITEM NO.	COR-RELA-TION	ITEM	ITEM NO.
61	.182	Serious infectious diseases	4	.154	Degree of vision defect	7	.254	Degree of speech defect	6
62	.175	Early self-care	16	.144	Legal status	54	.252	Number of and position in siblings	52
63	.160	Degree of vision defect	7	.124	Playmates or companions	26	.217	Size for age	10
64	.134	Degree of speech defect	6	.099	Children's diseases	3	.194	Degree of ortho-pedic defect	9
65	.109	Size for age	10	.048	Convulsions, seizures	12	.154	Adjustments to siblings	53
66	.030	Children's diseases	3	.030	General home atmosphere	56	.117	Children's diseases	3

Probable error and significance of correlations.   In Table XIII and in most of the tables of this study where the number of cases is slightly less than two hundred, a correlation of .200 is approximately four times the probable error, which is considered to be a satisfactory degree of reliability for correlation coefficients. In Table XIII all but the last few correlations are apparently satisfactory in terms of reliability. Rugg (1) states that correlation coefficients have the following qualifications:

CORRELATION	SIGNIFICANCE
From 0 to .15 or .20	Negligible or indifferent
.15 or .20 to .35 or .40	Present but low
.35 or .40 to .50 or .60	Markedly present
.60 or .70 or higher	High
Above .70	Very high

In Table XIII about two thirds of the correlations are in the class of markedly present or higher.

Discussion of total-score correlations.   The factor of family recreation, No. 59, is interpreted so that within the behavior group it has the highest correlation with the total score, a correlation of .699. This correlation indicates that there is high parallelism between low total behavior scores and poor family recreation, and that better behavior scores have better family recreation. Within the non-behavior group, family recreation is only fortieth (.306) among the sixty-six items, which means that between the poorer and better non-behavior cases there is relatively less difference than between the extreme behavior cases. When both groups are combined, this correlation is .684, ranking fifteenth from the highest. There is a high correlation between family recreation and total behavior score when both groups are combined; it is even higher for the behavior group alone and considerably less in the non-behavior group alone. In Table XIII the physical and sensory items tend to be among the lower in correlations with total score within all three groups. All sixty-six of the items may be interpreted individually in the manner of the family recreation which has just been cited.

Intercorrelations of Factors

Within the main behavior group of 189 cases, correlation coefficients have been computed for all sixty-six factors with each of the sixty-five remaining factors, a total of 2145 correlations. In Table XIV the average correlation of each factor with the remaining sixty-five is given, and the five highest individual correlations are also given. The results shown in this table merit more discussion than can be presented here. When interpreting the factors for any particular case, the correlations of Table XIV should be consulted as well as the discussion in Part III. The correlations for Item 10 (size) are typical of what can be learned about these factor relations. The average correlation with all sixty-five factors is .043, which is not a very significant correlation. The best correlation with size is initiative and ambition, with a correlation of .448, which is interpreted to mean that the more ideal the size the better are the vocational interests and the more unusual and undesirable the size the poorer the initiative and ambition. On the basis of guesswork alone this relationship between size and vocational interests might not be suspected. The second correlation with size is child's attitude toward home, .384; the more nearly usual the size for age the better the attitude and the poorer the size adjustment the poorer the attitude toward the home. The degree of orthopedic defect is third, .310; motor control is fourth, .277; and convulsions and seizures is fifth, with .266.

It will be noted from the average correlations in Table XIV that most of the correlations between causes are comparatively low aside from the five best, which have been listed for each item. These low correlations tend to show that behavior causes are a large number of factors more or less independent of each other rather than a high correlation of a few factors. But there are some combinations of factors which merit attention.

Correlations of combinations of factors with total score. From the last part of Table XIII, in which both groups are combined, three sets of five items have been selected for special study,

TABLE XIV. INTERCORRELATIONSHIPS OF FACTORS
189 BEHAVIOR CASES [1]

1. Child's early health .094			2. Child's present health .138		
	No.	ITEM		No.	ITEM
.347	57	Ideals of home	.373	9	Degree of orthopedic defect
.320	6	Degree of speech defect	.296	30	Fear, dread, anxiety, etc.
.319	4	Serious infectious diseases	.279	12	Convulsions, seizures
.260	3	Children's diseases	.275	4	Serious infectious diseases
.209	11	Motor control and muscular co-ordination	.274	33	Intelligence

3. Children's diseases .073			4. Serious infectious diseases .057		
	No.	ITEM		No.	ITEM
.260	1	Child's early health	.319	1	Child's early health
.181	30	Fear, dread, anxiety, etc.	.294	6	Degree of speech defect
.180	8	Degree of hearing defect	.275	2	Child's present health
.167	2	Child's present health	.270	13	Nervousness
.163	9	Degree of orthopedic defect	.207	42	Father's age at birth of child

5. Accidents .097			6. Degree of speech defect .083		
	No.	ITEM		No.	ITEM
.447	9	Degree of orthopedic defect	.350	28	Personality type
.297	25	Later recreational facilities	.320	1	Child's early health
.249	6	Degree of speech defect	.294	4	Serious infectious diseases
.220	8	Degree of hearing defect	.262	11	Motor control and muscular co-ordination
.219	10	Size for age	.249	5	Accidents

7. Degree of vision defect .049			8. Degree of hearing defect .088		
	No.	ITEM		No.	ITEM
.229	8	Degree of hearing defect	.360	11	Motor control and muscular co-ordination
.226	31	Excitement, shock, uneasiness, etc.	.252	6	Degree of speech defect
.194	11	Motor control and muscular co-ordination	.229	7	Degree of vision defect
.185	1	Child's early health	.226	50	Home language
.184	6	Degree of speech defect	.220	5	Accidents

9. Degree of orthopedic defect .103			10. Size for age .043		
	No.	ITEM		No.	ITEM
.447	5	Accidents	.448	35	Initiative and ambition
.377	11	Motor control and muscular co-ordination	.384	63	Child's attitude toward home
			.310	9	Degree of orthopedic defect
.373	2	Child's present health	.277	11	Motor control and muscular co-ordination
.367	12	Convulsions, seizures			
.331	33	Intelligence	.266	12	Convulsions, seizures

11. Motor control and muscular co-ordination .134			12. Convulsions, seizures .099		
	No.	ITEM		No.	ITEM
.377	9	Degree of orthopedic defect	.367	9	Degree of orthopedic defect
.360	8	Degree of hearing defect	.310	11	Motor control and muscular co-ordination
.322	33	Intelligence			
.310	12	Convulsions, seizures	.282	31	Excitement, shock, uneasiness, etc.
.295	30	Fear, dread, anxiety, etc.	.279	2	Child's present health
			.266	10	Size for age

[1] The number after the item is the average correlation with all the other sixty-five factors; for example, a child's early health has an average correlation of .094 with all other factors.

13. Nervousness .091			14. Personal hygiene and clothing .155		
	No.	ITEM		No.	ITEM
.335	31	Excitement,shock,uneasiness,etc.	.375	19	Conditions of eating
.270	28	Personality type	.375	49	Economic status
.270	4	Serious infectious diseases	.340	57	Ideals of home
.269	30	Fear, dread, anxiety, etc.	.314	21	Time of sleeping
.257	23	Dreams	.314	24	Early recreational facilities

15. Looks or appearance .085			16. Early self-care .047		
	No.	ITEM		No.	ITEM
.258	17	Present self-care	.502	17	Present self-care
.196	34	Interests or hobbies	.294	20	Eating habits
.189	60	Parents' social adjustment	.253	18	Home duties
.179	24	Early recreational facilities	.208	35	Initiative and ambition
.176	21	Time of sleeping	.183	4	Serious infectious diseases

17. Present self-care .116			18. Home duties .146		
	No.	ITEM		No.	ITEM
.502	16	Early self-care	.405	20	Eating habits
.353	62	Attitude toward child	.395	61	Discipline
.322	18	Home duties	.356	62	Attitude toward child
.315	20	Eating habits	.325	56	General home atmosphere
.280	14	Personal hygiene and clothing	.322	17	Present self-care

19. Conditions of eating .195			20. Eating habits .167		
	No.	ITEM		No.	ITEM
.515	57	Ideals of home	.432	21	Time of sleeping
.505	59	Family recreation	.407	19	Conditions of eating
.485	21	Time of sleeping	.405	18	Home duties
.474	24	Early recreational facilities	.366	62	Attitude toward child
.460	49	Economic status	.333	44	Father's health

21. Time of sleeping .195			22. Sleeping conditions .127		
	No.	ITEM		No.	ITEM
.485	19	Conditions of eating	.409	49	Economic status
.434	63	Child's attitude toward home	.401	19	Conditions of eating
.432	20	Eating habits	.353	40	Father's education
.414	25	Later recreational facilities	.344	48	Occupation
.389	56	General home atmosphere	.312	39	Mother's intelligence

23. Dreams .097			24. Early recreational facilities .165		
	No.	ITEM		No.	ITEM
.268	43	Mother's age at birth of child	.474	19	Conditions of eating
.262	2	Child's present health	.393	64	School attendance
.257	13	Nervousness	.390	25	Later recreational facilities
.250	30	Fear, dread, anxiety, etc.	.369	50	Home language
.248	42	Father's age at birth of child	.366	56	General home atmosphere

25. Later recreational facilities .209			26. Playmates or companions .185		
	No.	ITEM		No.	ITEM
.500	26	Playmates or companions	.500	25	Later recreational facilities
.480	56	General home atmosphere	.429	27	Social type
.420	19	Conditions of eating	.358	59	Family recreation
.414	21	Time of sleeping	.341	41	Mother's education
.400	62	Attitude toward child	.340	28	Personality type

27. Social type .119		
	No.	Item
.429	26	Playmates or companions
.335	63	Child's attitude toward home
.308	28	Personality type
.303	25	Later recreational facilities
.271	29	Anger, rage, revenge, etc.

28. Personality type .122		
	No.	Item
.434	32	Pity, sympathy, enthusiasm, etc.
.356	29	Anger, rage, revenge, etc.
.350	6	Degree of speech defect
.347	31	Excitement, shock, uneasiness, etc.
.340	26	Playmates or companions

29. Anger, rage, revenge, etc. .114		
	No.	Item
.356	28	Personality type
.291	31	Excitement, shock, uneasiness, etc.
.282	37	General behavior
.271	27	Social type
.266	52	Number and position in siblings

30. Fear, dread, anxiety, etc. .170		
	No.	Item
.553	56	General home atmosphere
.370	31	Excitement, shock, uneasiness, etc.
.315	32	Pity, sympathy, enthusiasm, etc.
.296	2	Child's present health
.295	11	Motor control and muscular co-ordination

31. Excitement, shock, uneasiness, etc. .116		
	No.	Item
.370	30	Fear, dread, anxiety, etc.
.351	32	Pity, sympathy, enthusiasm, etc.
.347	28	Personality type
.335	13	Nervousness
.291	29	Anger, rage, revenge, etc.

32. Pity, sympathy, enthusiasm, etc. .108		
	No.	Item
.434	28	Personality type
.351	31	Excitement, shock, uneasiness, etc.
.315	30	Fear, dread, anxiety, etc.
.270	66	Child's attitude toward school
.250	11	Motor control and muscular co-ordination

33. Intelligence .157		
	No.	Item
.333	59	Family recreation
.331	9	Degree of orthopedic defect
.322	11	Motor control and muscular co-ordination
.307	50	Home language
.297	41	Mother's education

34. Interests or hobbies .127		
	No.	Item
.342	25	Later recreational facilities
.295	36	Vocational interests
.290	35	Initiative and ambition
.286	26	Playmates or companions
.279	33	Intelligence

35. Initiative and ambition .135		
	No.	Item
.448	10	Size for age
.435	46	Father's personality
.362	25	Later recreational facilities
.295	65	Scholarship
.290	34	Interests or hobbies

36. Vocational interests .120		
	No.	Item
.295	34	Interests or hobbies
.271	28	Personality type
.267	35	Initiative and ambition
.265	57	Ideals of home
.245	62	Attitude toward child

37. General behavior .128		
	No.	Item
.310	56	General home atmosphere
.309	66	Child's attitude toward school
.300	63	Child's attitude toward home
.292	51	Other adults in home
.282	29	Anger, rage, revenge, etc.

38. Father's intelligence .069		
	No.	Item
.339	19	Conditions of eating
.311	40	Father's education
.267	22	Sleeping conditions
.262	25	Later recreational facilities
.243	34	Interests or hobbies

39. Mother's intelligence .192

	No.	ITEM
.513	40	Father's education
.506	41	Mother's education
.433	47	Mother's personality
.373	21	Time of sleeping
.367	48	Occupation

40. Father's education .168

	No.	ITEM
.724	41	Mother's education
.513	39	Mother's intelligence
.492	48	Occupation
.447	50	Home language
.410	32	Pity, sympathy, enthusiasm, etc.

41. Mother's education .158

	No.	ITEM
.724	40	Father's education
.506	39	Mother's intelligence
.481	48	Occupation
.475	50	Home language
.393	49	Economic status

42. Father's age at birth of child .171

	No.	ITEM
.738	43	Mother's age at birth of child
.419	44	Father's health
.410	40	Father's education
.366	46	Father's personality
.344	59	Family recreation

43. Mother's age at birth of child .136

	No.	ITEM
.738	42	Father's age at birth of child
.402	47	Mother's personality
.319	44	Father's health
.268	23	Dreams
.266	27	Social type

44. Father's health .149

	No.	ITEM
.422	46	Father's personality
.419	42	Father's age at birth of child
.333	20	Eating habits
.319	43	Mother's age at birth of child
.308	58	Religion

45. Mother's health .133

	No.	ITEM
.308	39	Mother's intelligence
.253	11	Motor control and muscular co-ordination
.253	61	Discipline
.247	56	General home atmosphere
.244	58	Religion

46. Father's personality .154

	No.	ITEM
.435	35	Initiative and ambition
.422	44	Father's health
.366	42	Father's age at birth of child
.364	54	Legal status
.364	59	Family recreation

47. Mother's personality .167

	No.	ITEM
.433	39	Mother's intelligence
.402	43	Mother's age at birth of child
.387	45	Mother's health
.379	56	General home atmosphere
.359	62	Attitude toward child

48. Occupation .142

	No.	ITEM
.539	49	Economic status
.492	40	Father's education
.481	41	Mother's education
.430	19	Conditions of eating
.367	39	Mother's intelligence

49. Economic status .165

	No.	ITEM
.539	48	Occupation
.460	19	Conditions of eating
.429	59	Family recreation
.409	22	Sleeping conditions
.403	40	Father's education

50. Home language .132

	No.	ITEM
.475	41	Mother's education
.447	40	Father's education
.369	24	Early recreational facilities
.357	19	Conditions of eating
.316	59	Family recreation

51. Other adults in home .117

	No.	ITEM
.333	54	Legal status
.299	46	Father's personality
.299	55	Broken home
.292	37	General behavior
.257	44	Father's health

52. Number of and position in siblings .073

	No.	ITEM
.266	28	Personality type
.209	53	Adjustments to siblings
.193	54	Legal status
.192	26	Playmates or companions
.192	61	Discipline

53. Adjustments to siblings .041

	No.	ITEM
.312	26	Playmates or companions
.245	11	Motor control and muscular co-ordination
.209	52	Number and position in siblings
.204	51	Other adults in home
.191	54	Legal status

54. Legal status .111

	No.	ITEM
.555	55	Broken home
.364	43	Mother's age at birth of child
.333	51	Other adults in home
.320	41	Mother's education
.307	44	Father's health

55. Broken home .092

	No.	ITEM
.555	54	Legal status
.318	58	Religion
.287	47	Mother's personality
.254	66	Child's attitude toward school
.233	60	Parents' social adjustment

56. General home atmosphere .213

	No.	ITEM
.571	61	Discipline
.553	30	Fear, dread, anxiety, etc.
.494	60	Parents' social adjustment
.483	62	Attitude toward child
.480	25	Later recreational facilities

57. Ideals of home .207

	No.	ITEM
.515	19	Conditions of eating
.479	56	General home atmosphere
.459	60	Parents' social adjustment
.412	61	Discipline
.408	59	Family recreation

58. Religion .141

	No.	ITEM
.401	60	Parents' social adjustment
.400	56	General home atmosphere
.392	57	Ideals of home
.333	59	Family recreation
.318	55	Broken home

59. Family recreation .214

	No.	ITEM
.505	19	Conditions of eating
.494	56	General home atmosphere
.429	49	Economic status
.422	63	Child's attitude toward home
.408	57	Ideals of home

60. Parents' social adjustment .171

	No.	ITEM
.459	57	Ideals of home
.410	46	Father's personality
.401	58	Religion
.398	59	Family recreation
.373	56	General home atmosphere

61. Discipline .180

	No.	ITEM
.571	56	General home atmosphere
.544	62	Attitude toward child
.516	63	Child's attitude toward home
.395	18	Home duties
.395	57	Ideals of home

62. Attitude toward child .196

	No.	ITEM
.544	61	Discipline
.483	56	General home atmosphere
.452	63	Child's attitude toward home
.412	57	Ideals of home
.407	19	Conditions of eating

63. Child's attitude toward home .176

	No.	ITEM
.516	61	Discipline
.476	56	General home atmosphere
.452	62	Attitude toward child
.434	21	Time of sleeping
.422	59	Family recreation

64. School attendance .143

	No.	ITEM
.393	19	Conditions of eating
.393	24	Early recreational facilities
.390	63	Child's attitude toward home
.357	59	Family recreation
.357	25	Later recreational facilities

65. Scholarship .120

	No.	ITEM
.314	64	School attendance
.312	33	Intelligence
.295	35	Initiative and ambition
.275	25	Later recreational facilities
.267	66	Child's attitude toward school

66. Child's attitude toward school .065

	No.	ITEM
.309	37	General behavior
.270	31	Excitement, shock, uneasiness, etc.
.267	65	Scholarship
.259	64	School attendance
.254	55	Broken home

to determine the correlations of combinations of factors with total score. The results are shown in Table XV.

TABLE XV. CORRELATIONS OF COMBINATIONS OF FACTORS WITH TOTAL SCORE

FIVE HIGH ITEMS			FIVE AVERAGE ITEMS			FIVE LOW ITEMS		
CORRELATION	ITEM NO.	ITEM	CORRELATION	ITEM NO.	ITEM	CORRELATION	ITEM NO.	ITEM
.800	61	Discipline	.588	17	Present self-care	.273	12	Convulsions, seizures
.791	63	Child's attitude toward home	.566	38	Father's intelligence	.252	52	Number of and position in siblings
.751	62	Attitude toward child	.558	44	Father's health	.217	10	Size for age
.733	37	General behavior	.557	64	School attendance	.194	9	Degree of orthopedic defect
.728	65	Scholarship	.543	15	Looks or appearance	.117	3	Children's diseases
.751		Median correlation	.558		Median correlation	.217		Median correlation
.909		Combined correlation with total	.771		Combined correlation with total	.419		Combined correlation with total

Table XV shows that, when the five factors, discipline, child's attitude toward home, attitude toward child, general behavior, and scholarship, are combined, the correlation with total score is .909, which is a high correlation. When the five factors of a second set, present self-care, father's intelligence, father's health, school attendance, and looks or appearance, are combined, the correlation with the total is .771; and when the five factors of a third set, convulsions and seizures, number of and position in siblings, size for age, degree of orthopedic defect, and chilren's diseases, are combined, there is a correlation of only .419 with the total score.

In the practical diagnosis of individual problems it will undoubtedly be found that poor factors occurring in combination in Table XIII at the top of the last column create chronic and aggravated problems, whereas those with combinations of factors near the lower part of that table will be less serious problems.

Parental characteristics in combinations. There are five items for each parent, Items 38 to 47 inclusive, which characterize parents as to intelligence, education, age, health, and personality. In the last part of Table XIII these items fall near the middle of the sixty-six factors in distinguishing between behavior and non-behavior groups of children. The personality of the mother is most important, next her intelligence, and third the father's personality. Next in order are the father's intelligence, the father's health, the father's education, and the mother's education. The last three in order are the father's age, the mother's age, and the mother's health.

Each of these five parental traits has been correlated with the corresponding trait in the other parent for the behavior group, for the non-behavior group, and for both groups combined, with the results shown in Table XVI.

TABLE XVI. CORRELATIONS OF PAIRED TRAITS IN PARENTS

BEHAVIOR GROUP			NON-BEHAVIOR GROUP			BOTH GROUPS		
RANK ORDER	COR-RELA-TION	FACTOR	RANK ORDER	COR-RELA-TION	FACTOR	RANK ORDER	COR-RELA-TION	FACTOR
1	.738	Age	1	.715	Education	1	.742	Education
2	.724	Education	2	.545	Intelligence	2	.680	Age
3	.303	Health	3	.497	Age	3	.484	Personality
4	.278	Personality	4	.384	Personality	4	.464	Intelligence
5	.162	Intelligence	5	.089	Health	5	.242	Health

Table XVI shows that within the behavior group, intelligence of parents is most poorly correlated, personality is next in low relationship, with age most nearly uniform. The clashes between parents arising from these discrepancies may be general causes of children's malbehavior. In the non-behavior group, parents resemble each other most in education, second in intelligence, third in age, fourth in personality, and fifth in health. When both groups are combined, education has the closest relationship, age second, personality third, intelligence fourth, and health fifth. When all three groups are considered, it appears that the education of the two parents tends to be generally alike, showing high correlations, and that the intelligence of the parents is very highly related.

The five parental factors were also grouped together for the fathers and mothers separately and correlated with the total score. Within the behavior group the fathers' five scores correlated .798 and the mothers' five scores .596, which seems to indicate that fathers have more influence than mothers on behavior maladjustments of children. In the non-behavior group the five fathers' items are again high, with a correlation of .593, and the mothers' .385; and in the combined behavior and non-behavior groups the fathers' items correlate .786 with the total score and the mothers' .668. From this evidence it would seem that fathers have slightly more effect upon children's behavior, which is contrary to the popular opinion that the mother has more influence because she spends more hours than the father with the children in the home.

Reports of Other Behavior Surveys

From the tables and discussion of this chapter it is evident that there are some combinations of factors which tend to produce behavior problems. The analysis of behavior problems will become a science and will be removed from the realm of subjective opinion and mere guesswork when these relationships are known and can be interpreted. In the remainder of this chapter other studies will be discussed in which attempts have been made to relate causes or to discover the most frequent types of malbehavior symptoms.

Minneapolis and Cleveland Surveys.   Wickman (2)[1] made a study of the behavior problems of the children in an elementary school of Minneapolis and later, one in Cleveland. For the Minneapolis investigation the total of behavior problems in 801 children is shown in Table XVII, page 370.

In the Cleveland Survey twenty-seven teachers were asked to list behavior problems and reported 428 items, which reduced to 185 items when duplications were eliminated. In Table XVIII are shown the number of times and the frequent or habitual occurrence of the forty-nine most common traits. Eight hundred seventy-four children are included in this report, pages 371-372.

[1] These distributions are quoted by permission from the publisher.

TABLE XVII. TOTAL INCIDENCE OF BEHAVIOR PROBLEMS
IN 801 CHILDREN, REPORTED BY TEACHERS
OF AN ELEMENTARY PUBLIC SCHOOL, MINNEAPOLIS, 1924

TYPE OF PROBLEM	PER CENT OF 801 PUPILS
Lack of interest	21.6
Cheating	17.6
Unnecessary tardiness	15.7
Lying	15.5
Defiance of discipline	10.9
Marked overactivity	9.4
Unpopularity with children	7.9
Temper outbursts	6.5
Bullying	6.1
Speech difficulties	5.1
Imaginative lying	3.6
Stealing	2.7
Masturbation, suspected	2.6
Truancy	2.4
Obscene talk, notes, etc	1.1
Masturbation, known	0.7

This report, interpreted, shows that 74.7 per cent of all the 874 pupils whispered, and that 41.0 per cent of them whispered frequently or habitually. The items with the greater frequencies are common phenomena in the classroom, whereas the less frequent items such as profanity or smoking, naturally are not of such common occurrence in and about the school. Wickman's study of this particular group was limited to items observed at school; but if the study had been extended to the home life and outside activities, there would probably have been a greater incidence of items toward the bottom of Table XVIII.

Detroit Behavior Survey. Wickman's report rated or listed all the pupils of the school with their types of problems. In the Detroit Survey which we shall now discuss, only the characteristics of those who were considered to be problems were known or reported.

In June, 1929, under the auspices of the Psychological Clinic a survey was made of behavior cases enrolled in the Detroit public

TABLE XVIII. TOTAL INCIDENCE AND FREQUENT OR HABITUAL INCIDENCE IN 874 PUPILS OF A CLEVELAND SCHOOL[1]

TYPE OF PROBLEM	PER CENT OF INCIDENCE IN 874 PUPILS	
	TOTAL INCIDENCE	FREQUENT OR HABITUAL INCIDENCE
Whispering	74.7	41.0
Inattentive	59.0	29.1
Careless in work	44.4	23.9
Tattling	42.0	11.5
Disorderly in class	38.8	18.4
Interrupting	38.7	18.6
Failure to study	36.2	17.5
Shy, withdrawing	35.2	18.2
Daydreaming	33.4	13.5
Lack of interest	31.8	10.8
Overactive	30.9	16.5
Cheating	29.5	8.7
Oversensitive	25.5	8.3
Neglectful	25.4	9.9
Physically lazy	20.8	10.7
Lying, untruthful	19.6	3.3
Unnecessary tardiness	17.6	3.5
Acting "smart"	14.6	7.4
Overcritical	14.2	5.3
Imaginative tales	13.3	3.7
Meddlesome	12.6	4.2
Sullen, sulky	12.5	2.5
Domineering	12.1	5.9
Slovenly appearance	11.8	4.8
Suggestible	9.4	4.5
Fearful	9.3	1.8
Physical coward	8.8	1.2
Nervous	8.7	3.5
Willfully disobedient	8.2	3.7
Destroying property	8.2	1.2
Unhappy, depressed	8.0	1.4
Quarrelsome	7.9	2.5
Stubborn in group	7.5	1.8
Rude, impudent	6.7	3.8
Impertinent, defiant	5.6	1.7
Carrying grudges	4.9	0.8
Stealing articles	4.0	0.6
Masturbation	3.9	0.9
Enuresis	3.9	0.8
Sissy (or tomboy)	3.6	1.2

[1] After Wickman.

371

TABLE XVIII.   TOTAL INCIDENCE AND FREQUENT OR HABITUAL INCIDENCE
IN 874 PUPILS OF A CLEVELAND SCHOOL—*Continued*

TYPE OF PROBLEM	PER CENT OF INCIDENCE IN 874 PUPILS	
	TOTAL INCIDENCE	FREQUENT OR HABITUAL INCIDENCE
Suspicious	2.1	0.3
Cruel, bullying	1.7	0.7
Profanity	1.7	0.0
Truancy	1.6	0.2
Temper outbursts	1.5	0.3
Stealing money	0.7	0.3
Stealing food, sweets	0.7	0.2
Obscene notes, talk	0.3	0.0
Smoking	0.2	0.1

elementary schools. As a different method of approach was used from that for the Behavior Scale, it seems desirable to report some unpublished findings and techniques for the analysis of results.

The 1357 cases comprised approximately one per cent of the total elementary-school enrollment; the average number of cases per school was 7.5. They ranged in age from five to fourteen years, with a fairly uniform distribution from ages eight to twelve inclusive and with fewer at the extremes. There were 1145 boys and 212 girls, with the boys comprising 84.4 per cent and the girls 15.6 per cent of the total.

A recording form for the listing of the pupils was furnished which contained an alphabetical list of twenty-six items, such as "argues, talkative" and "avoids others, timid." Teachers were instructed to check the items which applied to each pupil listed. The distribution of the number of items checked against each pupil is shown in Table XIX.

Table XIX shows that a few cases were considered to be of little consequence by the teachers, but that others with as many as nineteen of the twenty-six items appeared to be really serious problems. An average of 6.8 items was checked per pupil.

TABLE XIX.   DISTRIBUTION OF NUMBER OF BEHAVIOR ITEMS PER PUPIL

SERIAL NUMBER OF ITEMS CHECKED	NUMBER OF PUPILS	TOTAL NUMBER OF ITEMS
1	18	18
2	78	156
3	125	375
4	156	624
5	178	890
6	152	912
7	140	980
8	120	960
9	109	981
10	82	820
11	56	616
12	60	720
13	31	403
14	18	252
15	7	105
16	15	240
17	6	102
18	4	72
19	2	38
Totals.............	1357	9264

Average number of items per pupil 6.8

Table XX shows that the item "interferes, disturbs" is the most frequent and is marked 871 times in the 1357 cases, or that 64.2 per cent of all the cases were checked in this particular item. There was a total of 9264 markings of all items on all cases, and the 871 marks for "interferes, disturbs" comprise 9.4 per cent of the total items marked. In this table the items are arranged in the order of the greatest frequency of their markings.

It should be noted from Table XX that the aggressive and positive types of behavior are more frequently reported than are the recessive and negative traits, such as "quiet, seclusive." There is no certain guarantee that the less frequent items, such as "sets fires," are actually less common than the aggressive ones, but merely that they are not known to the teachers. These items are, on the whole, "symptoms" rather than causes of behavior

TABLE XX. FREQUENCIES OF THE BEHAVIOR ITEMS

ITEMS OR TRAITS	NUMBER	PER CENT OF MAXIMUM POSSIBLE OCCURRENCE	PER CENT OF TOTAL OF ALL ITEMS OCCURRING
Interferes, disturbs............	871	64.2	9.4
Argues, talkative.............	848	62.5	9.2
Fights, quarrelsome...........	810	59.7	8.7
Defiant, stubborn.............	647	47.7	7.0
Lies, deceitful................	556	41.0	6.0
Bullies, boasts................	549	40.5	5.9
Resents correction............	520	38.3	5.6
Cruel, teases.................	473	34.9	5.1
Cheats in school or at play.....	469	34.6	5.1
Obstinate, sullen.............	465	34.3	5.0
Smart aleck..................	333	24.5	3.6
Impulsive, erratic............	324	23.9	3.5
Daydreams, absent-minded....	305	22.5	3.3
Overactive, nervous...........	295	21.7	3.2
Steals.......................	292	21.5	3.2
Disliked, repulsive............	252	18.6	2.7
Truant (school)...............	231	17.0	2.5
Temper tantrums, rage........	204	15.0	2.2
Profane, vulgar, obscene.......	182	13.4	2.0
Selfish......................	135	9.9	1.5
Hysterical, cries..............	124	9.1	1.3
Quiet, seclusive..............	97	7.1	1.0
Truant (home)...............	97	7.1	1.0
Sex abuse....................	87	6.4	0.9
Avoids others, timid..........	84	6.2	0.9
Sets fires....................	14	1.0	0.2
Totals....................	9264	....	100.0

difficulties. The Detroit Behavior Scale is an instrument for the diagnosis of causes behind symptoms such as are reported in this survey. There are a few additional features of this behavior survey which merit discussion.

Differences in traits by age. In the 1357 cases there were 141 seven-year-olds and 157 twelve-year-olds. The percentages of frequency of occurrence of each item were computed for these two age groups, and the differences in frequency of occurrence are listed in Table XXI.

TABLE XXI. DIFFERENCES IN PERCENTAGES OF FREQUENCY BETWEEN SEVEN-YEAR-OLD AND TWELVE-YEAR-OLD PUPILS

SEVEN-YEAR-OLD WORSE		TWELVE-YEAR-OLD WORSE
15 per cent	to	19.99 per cent
		Argues, talkative Resents correction Cheats in school or at play
10 per cent	to	14.99 per cent
		Smart aleck Impulsive, erratic
5 per cent	to	9.99 per cent
Overactive, nervous Hysterical, cries Avoids others, timid		Defiant, stubborn Bullies, boasts Disliked, repulsive Truant (school) Temper tantrums, rage
0 per cent	to	4.99 per cent
Fights, quarrelsome Selfish Quiet, seclusive Sex abuse Sets fires		Interferes, disturbs Lies, deceitful Cruel, teases Obstinate, sullen Steals Profane, vulgar, obscene Truant (home) Daydreams, absent-minded

The numbers in Table XXI show differences between percentages of frequency of occurrence. The term "argues, talkative" occurs for 55.3 per cent of the seven-year-olds and for 70.7 per cent of the twelve-year-olds, which is a difference of 15.4 per cent; hence it falls in the first or higher group in Table XXI. It should be noted that in eighteen of the twenty-six traits the twelve-year-olds are worse than are the seven-year-olds. The more aggressive physical traits characterize the older group, although one might expect that "temper tantrums, rage" would occur more frequently with younger than with older children—the opposite of what actually was found.

Difference in traits by intelligence. A tabulation of traits was made between bright children and dull children, with the results shown in Table XXII. Bright children were selected from the highest 20 per cent in intelligence for any age, the dull from the poorest 20 per cent.

TABLE XXII. DIFFERENCES IN PERCENTAGES OF FREQUENCY BETWEEN BRIGHT AND DULL PUPILS

BRIGHT WORSE		DULL WORSE
15 per cent	to	19.99 per cent
Interferes, disturbs Smart aleck		Cheats in school or at play
10 per cent	to	14.99 per cent
Argues, talkative Bullies, boasts		Fights, quarrelsome
5 per cent	to	9.99 per cent
Cruel, teases Selfish		Obstinate, sullen Daydreams, absent-minded Steals Hysterical, cries Quiet, seclusive Truant (home)
0 per cent	to	4.99 per cent
Impulsive, erratic Overactive, nervous Truant (school) Temper tantrums, rage Profane, vulgar, obscene		Defiant, stubborn Lies, deceitful Resents correction Disliked, repulsive Sex abuse Avoids others, timid Sets fires

Bright children are worse than dull ones in traits involving the use of their intelligence for undesirable purposes. They tend to show more aggressiveness in mental action. Dull children are worse in the physical aspects of malbehavior, such as fighting. They are also oftener found to be equipped with antisocial tendencies, such as obstinacy, cheating, and similar traits.

Relationship of traits to one another. In studying the traits checked against individual children it was noted that certain items such as "argues, talkative" were frequently checked when "fights, quarrelsome" was also checked. The extent of these coincidences was computed on five hundred of the cases, and the frequency of occurrence of each of the twenty-six traits was found with respect to the twenty-five other traits. From the results of the more common coincidences, shown in Table XXIII, it is possible to predict some of the traits which might be expected to exist when one trait is known to be present in an individual. Such a series of relationships is valuable in understanding the problem of any child and furnishes some basis of what appears to be "detective" work on the part of the psychologist or investigator. For example, of the children who argue, about 75 per cent fight or interfere with others. Eighty per cent of those who lie also steal. One half of those who daydream use arguing as a means of shutting out those who would interfere with daydreaming. This table of relationships is presented for whatever value it may have of itself and as an illustration of an approach to the study of behavior which has been much neglected to date. It might appropriately be named the "Psychology of Behavior Patterns." In Table XXIII the twenty-six behavior traits and the frequency of occurrence of the twenty-five other traits are shown in ten-point steps of percentages, from 40 per cent through 89.9 per cent. (See pages 378 to 382.)

The material in this chapter has been presented to show the possibilities of statistical treatment in determining the composition of behavior patterns. With the improvement of techniques for the measurement of behavior tendencies, such as the Detroit Scale for Behavior, the authors believe that many of the problems of delinquency will eventually be solved.

BIBLIOGRAPHY

1. RUGG, HAROLD O.—*Statistical Methods Applied to Education.* Boston: Houghton Mifflin Co., 1917. 410 pp.
2. WICKMAN, E. KOSTER—*Children's Behavior and Teachers' Attitudes.* New York: Commonwealth Fund, 1928. 247 pp.

TABLE XXIII. PERCENTAGE OF GREATEST FREQUENCY OF ITEMS WITH ONE ANOTHER

TRAIT	PERCENTAGE				
	80.0 TO 89.9	70.0 TO 79.9	60.0 TO 69.9	50.0 TO 59.9	40.0 TO 49.9
Argues, talkative		Fights, quarrelsome Interferes, disturbs	Defiant, stubborn		Resents correction Lies, deceitful Cheats in school or at play Obstinate, sullen Cruel, teases
Avoids others, timid			Daydreams, absent-minded		Quiet, seclusive
Bullies, boasts	Fights, quarrelsome	Argues, talkative	Interferes, disturbs Defiant, stubborn	Cruel, teases	Resents correction Lies, deceitful Obstinate, sullen Cheats in school or at play
Cheats in school or at play		Fights, quarrelsome Lies, deceitful	Argues, talkative Interferes, disturbs Defiant, stubborn		Resents correction Cruel, teases Bullies, boasts Obstinate, sullen
Cruel, teases	Fights, quarrelsome	Interferes, disturbs Argues, talkative	Defiant, stubborn	Bullies, boasts Cheats in school or at play Lies, deceitful	Resents correction Obstinate, sullen
Daydreams, absent-minded				Argues, talkative	Fights, quarrelsome Interferes, disturbs

TABLE XXIII. PERCENTAGE OF GREATEST FREQUENCY OF ITEMS WITH ONE ANOTHER—*Continued*

TRAIT	PERCENTAGE				
	80.0 TO 89.9	70.0 TO 79.9	60.0 TO 69.9	50.0 TO 59.9	40.0 TO 49.9
Defiant, stubborn		Fights, quarrelsome	Argues, talkative Interferes, disturbs	Resents correction Obstinate, sullen Lies, deceitful	Bullies, boasts Cheats in school or at play
Disliked, repulsive		Fights, quarrelsome Interferes, disturbs Argues, talkative	Defiant, stubborn Lies, deceitful	Cheats in school or at play Bullies, boasts Cruel, teases	Resents correction Obstinate, sullen
Fights, quarrelsome		Argues, talkative Interferes, disturbs	Defiant, stubborn		Cruel, teases Lies, deceitful Resents correction Bullies, boasts Cheats in school or at play Obstinate, sullen
Hysterical, cries			Interferes, disturbs	Argues, talkative Lies, deceitful Fights, quarrelsome	Cheats in school or at play Defiant, stubborn Overactive, nervous
Impulsive, erratic	Interferes, disturbs	Argues, talkative Fights, quarrelsome		Defiant, stubborn Cruel, teases	Bullies, boasts Lies, deceitful Overactive, nervous Resents correction Cheats in school or at play

379

TABLE XXIII. PERCENTAGE OF GREATEST FREQUENCY OF ITEMS WITH ONE ANOTHER—*Continued*

TRAIT	PERCENTAGE				
	80.0 TO 89.9	70.0 TO 79.9	60.0 TO 69.9	50.0 TO 59.9	40.0 TO 49.9
Interferes, disturbs		Fights, quarrelsome Argues, talkative		Defiant, stubborn	Cruel, teases Resents correction Lies, deceitful Cheats in school or at play Bullies, boasts
Lies, deceitful			Fights, quarrelsome Argues, talkative Cheats in school or at play Interferes, disturbs	Defiant, stubborn	Steals Resents correction Cruel, teases
Obstinate, sullen	Defiant, stubborn	Fights, quarrelsome Argues, talkative	Resents correction Interferes, disturbs		Cruel, teases Cheats in school or at play Bullies, boasts Lies, deceitful
Overactive, nervous		Interferes, disturbs	Argues, talkative Fights, quarrelsome	Impulsive, erratic	Defiant, stubborn Bullies, boasts
Profane, vulgar, obscene	Fights, quarrelsome	Argues, talkative Interferes, disturbs Lies, deceitful	Cheats in school or at play Defiant, stubborn	Cruel, teases	Bullies, boasts Resents correction Obstinate, sullen
Quiet, seclusive			Daydreams, absent-minded	Avoids others, timid	

TABLE XXIII. PERCENTAGE OF GREATEST FREQUENCY OF ITEMS WITH ONE ANOTHER—*Continued*

TRAIT	PERCENTAGE				
	80.0 TO 89.9	70.0 TO 79.9	60.0 TO 69.9	50.0 TO 59.9	40.0 TO 49.9
Resents correction		Argues, talkative Defiant, stubborn Fights, quarrelsome	Interferes, disturbs	Obstinate, sullen	Lies, deceitful Cheats in school or at play Bullies, boasts Cruel, teases
Selfish	Fights, quarrelsome	Argues, talkative Defiant, stubborn Interferes, disturbs Resents correction	Obstinate, sullen Bullies, boasts Lies, deceitful Cheats in school or at play	Cruel, teases	Smart aleck
Sets fires	Argues, talkative Bullies, boasts Fights, quarrelsome Lies, deceitful Interferes, disturbs	Steals		Cheats in school or at play Cruel, teases Defiant, stubborn Impulsive, erratic Obstinate, sullen Sex abuse	
Sex abuse		Argues, talkative Interferes, disturbs	Lies, deceitful Fights, quarrelsome	Defiant, stubborn	Cheats in school or at play Daydreams, absent-minded Profane, vulgar, obscene

381

TABLE XXIII. PERCENTAGE OF GREATEST FREQUENCY OF ITEMS WITH ONE ANOTHER—*Continued*

TRAIT	PERCENTAGE				
	80.0 TO 89.9	70.0 TO 79.9	60.0 TO 69.9	50.0 TO 59.9	40.0 TO 49.9
Smart aleck		Argues, talkative Fights, quarrelsome Interferes, disturbs	Defiant, stubborn Bullies, boasts	Cruel, teases Lies, deceitful Resents correction	
Steals	Lies, deceitful		Argues, talkative Cheats in school or at play	Fights, quarrelsome Defiant, stubborn Interferes, disturbs	
Temper tantrums, rage	Defiant, stubborn	Fights, quarrelsome Argues, talkative	Interferes, disturbs Resents correction Obstinate, sullen	Bullies, boasts Cruel, teases Lies, deceitful	Cheats in school or at play
Truant (school)				Interferes, disturbs Lies, deceitful Fights, quarrelsome Argues, talkative	Bullies, boasts Defiant, stubborn Cheats in school or at play
Truant (home)			Truant (school)	Lies, deceitful Argues, talkative Bullies, boasts Defiant, stubborn Interferes, disturbs	Cheats in school or at play Fights, quarrelsome Steals

CHAPTER XIV

GENERAL CONSIDERATIONS AND CONCLUSIONS

THE diagnosis and treatment of behavior problems are among the most timely and important issues for education and for social work. In Chapter I many of the costs of juvenile delinquency and of adult crime were cited. The costs are not only in terms of the actual money expense to society for protective or remedial work, but also in terms of the loss of human energy diverted from production. The costs in terms of individual happiness, in terms of family disgrace and shame, and in terms of loss of life cannot be measured in dollars and cents; but they are to be reckoned as appalling losses. Not long ago a news editorial openly stated that it was becoming dangerous for anyone, particularly women, to go for a stroll in their residential neighborhoods. Government and indeed society have serious problems in the lessening and curbing of delinquency and crime.

Not all adult criminals were delinquents in youth, but many of them were. Studies by Glueck (see Chapter IV) show that four out of five who were problems of behavior maladjustment in childhood or youth repeat within a five-year period. In a short space of a few months in the Detroit clinic one hundred cases between the ages of twenty and thirty who were the subjects of news stories of stealing, murdering, or attacking women were checked in the clinic records as problem cases in their school careers from five to ten years before. Most of them were of dull intelligence but not feeble-minded. They were retarded in school, chronically truant, and eventually evicted from regular grades, some of them still unadjusted when they left the school for behavior problems, where they had remained too short a time for permanent improvement. The story can be duplicated in any city if the records are available. Since adult delinquencies often had their origins in childhood, it is extremely important that the maladjustments of children be analyzed and treated in their early years. The Detroit Scale of Behavior Factors is offered as a means of making such analysis and treatment.

COMPLEXITY OF BEHAVIOR FACTORS

The results of the Detroit Scale show that behavior problems have many causes which are not correlated very highly with each other except in a few instances for each factor. These higher correlations were listed in detail for each of the sixty-six items in Table XIV of Chapter XIII. But within the lower correlations it is probably true that there are subtle relationships between causes which develop a generally poor attitude, and justify a dubious outlook on all of a child's activity. It is necessary to find as many of these minor causes as possible and to treat all of them. Reference might be made to the parallel case of the faulty operation of the family car when three or four mechanisms are slightly out of adjustment, such as poor gas, dirty spark plugs, faulty timing, and a zero temperature. In children a combination of illnesses or slight sensory defects may produce a low achievement record at home and in school. Eventually these poor records become a source of worry. Antagonisms and antipathies develop so that it is difficult to discover what is original cause and what is derived cause. Possibly it is not important to know the sequence of causes after they have occurred; it is more vital to unravel the whole tangle as happily, rapidly, and completely as possible.

Many times it has been stressed that the overt acts of children, such as lying and stealing, are not positive vices to be cured by direct action, but that they are indirect and unusual results of worry, fear, insecurity, and home conflicts. On account of these hidden mechanisms and the necessity for long-time cure, the adjustment worker and the teacher or parent seem to be operating in opposition or conflict because of impatience and mutual misunderstanding. If the parent and teacher can understand more of the real nature of behavior mechanisms, greater progress will be made in all behavior programs.

Uses of the Behavior Scale

There are many clinics and adjustment agencies dealing with the problems of maladjusted children. It is hoped that the Detroit Behavior Scale will prove valuable in analyzing their problem cases. From the experience of the authors in studying behavior cases as well as in having model children rated, it is evident that specific scores are valuable in determining just how bad a case actually is and just what factors are operating in detrimental ways on the child. Nothing is quite so unsatisfactory in social work as to be expected to make an immediate diagnosis from a few hurried questions, or from looking at the child, or from hearing what complaints are lodged against him.

Throughout this presentation there has always been foremost in thought the use of all the facilities of a community in making complete and final diagnosis and treatment of cases. Certain physical factors, such as defective vision, have been treated somewhat at length by describing the various types of visual defects and the results in terms of emotional and psychological handicaps; but the final diagnosis of the visual status is to be referred to reputable oculists. It is expected and hoped that more importance will be attached to the correction of physical and sensory defects, since the social significance of correction has been stressed. Among behavior cases there are many instances of emotional and volitional trends which will eventually lead to certain types of active psychoses; the incipient causes are already present. It is hoped that psychiatrists will find the scale useful in detecting these symptoms and in treating them as early as possible. It is not expected or hoped that any chronic or aggravated psychopathic case can be diagnosed by the lay social worker or teacher by use of this scale, but rather that their awareness of the problem will suggest the urgent need for adequate psychiatric treatment by competent specialists.

There are many cases of behavior difficulty in rural areas or in small towns, known to visiting teachers, health nurses, and teachers, in which adequate social, psychological, and psychiatric diagnoses are not available. If such workers conscientiously study this scale as to its administration and interpretation, they should be able to use it effectively to help children who are in difficulty. There is always the danger of tactless approach to behavior factors, particularly on the latter part of the scale, dealing with the home; but these errors are not limited to workers without training. If the scale is administered in a straightforward manner, without apology, with sympathetic understanding of children, and with friendliness to parents, worth-while results may be expected. Obviously better results should be obtained after several cases have been studied. The school administrator or administrative head of any diagnostic agency should find the scale useful in securing specific checks upon the detailed work of the staff. Definiteness will surely add effectiveness to a field that, regrettably, has long been characterized by its dependence upon personal opinion and subjective evaluation.

SIGNIFICANCE OF LOW SCORES

Educators and social workers have long been cognizant of the fact that certain children who were problems in youth continued to become more serious problems in adulthood. There were no diagnostic procedures, such as behavior scale scores, to aid them in their beliefs; but the obvious cases were certainly expected to appear later. If certain cases are long-time problems with the possibility of no final adjustment unless help is obtained, these facts should be known and faced by the adjustment agencies. If there is a certain residue of cases which can never be adjusted, society should be informed and policies should be set up to segregate them or render them harmless to themselves and to others.

The authors are strongly of the opinion that some of the cases with scores of 200 or less fall into this class. Just how many such cases there are or what scores are the crucial points below which maladjustments are quite prone to occur is not known. By measuring numerous cases of behavior maladjustment it is hoped that many will be benefited. If there are others who cannot be helped, they should be discovered and supervised so that their antisocial tendencies will be reduced to a minimum.

Extreme scores on a behavior-factor scale should approach in usefulness extreme scores in intelligence tests in determining certain outstanding cases of high or of low mental ability. The early detection, special training, and institutionalization of the low-grade feeble-minded have been tremendously aided by the use of intelligence tests. The behavior scale has possibilities of prognosis in a field as important as that of mental differences. In any event the behavior scale should help lift an unfair and unjust load from the field of mental measurement, which has been expected in some mysterious way to solve problems of delinquency. The true value of mental measurement should be increased rather than decreased by the establishment and maintenance of a better perspective toward it. Techniques originating in the field of mental measurement have been of untold value in setting up the present plan of measurement in a field where, also, it is difficult to ascertain facts.

NEXT STEPS

The Detroit Scale of Behavior Factors is only a beginning for a more comprehensive and intelligent approach to the problems of maladjustment and delinquency. There are many other phases of human relationships in which children grow up which should be evaluated in a manner similar to this technique. Society is demanding that education produce effective results, not only in terms of academic scholarship, but also in terms of successful social and vocational living. Education must find out where its weak spots are and what must be done to eliminate them in order to avoid making life failures of children. By the use of this scale the real work of behavior diagnosis and treatment is not ended but just begun.

GENERAL REFERENCES

1. BURT, CYRIL—*The Young Delinquent.* New York: D. Appleton-Century Co., 1925. 619 pp.
2. GORDON, R. G.—*Personality.* New York: Harcourt, Brace & Co., 1926. 302 pp.
3. GROVES, ERNEST R.—*Personality and Social Adjustment.* New York: Longmans, Green & Co., 1923. 126 pp.
4. HEALY, WILLIAM, and others—*Reconstructing Behavior in Youth.* Judge Baker Foundation Publication, No. 5. New York: Alfred A. Knopf, 1929. 325 pp.
5. LA RUE, DANIEL W.—*Mental Hygiene.* New York: The Macmillan Co., 1927. 443 pp.
6. MORGAN, JOHN J. B.—*The Psychology of the Unadjusted School Child.* New York: The Macmillan Co., 1924. 300 pp.
7. THOM, DOUGLAS A.—*Everyday Problems of the Everyday Child.* New York: D. Appleton-Century Co., 1927. 350 pp.
8. WATSON, MAUD E.—*Children and Their Parents.* New York: F. S. Crofts & Co., 1932. 362 pp.

INDEX